Praise for *Policing Higher Education*

"Eve Darian-Smith has written a book for our times. *Policing Higher Education* provides a primer on our driving issues today: free expression and academic freedom, the grounds of knowledge making, and the demands of critical social engagement in a world of interactively spiraling authoritarianism and repression. A probing analysis to think with." —**David Theo Goldberg, University of California, Irvine, author of *The War on Critical Race Theory: Or, the Remaking of Racism***

"*Policing Higher Education* brings an international perspective to contemporary debates about academic freedom. In response to attacks on both scholarship and constitutional democracy, Darian-Smith urges us to define and defend academic freedom as an ethical practice founded on social responsibility. This ambitious work will be essential reading for anyone concerned about the future of higher education in the US and around the world."
—**Henry "Hank" Reichman, author of *Understanding Academic Freedom***

"*Policing Higher Education* moves beyond the limitations of domestically focused analyses to place academic freedom in a global context. Connecting the dots between pressures on academic freedom, antidemocracy movements, and global economic powers, it gives readers indispensable tools for expanded understanding and action across disciplinary borders, institutions, and nation-states." —**Anne McCall, The College of Wooster; Scholars at Risk, United States Section**

"Eve Darian-Smith has produced a book of seminal importance. She offers a brilliant defense of the humanities, academic freedom, and scholars as critically engaged intellectuals. In addition, she integrates history, criticism, and a discourse of resistance and hope into essential reading for anyone concerned about the relationship between education and democracy. This book could not have appeared at a more crucial time." —**Henry Giroux, author of *Race, Politics, and Pandemic Pedagogy: Education in a Time of Crisis***

"In a time of severe ideological attacks on academic freedom and on higher education in general, books such as *Policing Higher Education* are even more necessary. Eve Darian-Smith's volume needs to be widely read and discussed by anyone who cares about what is happening to higher education today."
—**Michael W. Apple, author of *Can Education Change Society?***

"*Policing Higher Education* gives us hope for why we should care about what is happening in our universities and for how we can build resilience and momentum for justice through difficult conversations and coalitions. A must-read for all those engaged with higher education and for those who care about the state of the world." —**Swati Parashar, University of Gothenburg**

"Both a passionate manifesto and fact-based academic account, *Policing Higher Education* places the attacks on academic freedom and autonomy in the US in a global perspective and relates them to the importance of social responsibility for higher education." —**Hans de Wit, Center for International Higher Education, Boston College**

"Surveying the growing challenges in the US, including the corporate capture of universities, increased policing activities on university grounds, and the banning of so-called controversial topics, Darian-Smith makes a compelling case for society to defend the public mission of universities. This book shows a way forward."
—**Salvador Herencia-Carrasco, University of Ottawa; Coalition for Academic Freedom in the Americas**

"It is tempting to see Ron DeSantis's ransacking of New College, Christopher Rufo's attack on critical race theory, and Texas's defunding of offices for diversity, equity, and inclusion as exceptional acts of right-wing overreach. Darian-Smith, however, provides the much-needed tools to situate these attacks as local iterations of the creeping authoritarianism and societal fascisms spreading around the world. Defenders of democracy and academic freedom must enter the existential fight ahead with the clear analysis that Darian-Smith provides."
—**Isaac Kamola, Trinity College; director, Center for the Defense of Academic Freedom, American Association of University Professors**

"Eve Darian-Smith has produced a fresh take of vital importance for those who care about American and global democracy. This is a must-read book not only for new and seasoned scholars alike but for anyone concerned about backsliding democracies. What's especially original is the manner in which Darian-Smith foregrounds the link between rising antidemocracy and recent declines in academic freedom. The best part is that she provides a road map for fighting back!" —**Marc Spooner, coeditor of the forthcoming *What Are Universities For? Challenges and Re-imaginings***

"Scholars deeply desire the freedoms to learn, teach, investigate, and publish and to cooperate with each other in doing so. Unless they can practice truth and the common good in the public sphere, and unless governments everywhere respect their rights and listen to what they say, we cannot meet the climate-nature emergency and the other great challenges we face."
—**Simon Marginson, University of Oxford; editor, *Higher Education***

Policing Higher Education

CRITICAL UNIVERSITY STUDIES
Jeffrey J. Williams and Christopher Newfield, Series Editors

Policing Higher Education

The Antidemocratic Attack on Scholars
and Why It Matters

Eve Darian-Smith

JOHNS HOPKINS UNIVERSITY PRESS   BALTIMORE

© 2025 Johns Hopkins University Press
All rights reserved. Published 2025
Printed in the United States of America on acid-free paper
9 8 7 6 5 4 3 2 1

Johns Hopkins University Press
2715 North Charles Street
Baltimore, Maryland 21218
www.press.jhu.edu

Library of Congress Cataloging-in-Publication Data is available.

A catalog record for this book is available from the British Library.

ISBN 978-1-4214-5131-2 (hardcover)
ISBN 978-1-4214-5132-9 (ebook)
ISBN 978-1-4214-5291-3 (ebook o)

This work is available in an Open Access edition licensed under a Creative Commons Attribution-NonCommercial-NoDerivatives 4.0 International License: https://creativecommons.org/licenses/by-nc-nd/4.0/.

Special discounts are available for bulk purchases of this book. For more information, please contact Special Sales at specialsales@jh.edu.

To the enormously courageous scholars and students fighting, on behalf of us all, for the freedom to think, learn, know, be known, and imagine alternative futures

Education must enable one to sift and weigh evidence, to discern the true from the false, the real from the unreal, and the facts from the fiction.

—Rev. Dr. Martin Luther King Jr., civil rights activist, 1947

The most potent weapon in the hands of the oppressor is the mind of the oppressed.

—Steve Biko, South African anti-apartheid campaigner, 1996

Wherever fear dominates, true happiness vanishes and individual willpower runs dry. Judgments become distorted and rationality itself begins to slip away. Group behavior can become wild, abnormal and violent.

—Weiwei, artist barred from China, 2017

The road to authoritarianism begins when societies stop questioning themselves and when such questioning stops, it is often because intellectuals either have become complicit with such silence or actively produce it.

—Henry Giroux, public intellectual, 2021

We learned that the university is a fragile institution, that it is very dependent on the conditions under which it operates in order to retain its autonomy as an institution and its values of academic freedom. But it also reminded us that the university is a powerful institution—because were it not for that fact, an authoritarian regime would not spend so much time and energy.

—Shalini Randeria, president and rector of the dismantled Central European University, 2023

Contents

List of Figures xi
Preface xiii

Introduction 1

1 Intersecting Global Trends: Rising Antidemocracy, Declining Academic Freedom 25

2 The Politics of Knowledge Production 61

3 Classrooms as Global Battlegrounds 98

4 Higher Education and Democratic Dreams 135

5 Weaponizing Universities in the Twenty-First Century 178

6 Fighting Back: Revisioning Higher Education 216

Acknowledgments 239
Appendix. PEN America: Principles on Campus Free Speech 241
Notes 255
References 271
Index 295

Figures

Chapter 1

1. Brasilia attack, Brazil, January 8, 2023	34
2. Growing partisan divide in US views on higher education, 2019	38
3. Declines in respect for academic freedom internationally, 2022	40
4. Educational gag orders in the United States, January 1, 2021–November 1, 2023	58

Chapter 2

5. Cleaning of the *Pillar of Shame*, University of Hong Kong, 2021	68
6. Nazi book burning, 1933	75
7. Einstein with students, 1946	78

Chapter 3

8. Faculty protesting in silence at Boğaziçi University, Turkey, January 2021	125

Chapter 4

9. Police officers in riot gear, San Francisco State University (then College), 1968	147
10. Student teach-in, Santa Barbara wharf, 1970	152

11. Student protest at People's Park, University of
    California, Berkeley, 1969 — 154
12. Kent State student waving a flag before the Ohio
    National Guard, May 1970 — 155
13. Book burning, Santiago, Chile, 1973 — 163
14. UC Davis policeman pepper-spraying students,
    2011 — 169

Chapter 6

15. Rhodes Must Fall protest, University of Cape
    Town, 2015 — 226

Preface

The Center for Art, Architecture and Design at the University of Monterrey, Mexico, is a magnificent building set against the craggy cliffs that frame the city. Built by the famous Japanese architect Tadao Ando, the building was envisioned as a "portal of knowledge and a melting pot for creativity." Inside, students sprawl across the massive stairwells, drawing, dancing, talking. Looking down from the fourth floor through dramatically angled windows, other students are busy working at printing presses, industrial sewing machines, and at big tables laying out fabric, feathers and paint. A young woman bursts through a doorway with giant black headdresses balanced awkwardly on each arm. A testament to youthful energy, it is a powerful space where new worldviews can be imagined and embraced.

I was spending my days in quite different surroundings, inside an auditorium attending a conference discussing the global attack on higher education. Hosted by the organizations Scholars at Risk and the Coalition for Academic Freedom in the Americas, this meeting was a site for researchers, students, and activists to share their stories about harassment, persecution, and in some cases imprisonment or forced exile from universities and homelands. Participants came from across the Americas—from Brazil, Canada, Mexico, Venezuela, the United States, and elsewhere. What unfolded over a few days was a powerful and moving conversation about state interventions in classrooms and policing of critical inquiry—quite a contrast to the light-filled space where students talked outside. What I heard was expected but still shocking, underscoring that scholars, teachers, and students around the world are increasingly subject to surveillance, censorship, and potential imprisonment over the way they think, the way they teach, and the way they challenge those in power. Participants often evoked the words of the Brazilian educator Paulo Freire, particularly his writings in *Pedagogy of the Oppressed* (1968), which was published while he was in exile from a right-wing dictatorship supported by the United States. In his book Freire explored how colonial oppressors imposed "ideological hegemony" on the lower classes and argued that this oppression must be countered through collaborative learning between teachers and students. At the conference, some people noted that Freire's internationally acclaimed book had been banned by then-President Jair Bolsonaro of Brazil. As conference translators nimbly switched between Spanish, Portuguese, and English and attendees fiddled with their earphones trying to keep up with wide-ranging questions, it became clear that we had much to share and learn from one another.

This book is about the global attack on higher education and academic freedom in the early decades of the twenty-first century. Of course, universities have always been sites of political intervention, as governments and political figures have tried to impose ideological and religious values on scholars whose teachings shape the thinking of future generations. I argue, however, that today, unlike in the past, we are facing a global wave of antidemocratic governance and rise of extremist far-right political leaders. These political figures share tactics of oppression against ordinary citizens as they build their power base and chip away at the basic principles of representative government. In short, around the world there is a shift toward antidemocracy and growing authoritarianism. This is happening in powerful so-called liberal democracies across the global north and global south, such as Australia, India, Germany, Israel, Britain, and Brazil, and in economically less powerful countries, such as Turkey, Hungary, and the Philippines. And correspondingly, in each of these national contexts, we also see escalating attacks on higher education and academic freedom. These attacks happen in a variety of ways—for example, by defunding research, censoring curriculum, limiting publications, retracting jobs, denying tenure, harassing scholars in public, bullying them online, and doxing. In some places, the attacks may also involve prosecution, imprisonment, torture, being disappeared, being forced into exile, and even death.

This worldwide attack on higher education suggests we should take a comparative and global perspective when discussing academic freedom and the right to think critically. As argued in this book, attacks on universities shouldn't be thought of as discrete events contained within national borders. While playing out within unique state contexts that reflect country-specific cultural values, attacks on higher education around the world reflect a growing cadre of antidemocratic politicians who share common strategies and aspirations. One of these strategies is to prevent scholars questioning, challenging, and protesting their unjust and discriminatory regimes and authority to govern.

While taking a global perspective, the book foregrounds attacks on academic freedom in the United States for several reasons. First, the United States has played a major role in developing higher education at national and international levels since the mid-twentieth century. This leadership role is linked to the nation's dominant economic and political presence on the world stage. What goes on in US universities influences what is thought about and taught in other countries. This is an unfair and regrettable reality. As a result, many overseas universities model themselves on the US system, including elite private universities such as Harvard, Yale, and Stanford and flagship public universities such as the University of California, Los Angeles; the University of California, Berkeley; the University of Michigan; and the University of Texas. Together, these research universities command an enormous presence across higher education sectors, wherever you live in the world. So, understanding how academic freedom can be dismantled—even in these powerful academic institutions—offers insights about how other universities inside and outside the United States may be following the same trajectory.

The second reason for focusing on the United States is, in my view, more important because it speaks to the larger political context in which higher education operates. The United States is increasingly embracing antidemocracy and is joining a global drift toward authoritarianism. Emerging among some Americans is a shift in attitude devaluing the concept of democracy itself. This is expressed most clearly through the MAGA Republican Party, which has explicitly strategized to undermine free and fair elections, diminish policies that create equal opportunities for all, and install "loyalist" judges, public servants, and government agencies. Democratic principles, including academic freedom, are being whittled away in plain sight of the public, much to the explicit pleasure of radical Republican leaders and their core populist supporters. This dramatic swing in public opinion and political practice can be interpreted as an omen of what may happen—or is already happening—in other democracies as well.

The third reason for focusing on the United States is personal and reveals my own distress at what is happening. I am an Australian and now US citizen who has lived in the United States for three decades. I care very deeply about the extreme divisiveness blanketing the country. Core supporters of the far-right Republican Party represent about 25 percent of the population. Many of them practice deliberate ignorance that buttresses their racist, antisemitic, misogynist, and anti-immigrant worldviews. A smaller number of core supporters thrive on conspiracy theories promoted by QAnon and other extreme ideological, militaristic, and cultlike groups. What this adds up to is a very deep divide in the population between those who defend academic freedom, truth, expertise, and scientific knowledge as collective societal goods, on the one hand, and a powerful anti-intellectual minority that revels in falsehoods and see professors and students as the "enemy," on the other. This minority is led by far-right political figures who make no pretense about being financially supported by modern-day "captains of industry," such as Charles Koch, Rupert Murdoch, and Elon Musk, who dominate the energy, finance, media, and technology sectors.

Compounding this disturbing societal divide, more and more people are carrying guns and seem prepared to defend their personal worldviews through aggression. As a result, schools and universities in the United States are increasingly becoming the targets of violence. And the campus as a site of innovative knowledge production is under real and existential threat. As a sign of the times, my university mandates that I do emergency training that includes dealing with active shooters and securing student safety against violent attack. As we all know, however, threats to safety are more than physical. Increasingly, scholars, students, librarians, staff, and even some administrators are being harassed and censored, and their jobs and livelihoods are being threatened. State legislatures are vetting curricula for "nonpatriotic" material, and ideologies infused with anti-Black and antidemocratic sentiment are being promoted. On physical, ethical, and emotional fronts, the university campus is now experienced by many who walk the corridors and teach in classrooms as a conflict zone, if not yet an actual battleground.

Evidence of this escalating tension is the growing number of phone calls I receive from scholars in Republican-led states such as Florida and Texas. As a department chair in the University of California system, these scholars are asking me about possible jobs on my campus, which isn't yet subject to direct legislative interference and censorship. California also has strict gun controls that prohibit a person from bringing firearms into buildings of student housing, research, and administration. What I am seeing is that the differences in campus culture in red and blue states is already resulting in the movement of some faculty and students in search of more secure jobs and sites of learning where academic freedom is respected. There is an emerging "brain drain" as scholars move out of Republican-led states, further polarizing the general population and future generations (Zahneis and June 2023). Like the underground networks that enabled women to get abortions before the procedure was legalized (and are now being restored to help women in Republican states where abortion is again deemed illegal), informal networks are already emerging to help scholars fleeing censorship, harassment, and persecution. These informal networks share commonalities with the global academic community that is linked to organizations such as Scholars at Risk and the Institute of International Education's Scholar Rescue Fund (IIE-SRF), which help scholars fleeing oppressive homelands, such as

Iran, Syria, and Turkey, to find jobs at host universities in democratic countries such as Germany, Britain, Canada, and the United States. As many of these host countries are now experiencing the swing toward antidemocratic regimes, an ethics of refuge and new networks of intellectual sanctuary are emerging internally within them. In a perverse sense, host universities are increasingly resembling the repressive institutions they historically opposed. And organizations such as Scholars at Risk are playing a new role in responding to a wave of persecution of scholars across and within rich industrialized countries in the global north.

As I was finishing this book for publication, the Israel-Hamas war broke out on October 7, 2023. Across the United States and around the world, university and college campuses became sites of agitation, reflecting rising Islamophobia and antisemitism among wider societies. As university presidents scrambled to deal with angry students, faculty, alumni, and donors and politically charged investigations, there was suddenly a renewed focus on who has a right to speak freely on university grounds. In the fever pitch of the situation, with suspensions, prosecutions, and resignations of students, faculty, and administrators, the more nuanced concept of collective academic freedom was again reduced to a constitutional right to free speech. As discussed in this book, this simplistic reduction undermines the concept of academic freedom, which is a limited right of a collective faculty to research, think, and teach according to professional standards set by highly trained experts in the academy. Moreover, I argue that reducing academic freedom to free speech is a shared strategy among far-right politicians that plays to their advantage as they tip the world toward antidemocracy and new forms of oppression. In short, under the banner of free speech, fact-based evidence and critical thought are policed, censored, and silenced. The new "free speech tzar" appointed under the United Kingdom's Higher Education (Freedom of Speech) Act 2023 illustrates this reductionism explicitly.

My book explores the deeply concerning global trends of rising authoritarianism and declining academic freedom. This exploration raises all sorts of questions. What is to become of higher education in the United States, across the Americas and Europe, and in other so-called democracies around the world? Where will scholars fleeing persecution in universities in Turkey, China, Russia, Afghanistan, and other authoritarian regimes go? And as communities migrate to geopolitically coalesce around either democratic or antidemocratic cities and regions—as is already happening in the United States—how is the relationship between higher education and the nation-state being challenged and perhaps altered? More profoundly, if academic freedom is attacked on a global scale, who will be left to train future generations to think critically and ask hard questions that challenge antidemocratic regimes at home and abroad?

Policing Higher Education

Introduction

Higher education in the United States is again beset by bitter partisan politics. Attacking teachers, vetting and disinviting guest speakers, policing the curriculum, and denying tenure to outspoken faculty have become commonplace across the country, particularly since 2016. On the political left, these events are understood as part of a backlash against "woke" liberal scholars, supposedly intent on indoctrinating younger generations with progressive thoughts. On the political right, universities are seen as challenging the status quo and questioning foundational narratives of US exceptionalism and a traditional White national identity. Whatever the interpretation, one consequence of the former Trump administration is that universities have once again become intense battlegrounds over the concept of academic freedom and, by extension, the right to free speech and public expression.

In response to escalating attacks on scholars, teachers, and students, there has been an outpouring of scholarship on the value of academic freedom, its changing meaning over time, its relationship to the constitutional protection of free speech, and its central role in upholding democratic principles (Finkin and Post 2009; Chemerinsky and Gillman 2018; Whittington 2018, 2024; Scott 2019; Reichman 2021; Gordon 2023). Unfortunately, these commentaries are US-centric and can be hard to follow for students and faculty as well as the broader public. They often get bogged down in specific contexts and legal details, especially as they relate to state laws and legislatures that differ dramatically across the country. Even at the federal level, deeply polarized politics concerning higher education and constitutional discourse make it hard to follow the conversation.

In this book, I take a different approach by examining higher education in the United States within a comparative and global framework. I move beyond local institutional crises and detailed legal battles to explore transnational economic and political forces framing today's university politics. Specifically, I examine the intersecting global trends of rising antidemocracy and declining academic freedom and ask how the United States fits into these trajectories. My central argument is that attacks on higher education in the United States are connected to similar battles over higher education occurring around the world in other democracies such as Brazil, Germany, Britain, Thailand, Hungary, Australia, Canada, India, Israel, Poland, the Philippines, and Argentina. And I argue that these attacks are related to a global rise in extreme politics and authoritarian-leaning governments that includes the United States.

What I suggest is that Americans need to see conflict over education as much more than ongoing culture wars, although it certainly is that (Bunch 2022; Ben-Porath 2023; Whittington 2024). Rather, we should be thinking about educational conflict in terms of intensifying battles over economic, political, and social power associated with what the political theorist Wendy Brown calls the "crisis of neoliberalism" (Brown 2019). Today, after decades of relative hegemony in the global political economy, the neoliberal order is extremely unpredictable as China, Russia, India, and other forces challenge the hegemonic globalization of the United States. Mass migrations, planetary warming, pandemics, nuclear escalation, global famine, and unprecedented levels of inequality are all contributing to a very destabilized world.

In this context it is perhaps not surprising that controlling how people think and behave has become vitally important to many leaders across the global south and global north who are seeking to maintain their economic, political, and social dominance. Put differently, attacks on academic freedom are emblematic of a destabilized world order unfolding on a global stage yet fought in the everyday experiences of teachers and students inside lecture halls, research labs, and seminar classrooms. This means that we should interpret today's crisis in higher education—unlike earlier episodes of educational crisis in US history—as part of a global pattern that demands new analytical questions and approaches that transcend a nation-state framework and the limitations of methodological nationalism (Darian-Smith and McCarty 2017; Kaczmarska and Yıldız 2022; Shahjahan and Kezar 2013; Shahjahan and Grimm 2023).

In analyzing the intersecting global trends of rising antidemocracy and declining academic freedom, I foreground the US academy. The United States is where I work, and higher education in the United States provides an unlikely, and previously underused, lens through which to understand the crisis of academic freedom around the world. Moreover, the US academy has an outsize influence on the global knowledge economy, particularly in English-speaking countries (Readings 1996; Kamola 2019b, de Wit and Jones 2022; Altbach et al. 2019). Certainly, as global south scholars rightly point out, the production and translation of knowledge cannot always be presumed to be emanating unidirectionally out of the global north to the global south (Connell 2007, 2019; Collyer et al. 2019). In practice, global knowledge production is a much more nuanced, synergistic, and complex terrain than those in the global north generally appreciate.

Still, in a material sense, the US education system acts as a portent of what will happen, or is already happening, elsewhere.

We can see this in the attacks on public universities by Republican leaders whose anti-education legislation cannot be disentangled from similar assaults that have been made for years by antidemocratic politicians in countries such as Hungary, Nicaragua, India, Brazil, Mexico, and Poland. In other words, oppressive educational systems around the world are a forerunner for oppressive domestic action in the United States; similarly, attacks on academic freedom in the United States influence and reinforce oppressive practices in Europe and elsewhere (Goldberg 2023b).

This synergy across higher educational sectors suggests that attacking scholars is more than just a common feature of antidemocratic governance. In the current moment, it is a strategically shared practice among a global cohort of mostly far-right politicians who learn from one another and engage in a cross-pollination of ideas and strategies (Rachman 2022). These leaders form what political scholar Alberto Toscano calls "an international far right" that works together and "that's more than happy to combine revanchist nationalisms with international coordination."[1] This is why it's necessary to think about attacks on scholars as part of a global phenomenon. Comparing the United States with other countries highlights similar policy decisions that tighten controls over universities and that share elements, including the express targeting of scholars and students of color and LGBTQ+ identity.

Goals of the Book

My first goal is to explore the interconnected global trends of rising antidemocracy and its relationship to escalating attacks on scholars and students (chapter 1). Why are we seeing a rise in antidemocracy around the world? What are the historical and structural drivers of this drift toward authoritarianism? In the context of the United States, how does the planned

Republican campaign to promote anti-intellectualism and defund public education over decades fit into this history and the contemporary discussion? Relatedly, in addition to the current escalation of police officers carrying guns on university grounds, what new forms of policing and control are emerging that chill scholarly dialogue and the freedom to question and challenge the status quo?

My second goal is to foster new conversations about academic freedom that make it more meaningful and relevant to both scholarly and nonscholarly audiences within and across national contexts (chapter 2). A major problem in talking about academic freedom is that it is a highly contested, dynamic, and fragile concept that cannot be reduced to a singular formal definition. This is not surprising given that academic freedom means different things to different scholarly communities and takes on particular significance in specific cultural contexts, sometimes closely monitored by state or religious authorities. As a result, academic freedom is talked about in a variety of ways, such as the freedom to learn, freedom to think, right to education, and right to know and be known, as it changes over time according to prevailing social values. In times of peace and relative social stability, academic freedom has largely been taken for granted in democratic countries since the 1970s. But in times of political and economic instability and war, the concept of academic freedom usually becomes more limited as political forces try to suppress scholarly challenges to those in power. In the context of today's global rise of the far right amid worldwide economic and political instability, this helps explain the global attack on scholars that includes reducing their academic capacity for challenging antidemocratic laws and policies.

Historically, academic freedom emerged in the modern era, linked to a global capitalist system and the building of modern nation-states. The freedom to explore new knowledge and scientific inquiry was considered a common good that supposedly benefited the entire nation, though in practice it typically served the interests of powerful ruling classes. Its first formulations emerged at the University of Leiden in the Netherlands, which was known for its tolerance of diverse intellectual views and as a haven for scholars fleeing the censorship of the Catholic Church in the late sixteenth and seventeenth centuries. The University of Göttingen in Germany became well known for academic freedom in the eighteenth century, influencing the founding of the University of Berlin in 1811, which became widely admired for its education reforms that drew on Wilhelm von Humboldt's twin concepts of *Lehrfreiheit* (freedom to teach) and *Lernfreiheit* (freedom to learn) under the rubric of *Akademische Freiheit* (academic freedom).

This understanding of academic freedom was picked up across Western and Eastern Europe in the early decades of the twentieth century, particularly in the wake of World War I. In Latin America there was a wave of legal reforms that included academic freedom in the 1930s and 1940s. These regional reforms are often associated with the student-led Córdoba movement that sought to make universities "more accessible to the wider society and improve student welfare" (Spannagel 2024:15). In the United States, academic freedom was first articulated at the national level by the American Association of University Professors (AAUP) in 1915 and revised in its 1940 Statement of Principles on Academic Freedom and Tenure.[2] In part because the United States has played an outsize role in the expansion and internationalization of higher education since the middle of the twentieth century, the US position on academic freedom has influenced universities around the world. However, it is important to remember that the US definition of academic freedom established by the AAUP is not universal, even if most people presume this is the case. Moreover, even within the United States, it is interpreted and practiced unevenly across the country.

Despite these variations in the definition and practice of academic freedom, there is an aspirational consensus today that it protects scholars, teachers, and students' collective ability to research, teach, and disseminate evidence-based knowledge grounded in highly trained expertise, without fear of political or religious oversight, pressure, censorship, or punishment. This means that scholars have limits on what they say, which must accord with professionally determined academic standards as well as laws that apply to everyone, such as those on pornography, defamation, and treason. In short, academic freedom is not synonymous with the individual's right to free speech.

Notably, academic freedom is theoretically meant to protect scholars *and* universities from political intervention and censure by state and religious authorities. In other words, academic freedom is not just about the rights of scholars or students; it also necessarily includes the autonomy of the university to provide the intellectual space in which academic freedom can be practiced. This applies whether the university is public or private. As the political philosopher Judith Butler writes, "Academic freedom is both a right and an obligation. It allows faculty to pursue lines of research and modes of thought without interference from government or other external authorities." What's more, Butler continues, it obliges scholars to secure "the task of the university to preserve and support critical thought, even when it is not in line with official views of the state or other external institutions" (Butler 2017:857). In turn, notes David Kaye, former United Nations special rapporteur on freedom of expression, "states are under a positive obligation to create a general enabling environment for seeking, receiving and imparting information and ideas. Institutional protection and autonomy are a part of that enabling environment" (Kaye 2020:6).

What this brief description of academic freedom underscores is that it is a complex concept in meaning and application. Finding a way to talk about academic freedom that speaks to scholarly and nonscholarly communities, and that addresses how it can be applied within and across diverse national cultures and political contexts, is essential for explaining why it is important for flourishing societies that respect basic democratic principles, including the freedom to think and the freedom to learn.

My third goal for this book is to humanize the impacts of attacks on academic freedom, which, for readers, may be a rather abstract narrative of violence and fear among scholars and students. I do so by reflecting on stories from scholars who have been persecuted in the United States and elsewhere (chapter 3). Personal stories make plain what is at stake when people are punished for asking difficult questions and probing controversial subjects. My hope is that readers will reflect on what can be learned from these stories. What are the commonalities of persecuted scholars in Syria or Ethiopia with those now being policed in the United States, Canada, and the United Kingdom? How do these stories help us know what to look for, and possibly prepare for, on our own university campuses? Do these stories highlight a need for a more robust concept of academic freedom, and if so, what would that look like?

My fourth goal is to predicate the current conflicts in higher education, which may seem like an anomaly, on the past. I do so by following histories leading up to and informing the present. These histories are not just about the United

States but more correctly are global histories refracted through and framing the American context (chapter 4). In other words, today's aggressive assault by the far right on scholars and students did not appear out of nowhere; rather, it reflects both domestic and international battles over public higher education for the past 60 years under neoliberal logics and a conservative backlash. As James Baldwin reminds us, "History is not the past. It is the present." With that in mind, what can we learn from past efforts to control critical thinking and political dissent through the corporatization and bureaucratization of higher education? Does the past help us more fully understand efforts to weaponize universities and colleges today?

My fifth goal is to generate new insights into how oppressive practices—whether driven by racism, homophobia, misogyny, anti-intellectualism, fanaticism, religious fundamentalism, ideology, power, or greed—feature in attacks on higher education (chapter 5). In what ways are these drivers weaponizing university campuses and threatening the people who work and learn there? And how do current efforts to police "epistemic disobedience" connect to contemporary social and racial injustices as well as crises threatening human and planetary survival? (Mignolo 2010; Ghosh 2017). Reflecting on these intersecting and cumulative processes underscores how university campuses operate as a microcosm of the structural and material conditions that exist in the wider society. But campuses also function as a site for refracting, resisting, shaping, and translating social processes and for communicating back to people within and beyond the ivory tower. As a space of innovation, reflection, and, at times, agitation, the university context, I argue, opens pathways for thinking about how best to combat the global trend toward authoritarianism that threatens our most intimate social relations and how we can live collectively and ethically in the world.

Finally, my sixth goal is future-facing and explores how we can push back and take control over scholarship and learning in campus communities (chapter 6). How can we renew a societal appreciation for professional scholarship and scientific expertise? And how can this expertise inform and promote inclusive multiracial worldviews as well as methodological and pedagogical practices that ensure the freedom to "transgress" and think otherwise? (hooks 1994). Given that higher education is a privileged institution, how can we ensure that future generations of students—from all backgrounds, ethnicities, and socioeconomic classes—are able to think creatively about societal solutions and potentially sweeping change? Creative thinking is absolutely essential if we are to mitigate the global impacts of a warming planet that includes mass migrations, regional famine, and rising oceans. Relatedly, how can intellectual communities build alliances across state borders that challenge knowledge production framed by neocolonial economic logics, supremacist racist ideologies, and isolationist, self-serving national policies?

In many ways my argument builds on the work of Piya Chatterjee and Sunaina Maira in their edited volume, *The Imperial University* (2014), which convincingly shows that the United States' overseas "imperial interventions are linked to domestic repression, policing, and containment that penetrate the university" (Chatterjee and Maira 2014:8). However, that volume is of its time, reflecting the hegemonic power of the United States on the world stage. In contrast, I am suggesting that in the middle of the 2020s, US dominance is now being openly challenged economically, politically, and culturally—hence the escalation of insecurity that has led to the radical embracing of antidemocracy (and authoritarian allies) by the MAGA movement within the Republican Party. Extremist Republicans and their core supporters have turned their back on many of the policy prescriptions of the Washington Consensus in efforts to retain exclusive power at home and abroad and "Make America Great Again."

It is in this context that higher education has again become an explicit conflict zone, bombarded with massive disinformation campaigns and strategized efforts to denigrate scholarly expertise that include rewriting curricula; dismantling departments such as sociology and ethnic studies; removing policies that promote diversity, equity, and inclusion; and creating a university culture of censorship and fear. One of the goals of the far right is to return to a romanticized higher education that serves the best interests of young White men. The takeover of Florida's New College by Republican governor Ron DeSantis is an example of this process and a manifestation of "white resentment" in higher education (Anderson 2017). In sum, what we are facing today is a period in world history where multiple crises threaten the stabilization of the political economy, which was dominated for decades following World War II by the global north and, particularly, the United States. The reverberations of this destabilization are being felt through numerous public sectors, including higher education.

Together, my six goals in this book—linking the global drift toward antidemocracy with attacks on academic freedom, fostering new conversations, humanizing attacks on scholars, learning from the past, generating new insights, and re-envisioning curriculum and the constitution of intellectual communities—are ambitious. But I think it essential to think big for the following reasons.

First, connecting the dots between global geopolitics and increasing persecution and fear among scholars and students overcomes the limitations of thinking about higher education bound by national contexts (Shahjahan and Kezar 2013;

Shahjahan and Grimm 2023; Kaczmarska and Yıldız 2022). Second, it helps us better understand how attacks on academic freedom impact the local lives of ordinary people both on and off college campuses. And finally, and most importantly, it emphasizes that what may be happening over "there," in another part of the world, could also be happening "here," in our own environs, as well. Though I focus on attacks on academic freedom in the United States, placing the United States in a global context is the necessary analytical framework I explore in this book.

Reframing Academic Freedom

As already mentioned, among both university and nonuniversity communities, academic freedom is not well understood. Explanations of the concept often get bogged down in definitional and legal technicalities. This problem raises the need to reframe academic freedom so that it is legible to audiences within and beyond the academy. In this effort, my modest suggestion is that we should reframe academic freedom as a practice of social responsibility, which may have greater resonance with a wider public that may have little ambition or opportunity to go to university and may be focused on more immediate issues such as paying the rent, finding a job, and accessing health care.

Thinking about the university as an essential public institution for fostering social responsibility comprises spatial and temporal dimensions. Spatially, it helps break down the barriers between the university and the wider society in which institutions of higher education are situated. Temporally, it underscores that universities have a social responsibility both to immediate societies and to future generations. Universities, in other words, are socially responsible to students and nonstudents as well as their families and wider societies and are responsible also for promoting the well-being of our collective futures. Given rising authoritarianism facing populations around the world, coupled with the climate emergency that is already changing how many people live and work, the social responsibilities of scholars and universities are arguably more important today than ever before (Darian-Smith 2023c).

A reframing of academic freedom would help it to speak more effectively to a broader constituency including policy writers, administrators, legislators, judges, civil society organizations, and activists. Significantly, the idea of social responsibility resonates with thousands of environmental grassroots organizations and social movements such as Black Lives Matter and #MeToo. Social responsibility also speaks to the union activities on campuses that have "skyrocketed" in recent years,[3] along with off-campus labor mobilization and trade unionism among autoworkers, screenwriters, actors, Amazon employees, and health, transportation, hospitality, and postal workers—all of which suggests the existence of a wave of renewed political consciousness in the wider population (Darian-Smith 2024). Perhaps most importantly, a more legible concept of academic freedom may facilitate conversations between scholars, teachers, students, and educational communities that transcend ethnic, racial, class, gender, and religious divides, which in turn may overcome the many fraught debates about what academic freedom means within national contexts that currently plague the United States and many other countries around the world.

Talking about academic freedom as social responsibility and, in turn, exploring how it may promote social justice and societal equality have historically been more common in developing countries of the global south (Brandenburg et al. 2019; Choudry and Vally 2020; Hall and Tandon 2021). The words of the Brazilian educator Paulo Freire, particularly in

Pedagogy of the Oppressed (1968) (published while he was in exile from Brazil due to the activities of right-wing militants), are emblematic of the long-standing interconnectedness of public education and collective liberation in the public imaginary of many countries that grapple with postcolonial and decolonial histories (Ngũgĩ 1986; Federici, Caffentzis and Alidon 2000; Mamdani 2007; Kamola 2019a; Al-Bulushi 2023). I argue, however, that thinking about the role of higher education in furthering social responsibility is just as pertinent to the richer countries of the global north, particularly given increasingly oppressive conditions in higher education, where in practice colonial logics are deployed to police these countries' own citizenry. As noted by Steve Biko, a famous Black South African anti-apartheid campaigner, "The most potent weapon in the hands of the oppressor is the mind of the oppressed." Today's far-right extremists build on history lessons of colonial oppression and deploy them in new ways against the "enemy" scholar within.

While social responsibility may mean different things to different communities, it is possible to develop a generalizable concept applicable to higher education. A notable example is provided by Scholars at Risk (SAR), a nonprofit organization located in New York that helps scholars fleeing political persecution around the world and supports an extraordinarily diverse global academic community. SAR argues that one of the core values of higher education is social responsibility, defining this as a duty "to seek and impart truth, according to ethical and professional standards, and to respond to contemporary problems and needs of all members of society" (SAR 2020).

This definition of social responsibility, along with the idea that it is a core value in higher education, is echoed in various international treaties, academic organizations, and networks.

For instance, at the international level, social responsibility as a core value in higher education has long been promoted by the United Nations Educational, Scientific, and Cultural Organization (UNESCO) through its "Recommendation Concerning the Status of Higher-Education Teaching Personnel" (1997), which states that scholars have a set of rights that "carries with it special duties and responsibilities, including the obligation to respect the academic freedom of other members of the academic community and to ensure the fair discussion of contrary views." The document goes on to state that "teaching, research and scholarship should be conducted in full accordance with ethical and professional standards and should, where appropriate, respond to contemporary problems facing society." This sentiment is echoed in a recent report issued by the European Parliament in March 2023, *State of Play of Academic Freedom in the EU Member States*, which links academic freedom with academic responsibilities. According to the report, academia's responsibilities include "the handling of societal challenges and crises, such as climate change, growing inequality, or global pandemics" (Maassen et al. 2023:9). The report continues, "Overall, academia has the responsibility to use its higher education and research capacities to contribute, for example, to the adequate handling of challenges and crises, and in that way to the maintenance and enhancement of the democratic principles and institutions that form the political order of our societies" (Maassen et al. 2023:9).

Echoing European Union efforts to connect academia with wider societal concerns is the Talloires Network, an international group of universities from all over the world. Established in 2011, this network is a "growing global coalition of 431 university presidents, vice-chancellors and rectors in 86 countries who have publicly committed to strengthening the civic roles and social responsibilities of their institutions. It is the largest international network focused particularly on university civic engagement."[4] The Talloires Network partners with national and regional networks across Asia, Middle East, Africa and Europe in "building a global movement of civically engaged universities."[5]

Developing academic coalitions that transcend national borders is also endorsed in the *Inter-American Principles on Academic Freedom and University Autonomy* (2021), which sets out guidelines for defending scholars across the Americas, including Canada and the United States.[6] This innovative document also calls for rethinking knowledge production as "borderless" (Darian-Smith 2023a). Together UNESCO, SAR, the European Parliament, the Talloires Network, and the *Inter-American Principles* exemplify a range of efforts to promote a relationship between higher education and social responsibility that advances all members of society regardless of educational status or national identity.

Scholars would agree with these efforts to support higher education's social responsibility to fostering inclusive, multiracial, democratic societies. For instance, Emiliano Bosio and Gustavo Gregorutti, in their edited volume *The Emergence of the Ethically-Engaged University* (2023), explore how universities around the world can be involved in reconnecting learning to issues of politics and morality. They seek to move beyond market-driven priorities in higher education and to foster instead a philosophy centered on ethics and "informed by principles of mutuality, reciprocity and social responsibility" (Bosio and Gregorutti 2023:2). Necessarily, they argue, this change requires embracing non-Western perspectives, theories, and worldviews and engaging with non-Western ethics such as the concept of *ubuntu* in African universities (Waghid 2023; Waghid et al. 2023). This pluralist engagement is essential for reimagining the university as an institution whose support for the pursuit of global peace includes ensuring a sustainable planet on which all can live (Bosio and Gregorutti 2023:238).

Henry Giroux's work on critical pedagogy goes one step further. Building on the insights of Paulo Freire, he points to the emancipatory potential of knowledge sharing and argues that intellectuals have a special responsibility to examine how power operates "through institutions, individuals, social formations, and every life so as to enable or close down democratic values, identities, and relations" (Giroux and Bosio 2021:9; Giroux 2021). This responsibility, Giroux goes on, requires scholars to appreciate "why the tools we used in the past feel awkward in the present, often failing to respond to problems now facing the United States and other parts of the world." Moreover, he adds, it requires scholars to find a "new vocabulary for connecting not only how we read critically but also how we engage in movements for social change" (Giroux and Bosio 2021:10). I think these are very important points: the Euro-American academy needs not only to think with a different set of ethical and social priorities but also to find a better way to communicate to people, on and off campuses, why they should care about political attacks on universities and colleges.

Common to these international treaties, civil society networks, and scholarly interventions is a realization that a university's social responsibility is to local, national, and global communities. This is particularly relevant given that rising antidemocracy and declining academic freedom are interconnected global phenomena and that many societal problems (i.e., mass migration, planetary warming, biodiversity loss) have local, national, regional, and transnational impacts. Appreciating the global dimensions of local attacks on students and faculty opens up much-needed conversations about what the internationalization of higher education should look like in the future and what its aspirational goals should be (de Wit and Jones 2022).

Universities and Politics

Some readers may find linking academic freedom with social responsibility—and, by extension, social justice—to be problematic because it overtly politicizes the university community. My response is twofold. First, universities have always been political, despite efforts to distinguish academics from politics and despite the "traditional ivory tower conception of the academy as an institution devoted to the pursuit of truth" (Schrecker 2010:98; Apple 2010; Giroux 2021). Although some faculty try to distinguish scholarship from politics—as the AAUP understandably urged in 1915, in making a non-threatening case for academic freedom—the reality is that the "anti-politics orthodoxy" is not sustainable (Gordon 2023). Because it promotes innovative thinking, the university is intrinsically an institution of social inquiry and potential political change.

In the United States, for instance, the introduction of the GI Bill in the post–World War II era sought to redesign higher education for a less elite student body and pushed policies that increased the number of colleges and universities across the country. Although the plan was not totally successful, as discussed in chapter 4, it was nevertheless an explicitly political project. Even the Kalven Report, issued in 1967 by the University of Chicago and today often quoted in support of the view that faculty and students should remain neutral on political and social issues, conceded the intrinsic political nature of the university: "A university faithful to its mission will provide enduring challenges to social values, policies, practices, and institutions. By design and by effect, it is the institution which creates discontent with the existing social arrangements and proposes new ones. In brief, a good university, like Socrates, will be upsetting."[7]

My second response to those who object to linking academic freedom and social responsibility is more pragmatic. The university has again become the front of explicit political conflict, and the stark reality is that the far right is very much winning the fight over intellectual freedom in the United States and elsewhere. During the later 2010s and early 2020s in particular, conservatives aggressively undermined public trust in higher education and scholarly expertise. More generally, surveys show that people under 30 years of age are increasingly ambivalent about other institutions of democracy, such as a representative congress and an independent judiciary. Even the concept of democracy is being called into question as more and more people, influenced by disinformation and polarizing social media, turn in fear and desperation to strongman politicians and their authoritarian ideologies (Fisher 2023). The situation is very bleak, and educators can no longer hide behind the alleged objectivity of the microscope, dataset, or archive. Scholar of politics Timothy Kaufman-Osborn argues forcefully in his book *The Autocratic Academy* that "as the United States slides into authoritarianism, as antidemocratic forces gain in muscle and vitriol, the sector of our political economy called 'higher education' may contest or it may expediate this fate. What colleges and universities cannot do is remain aloof from this struggle over America's future, for they represent a key battleground on which this conflict is being and will continue to be fought" (Kaufman-Osborn 2023:8).

Public intellectuals such as Stanley Fish—who embraces the "anti-politics orthodoxy" and argues that scholars should stick to their job of research and teaching and should not engage in political conversation—are speaking from positions of privilege, safety, and complacency and do not fully realize the vulnerability of academic institutions to far-right political interference (Fish 2014; see Turk 2014). It is now very clear that the ivory tower that Fish holds so dear is being stormed and faculty jobs like those he has held over decades are under threat. Scholars in the social sciences and humanities are often targets, but scholars in the physical sciences are not immune, and it is naive to think otherwise. Today's extreme politicization of knowledge and the related "gig academy" should be haunting even tenured professors in elite research universities (Kezar et al. 2019).

What this means is that all educators, at all levels of job security, need to work together to face this threat, and the effort should be led by university administrators and tenured faculty, who have the greatest power to speak out (Altbach and Blanco 2024). Moreover, the full gamut of institutions needs to be involved—elite private universities and colleges, large public universities, small liberal arts schools, Historically Black Colleges and Universities (HBCUs), tribal colleges, and two-year community and city colleges. In other words, all educators need to start developing new strategies for showing people why they should be concerned about academic freedom in higher education and how it is connected to defending basic democratic principles such as the right to vote, fair wages, clean water, education, reproductive autonomy, and health care. I argue that talking about academic freedom as an ethic of social responsibility, which engages issues of equal opportunity and human dignity, points us in the right direction.

Why Care About Academic Freedom?

Clearly not everyone thinks a university education is important for their future goals. And for many young people, it is just too expensive to even dream about. The notion that college is available to everyone is simply not true, especially in the United States, which has the most expensive education system in the world (Goldrick-Rab 2017). Yet even with major economic and social obstacles, 50.2 percent of the US population have attended college (57 percent of women and 43 percent of men).[8] And despite the educational challenges presented by the COVID-19 pandemic, 61.8 percent of high school graduates enrolled in college in October 2021. A 2023 national survey conducted by the *Chronicle of Higher Education* found that overall, 78 percent of respondents would recommend that a relative or close friend pursue a bachelor's degree, and 79 percent said that getting a degree was worth the high cost. On the issue of educational quality, Democratic respondents were inclined to see colleges as providing a good education, while Republican respondents were less impressed.[9] What these figures suggest is that a robust majority of the population see value in attending college or university. However, most students who do attend college are from White middle- and upper-class socioeconomic backgrounds, with far fewer being members of racial and ethnic minorities, and even fewer still being first-generation and immigrant students. Despite the lack of diversity in student populations, those who do go to college clearly perceive some value in the higher education experience.

What about the many millions of young Americans who don't go to college? Today, as inequality and poverty escalate within the United States and around the world, it is understandable why many people see higher education as irrelevant to more pressing concerns such as feeding the family and providing basic housing, heating, and health care. Why should people, especially those from lower-income and minority backgrounds, care about attacks on academic freedom? If we broaden the conversation beyond class and demographic issues, what value does higher education have for the wider society and its taxpaying citizens? What is the common good that academic freedom supposedly provides?

These questions have long been neglected in the public domain. Since the 1950s and 1960s, higher education has often been regarded as a private good—an individual choice for those who can afford it. Jon Shelton calls this the "education myth": education was misguidedly promoted as the key solution to a vast array of social and economic problems (Shelton 2023; see also Kraus 2023). In other words, people falsely believed that society could educate itself out of structural racism and poverty. Despite Shelton's convincing argument, most people would say the opposite. For many people, the purpose of college is to train young people in skill sets that can make them more competitive in the job market. In this understanding, higher education has little to do with developing a common good for society. Rather, a college education is seen as an individualist enterprise, a ticket to upward mobility through better-paying jobs. And jobs in turn often determine why some undergraduate degrees are widely perceived as better than others—for instance, economics, business, and accounting are seen as more valuable or useful than history, literature, and languages. This profit-driven logic is endorsed through the redistribution of resources in favor of STEM (science, technology, engineering, and mathematics) research and teaching on almost all college and university campuses. And it is expressed in turn by the widespread popularity of STEM degrees among students in recent decades, who enter career paths they think will get them better employment and enable them to pay off their massive student loan debt.

Against this instrumental approach that sees higher education as job preparation, other commentators argue that going to college is about encountering new ideas. This approach fosters intellectual engagement and curiosity, pushing students outside their comfort zone and teaching them how to be critical and flexible thinkers. It also promotes innovation, new inventions, and ultimately new jobs.[10] Moreover, this approach argues that teaching students how to be critical thinkers better prepares the next generation to find solutions to society's pressing issues. Critical thinking of this kind is associated with a humanities-based education, often referred to as the liberal arts (Roth 2015). Humanities education is based on the idea that all members of society, irrespective of class, race, ethnicity, religion or gender, should be able to participate in general education and attain a well-rounded understanding of politics, history, economics, art, science, mathematics, and literature. This knowledge, at least historically, was regarded as vital for producing thoughtful and innovative thinkers who would benefit society in general and might one day become social leaders.

Despite declining student enrollments in the humanities, many commentators, quite rightly, regard this form of education as essential for developing a thriving and inclusive society (Fitzpatrick 2021; Lewis 2024). And arguably, education in the humanities is more essential than ever before. Notes one former educator:

> During a time of immense technological change, war and political division, nothing is more important than having the intellectual confidence to challenge what you see, hear and read with thoughtful questions. Humanistic study provides your students with an opportunity to develop their intellectual confidence. We should want our students to graduate intellectually and emotionally confident. That confidence is the foundation for success in the workplace. Too often, we think that skills solve problems, but, in fact, problem-solving starts by asking the right question first.[11]

A humanities-based education includes, among other things, training young people for engaged citizenship and "participatory readiness" for such tasks as serving on the jury in a complicated trial and understanding voting ballots (Allen 2016; also see Ferrall 2011; Zakaria 2016; Nussbaum 2016). I would add that participatory readiness should also include training people in media literacy and the ability to recognize disinformation, political propaganda, and conspiracy theories as opposed to evidence-based news and events.

Whether you support the humanities or not, my book seeks to transcend prevailing debates about whether college is for job training or intellectual innovation that, among other things, creates new kinds of jobs for students to train for. These debates are important and, in the context of artificial intelligence and ChatGPT, may attract renewed attention. But these arguments have been rehashed many times and rarely speak beyond anxious humanities scholars and college administrators to the wider public. In contrast, I want to open the conversation up to a much bigger audience, because what is at stake unquestionably affects everyone—Black, Brown, White, educated and uneducated, rich and poor. There is an immediate and pressing reason why higher education is important, why it should be considered a core and collective benefit to society, and why we should all care about attacks on universities and colleges in the United States and around the world. This is the global—and historically unique—rise of antidemocracy, which threatens to reorganize our entire social, political, and economic ways of relating to one another and experiencing the natural world.

Chapter One

Intersecting Global Trends: Rising Antidemocracy, Declining Academic Freedom

Today there is escalating concern about emerging antidemocratic regimes of governance, many of them veering toward outright authoritarianism and neofascism. This global political trend is typically examined to explain shifts in the global economy and geopolitical realignments at the international level. Rarely is this global trend connected with widespread attacks on scholars and students around the world, nor is it often traced to the ways extremists are both dismantling and rebuilding universities and colleges to better serve their oppressive antidemocratic aspirations. However, linking these two intersecting global trends is essential if we are to fully understand the global political economy of academic freedom. This chapter explicitly examines these two trends and explores how they are informing old and new forms of policing scholars and their research, teaching, and critical thinking, wherever one lives in the world.

Rising Antidemocracy

Global antidemocracy is evident in the widespread dismantling of democratic principles in many countries across the global south and global north. Of course, antidemocratic governance differs within specific countries, from outright autocrats who throw their political opponents into prison to those who employ more subtle modes of control, such as censoring social media or using it to further disinformation campaigns.

And not all antidemocratic leaders can be classified as technically fascist, though many do in fact fit the fascist profile and show fascist tendencies.

According to Walden Bello, a leading Filipino academic and political figure, a fascist leader is "a charismatic individual with strong inclinations toward authoritarian rule, who is engaged in or supports the systematic violation of basic human, civil, and political rights; who derives strength from a heated multiclass mass base; and who pursues a political project that contradicts the fundamental values and aims of liberal democracy or social democracy" (Bello 2019). Building on this general definition, sociolegal scholar Boaventura de Sousa Santos writes that the real danger lies in "the rise of fascism as a societal regime. Unlike political fascism, societal fascism is pluralistic, coexists easily with the democratic state, and ... rather than being national, is both local and global" (Santos 2001:186). What Bello and Santos emphasize is that various forms of societal fascism that privilege some human life over others have emerged as a global trend. While today's far-right leaders may not fit conventional political categories of "authoritarian," "totalitarian," or "fascist" regimes precisely because they emerge within democratic societies, the insidious rise of antidemocratic leaders demands our immediate attention (Glasius 2018; Beetham 2015).

In the United States and across Latin America, Europe, South Asia, Southeast Asia, Africa, and the Middle East, many far-right extremists and their political parties (along with a few far-left regimes) have gained increasing control. V-Dem, an independent research group based in Sweden, stated in its *Democracy Report 2022* that democratic advances since the 1990s have now been "eradicated." According to the report, 70 percent of the world's population now lives under dictatorships (V-Dem 2022a). This shocking statistic is confirmed by

Freedom House, a Washington-based nonprofit organization. Significantly, it notes that "antidemocratic politicians are also sharing practices and learning from one another, accelerating the turn toward alternatives" (Freedom House 2021). This comment underscores that, in contrast to earlier historical moments, today the lean toward authoritarianism is led by a transnational cadre of extremists and, as a global phenomenon, transcends national borders and continental divides.

The global lean toward "strongman" leadership in recent years has been the subject of much scholarship and commentary (Ben-Ghiat 2020; see also MacLean 2018; Bello 2019; Brown 2019; Applebaum 2020; Berberoglu 2020; Repucci 2020; Tobias and Stein 2022). A notable contribution to the literature is Gideon Rachman's book *The Age of the Strongman* (2022), which draws on interviews with many extremist leaders to present a global analysis of the phenomenon and the ways leaders share political tactics and similar policies that make it "harder to maintain a clear line between authoritarian and democratic worlds" (Rachman 2022:9). Notes the political analyst Moisés Naím, "Such [autocratic] drift is not the marginal phenomenon it looked like a decade ago." Naím continues, "The threat to global democracy could not be more real. The assaults on freedom are global, sustained, and formidable" (Naím 2022:228–245). This trend became even more evident during the COVID-19 pandemic, when many governments used the health crisis to ramp up civilian surveillance and monitoring of political activism in what scholars have called "governing through contagion" (Chua and Lee 2021).

Common to strongman leadership is the ability to rouse an emotional response among core supporters, which is often linked to anger against elites and hostility toward immigrants and other marginalized groups. The legal scholar Richard Falk calls this a cultlike "passion . . . that eludes rational analysis and argumentation."[1] Notably, argues Vijay Prashad, a leading political scholar and journalist, "the ascendancy of the far right across the world" rests on a strongman style. Discussing Javier Milei, the newly elected far-right leader of Argentina in November 2023, Prashad argues:

> It is not *what* they say they will do to solve the world's actual problems that matters so much as *how* they say it. In other words, for politicians like Milei (or Brazil's former President Jair Bolsonaro, India's Prime Minister Narendra Modi, and former US President Donald Trump), it is not their policy proposals that are attractive but their style—the style of the far right. People like Milei promise to take the country's institutions by the throat [including education] and make them cough up solutions. Their boldness sends a frisson through society, a jolt that masquerades as a plan for the future. (Prashad's italics)[2]

Antidemocratic leaders diminish society's best interests, promoting instead their own political power and economic profits. Most do not grab control through military coups or violent insurrection, as often occurred in the 1960s and 1970s under US-led campaigns such as Operation Condor.[3] Rather, current leaders typically rise to power by incrementally changing laws and policies in their favor (Levitsky and Ziblatt 2018).[4] Historically, transforming the law to best serve political leaders was a core strategy in institutionalizing Italian and German fascism in the interwar years. As political theorist H. Arthur Steiner wrote in "The Fascist Conception of Law," Italy's fascist revolution of 1922 "established its position within the frame-work and substance of public and private law." In fascist regimes, "legal transformation not only insures the revolution, but actually *makes* it" (Steiner 1936:1267; Steiner's italics).

Similarly, today's antidemocracy political figures adopt "lawfare" strategies that include "a cynical manipulation of the rule of law" against perceived enemies of the state (Dunlap 2001; Kittrie 2016; Santos 2023:205–238).[5] In most cases, lawfare is used as a weapon of oppression by powerful actors over less powerful and often marginalized actors, limiting their access to law and the ability to implement legal outcomes. Lawfare strategies include rewriting constitutions and presidential term limits, censoring journalists and evidence-based news media, dismantling judicial independence, attacking lawyers, and preventing citizens from voting freely without intimidation (Zanin et al. 2022).

At the same time, while undermining democratic principles, the state retains the veneer of legitimacy in its ostensible commitment to the rule of law. This is how Singapore's prime minister Lee Hsien Loon, now in his fifth term in office, imposed a highly repressive government that has dismantled human rights protections (Rajah 2012). This is how Israel's prime minister Benjamin Netanyahu justified the country's settler-colonial occupation of Gaza and the West Bank and why his far-right government diminished the power of Israel's Supreme Court to block government decisions (Erakat 2020). And this is how Turkey's president Recep Erdoğan, elected in 2014, revised laws and policies in his favor so that he now leads a hybrid regime that comprises "both authoritarian and democratic elements": "On the one hand Erdoğan has destroyed the bureaucracy and reduced state agencies into his own party branches. On the other hand, he has used bureaucracy to maintain his power against his opponents, such as intellectuals, through investigations, disciplinary punishments, detention and humiliations.... Erdoğan's authority is based on police power and its anti-constitutionalist character.... In this new system, the president holds all powers" (Doğan and Selenica 2022:164).

Scholars call this process of using lawfare strategies to undermine checks and balances on political power "autocratic legalism." This term highlights how leaders today often come to office through democratic elections but, once elected, work to dismantle established legal processes and institutions to serve their own objectives (Corrales 2015). According to legal scholar Kim Lane Scheppele, these leaders "use liberal methods to achieve their illiberal results," coming "to power not with bullets but with law." Notably, she adds, these autocrats often borrow strategies and tactics from one another (Scheppele 2018:571, 582). According to historian Ruth Ben-Ghiat, the tool kit of authoritarian-style governance includes extreme forms of nationalism, propaganda, virility, corruption, and varying degrees of violence (Ben-Ghiat 2020). Together, these processes point to an increasing militarization of daily life, which the historian Michel Geyer defines as the "tense social process in which civil society organizes itself for the production of violence" (quoted in Giroux 2021:41–42; see also Passavant 2021).

In addition to manipulating laws in their favor, antidemocratic leaders also come to power by working with corporate allies that finance their political campaigns and promote their party leadership. In exchange for corporate support from certain sectors such as energy, finance, and technology, politicians typically promise tax cuts as well as deregulation that dismantles accountability and oversight (Mayer 2017). This relationship is explicit with the oil and gas mining industry, which has effectively captured the political process in countries such as the United States, Australia, and Canada, in turn leading to increased levels of corruption (Darian-Smith 2023c; Nyberg 2021). In effect, many antidemocratic leaders function as the puppets of huge transnational corporations. Although this compromised relationship has been going on for decades, today there is little attempt to hide it. Put differently, what we are currently seeing is open collusion between antidemocratic leaders and the corporate sectors that finance and support them. I call this collusion "free-market authoritarianism," emphasizing that extreme politicians no longer see the need to pretend they support democratic principles (Darian-Smith 2022).

Examples of this radical antidemocratic trend are numerous. For instance, in the United States, the House Select Committee to Investigate the January 6th Attack on the United States Capitol issued a final report holding President Donald Trump solely responsible for inciting a violent attack to stop the peaceful and constitutional transfer of presidential power in 2020. More broadly, voting rights have been severely compromised by Republican legislation, the Supreme Court has been deliberately stacked with conservative judges, the Environmental Protection Agency has been undermined, and women's rights have been taken away with the overturning of *Roe v. Wade*. Ben-Ghiat writes, "Four years of an authoritarian-style presidency cemented the GOP's abandonment of consensus politics and the norms and customs of democracy" (Ben-Ghiat 2020:66). And President Joe Biden, on the campaign trail in September 2023, argued fiercely against Trump's authoritarian actions, stating that "there is something dangerous happening in America now. There is an extremist movement that does not share the basic beliefs in our democracy: the MAGA Movement.... Their extreme agenda, if carried out, would fundamentally alter the institutions of American democracy as we know it."[6]

Trump himself openly confirmed the basis of Biden's dire warning. In Trump's campaign speeches that led up to the

2024 presidential election, he reminded the world that if he was reelected, he would bring a fascist sensibility to the White House. Specifically, he claimed that he would seek vengeance on his critics and political opponents by resurrecting the Insurrection Act (1807), which enables the president to deploy troops to round up individuals and break up public protests. In a television interview, Trump said, "If I happen to be president and I see somebody who's doing well and beating me very badly, I say go down and indict them, mostly they would be out of business. They'd be out. They'd be out of the election."[7]

Trump also mentioned building huge camps for immigrants and implementing widespread deportations, weaponizing the civil service by populating it with "loyalists" to serve his bidding, and dismantling the Department of Education. As noted by Tom Nichols, a former Republican and a national security expert, these alarming indicators show "plans for a dictatorship that would appall every American."[8] Adding to these political warnings, legal scholars gloomily remind us that given the peculiarities of the US Constitution, which enables someone to become president without winning the popular vote, the Republican Party has promoted a "tyranny of the minority" (Levitsky and Ziblatt 2023).

Beyond the United States, in 2022 and 2023, radical far-right parties in France, Germany, and Denmark and across Europe gained widespread popularity. Other ultranationalist populist political leaders were electorally successful in Italy, Sweden, Spain, and the Netherlands, often coming to power through political coalitions promoting racist, misogynist, antisemitic, Islamophobic, and anti-immigrant ideas (Haynes, 2019; Miller-Idriss 2019). This means that most of the 27 member states of the European Union are now formally ruled by or strongly influenced by extremists and far-right populist parties. As one journalist noted, "Extremist ideology [is] spreading like an oil spill in Europe."[9] These newly elected heads of state joined a cadre of existing far-right political figures in India, Turkey, Russia, Nicaragua, Hungary, Israel, Poland, the Philippines, and elsewhere.

Outside formal party politics, there are many instances of activist groups and social movements, some of them revolving around conspiracy theories, that openly denigrate democracy. For example, in late 2022, German police uncovered an extensive terrorist movement called Citizens of the Reich, which was attempting to seize power and murder political opponents. The police arrested 25 members of the organization, but according to intelligence reports, this underground neofascist movement has approximately 23,000 members who are "united in their nostalgia for pre-WWII Germany."[10] On the other side of the world, in Brazil in early 2023, 5,000 extremist demonstrators stormed the state capital of Brasilia in support of former far-right president Jair Bolsonaro, who had been voted out of office. Bolsonaro stirred the crowd by arguing the election was stolen, modeling his narrative on Trump's "Big Lie." Notably, both German and Brazilian groups drew inspiration from the insurrectionary assault on the US Capitol on January 6, 2020 (figure 1).

Both within and outside formal government processes, the world is experiencing a global lean toward antidemocracy and authoritarianism. Most political commentators, however, overlook the impact of this tendency on higher education and the role universities play in the mounting assault on democracy (i.e., Sunstein 2018; Levitsky and Ziblatt 2018). Conversely, scholars of higher education, at least in the United States, generally don't engage with the far-right's aggressive antidemocratic attack on universities and colleges (i.e., Levine and Pelt 2021; Teays and Renteln 2022).[11] The silence about

Figure 1. Far-right protestors attacking Brazil's state capital buildings in Brasilia on January 8, 2023, in a staged event echoing Trump's insurrection and violent attack on the US Congress on January 6, 2020. Wikimedia Commons. Licensed under the Creative Commons Attribution 3.0 Unported license. https://creativecommons.org/licenses/by/3.0/deed.en.

extremist education politics seems remarkable given that attacks on higher education have been escalating rapidly since 2016, sending campuses into turmoil and being regularly reported in the *Chronicle of Higher Education*. It appears that analyses of extremist politics, on the one hand, and analyses of evolving practices in higher education, on the other, are not typically put into conversation with each other—precisely the effort that I argue must be made.

Declining Academic Freedom

Common to today's antidemocratic leaders is their effort to control higher education (Spooner 2023). These leaders, and the corporate sectors that support them, are acutely aware of the practical role universities can play in furthering their far-right ideologies and maintaining their power base. They know that controlling the wider society includes policing what scholars—and the future generations they teach—can and do think. The value in controlling universities is a lesson that has been learned and practiced over decades.

For instance, the libertarian economist Friedrich Hayek, in his much-cited essay "The Intellectuals and Socialism" (1949), explicitly talked about using scholars to spread ideology to students and the wider society. Hayek called scholars the "middlemen of ideas" and deeply influenced Milton Friedman in the 1970s at the University of Chicago, where he trained future generations of economists to spread free-market neoliberalism around the world. The increasing dominance of neoliberal thinking in turn shaped higher education throughout the 1980s and 1990s. This was helped by organizations such as the Heritage Foundation (established 1974), the Charles G. Koch Charitable Foundation (1980), Atlas Economic Research Foundation (1981) and the David Horowitz Freedom Center (1988), which together set an agenda to structurally change society through the production of certain kinds of knowledge and expertise (MacLean 2018; Mayer 2017; Wilson and Kamola 2021). These groups infiltrated universities by means of philanthropic donations, the construction of new buildings, and the financing of new faculty hires. In some cases, these groups worked with foreign investors in countries such as China and Saudi Arabia.

Of note is that this international network helped launch the new field of law and economics, which quickly became established in law schools, economics departments, business schools, and centers such as the Law and Economics Center at George Mason University (established 1974) (Priest 2020). The dramatic rise of the law and economics field and the spreading of its ideas to universities in Latin America, in Africa, and across Europe trained a new generation of conservative lawyers, judges, economists, and entrepreneurs. The founding of the American Law and Economics Association in 1991 underscored its consolidation as a legitimate field of inquiry and vividly illustrates the strategic transforming of education and scholarly ideas. This was a carefully crafted plan that involved, among other things, controlling any critical thought that could challenge for-profit agendas and economic, environmental, and legal deregulation. In sum, conservatives and libertarians intentionally used universities as instruments in promoting neoliberal economic ideology and related legal and political policy from the 1970s on (Schrum 2019; see chapter 4).

Today, conservatives continue to use higher education to further their own agenda, which includes pushing free-market ideology, censoring climate science, and training the next generation of conservative lawyers and judges (chapter 5). But with the global turn against democratic governance, we have entered a new phase of restraining critical thought. As Henry Giroux, renowned cultural critic and scholar of critical pedagogy, notes:

> Across the globe, a new historical conjuncture is emerging in which attacks on higher education as a democratic institution and on dissident public voices in general—whether journalists, whistleblowers, or academics—are intensifying with alarming consequences for both higher education and the formative public spheres that make democracy possible. Hyper-capitalism or market fundamentalism has put higher education in its cross hairs and the result has been the ongoing transformation of higher education into an adjunct of the very rich and powerful corporate interests. . . . In fact, the right-wing defense of the neoliberal dismantling of the university as a site of critical inquiry is more brazen and arrogant than anything we have seen in the past. (Giroux 2016)

In the United States, as recently as a decade ago, it would have been unheard-of for politicians to openly condemn higher education as a public institution. In the past, of course, scholars were often attacked for being communist, homosexual, unpatriotic, Jewish, or "extremists on the left." But today's Republican politicians openly encourage broad criticism of higher education by pointing to the entire "education establishment" as the problem and declaring that all "professors are the enemy." These broad attacks echo those of Ronald Reagan in the late 1960s, when as governor of California he openly condemned scholars and students and radical campus politics (Schrecker 2010:93). But today the attacks have gone much further than the conservative backlash of that era. What we are now seeing is the replacement of boards of trustees with political allies and the entire overhauling of some colleges (i.e., New College, Florida), as well as the defunding and disaccreditation of other colleges in an effort to close them down altogether. As Republican lieutenant governor Dan Patrick of Texas tellingly declared, "Tenured professors must not be able to hide behind the phrase 'academic freedom,' and then proceed to poison the minds of our next generation." This denigrating rhetoric is picked up, shared, and amplified by AI algorithms across social media platforms, filtering out into public discourse and shaping decision-making at many levels, including the banning of books at local libraries and the closing down of some departments (mainly in the humanities) at colleges and universities.

A public turn against public education is somewhat predictable given that a conservative onslaught on higher education has been taking place for years. Republican leaders, conservative think tanks, and political networks have collectively sown distrust in the academy. Specifically, this coordinated attack has presented universities and colleges as elite institutions run by progressives who indoctrinate younger generations with "woke" ideology. This strategy has proved immensely effective, and survey statistics show that since 2012 the Republican Party has successfully promoted an anti-education narrative that has reversed attitudes among its core supporters from regarding colleges positively to now thinking colleges have a negative impact on society (figure 2). This attitudinal turnaround is even more startling given that as recently as 2006, only a small number of Americans (8.2 percent) thought there was political bias and indoctrination in the classroom (Gross and Simmons 2006).

Far-right anti-education campaigns and strategies in the United States are shared transnationally among antidemocratic leaders who point to universities as sites of indoctrination and propaganda. This happened in Brazil under former president Bolsonaro as well as in Egypt, India, Canada, Italy,

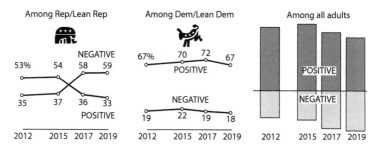

Figure 2. The growing partisan divide, over time, in US adults' views on higher education, 2012–2019: percentages of respondents who said that higher education had either a positive or a negative effect on the present state of affairs in the United States. Dem / Lean Dem = Democratic or leaning Democratic. Rep / Lean Rep = Republican or leaning Republican. Reproduced with permission from Pew Research Center. "The Growing Partisan Divide in Views of Higher Education." Pew Research Center, Washington, DC, 2019. https://www.pewresearch.org/social-trends/2019/08/19/the-growing-partisan-divide-in-views-of-higher-education-2/.

and Britain—in fact, in every country experiencing far-right governance. Given the surge in attacks on students and scholars, it should not come as a surprise that, according to V-Dem,

> all world regions except Sub-Saharan Africa show substantial declines in academic freedom. Asia and the Pacific has been thrown back to a level of academic freedom last registered in the region around 1978; Latin America returns to a situation last recorded in 1987; while Eastern Europe and central Asia has fallen to a record low since the fall of the Iron Curtain. Populous countries such as Brazil, China, India, and Russia exhibit substantially less academic freedom today than in 2011. They were recently joined by the United States of America, which has lost more than 0.15 points on the AFI scale (0–1). Thus, 37% of the world's population now live in countries with recent drops in academic freedom: almost two in five people globally. (V-Dem 2022b:3)

These alarming statistics are supported by Scholars at Risk (SAR), an international nonprofit organization based in New York. Its report *Free to Think 2023* gives evidence of 409 attacks on 66 higher education communities around the world between July 2022 and June 2023. These include nearly 200 killings, violent attacks, and disappearances of scholars and students in countries such as Nigeria, Pakistan, and Turkey. Significantly, the SAR report also includes the United States and other open societies such as Australia and Japan, where there has been a "spread of illiberalism" that diminishes quality education and threatens the foundations of democracy (Gueorguiev 2023). According to the report: "Around the world, executive authorities and lawmakers used the power of their respective offices in ways that undermine institutional autonomy, academic freedom, and quality higher education. While such efforts did not necessarily target individual scholars or students, they laid the groundwork for attacks on higher education by providing a veneer of legitimacy for curtailing and punishing those who engaged in disfavored academic work or expression. Perhaps nowhere among open societies was this trend more striking than in the United States" (SAR 2023:3–4).

According to law professor Michael Lynk, the statistics reported by V-Dem and SAR correlate to declines in democratic societies as measured in terms of political rights and civil liberties. Lynk notes unequivocally that "there is an exact parallel between the rise of illiberal democracy and authoritarian governments, and the crackdown on academic freedom and the independence and autonomy of universities. They go hand in hand. In fact, it's one of our best barometers for assessing how much respect or how little respect there is for democracy and the rule of law" (quoted in Lorinc 2023; figure 3).

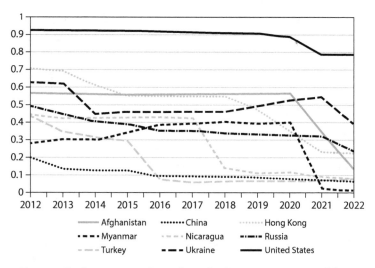

Figure 3. Declines in respect for academic freedom in countries around the world, as measured by the Academic Freedom Index. Reproduced with permission from Scholars at Risk. Scholars at Risk report *Free to Think 2023*, figure 1. https://www.scholarsatrisk.org/resources/free-to-think-2023/.

While direct physical violence is not something most scholars or students in the United States anticipate, the expectation that campuses are safe places is shifting. A combination of extreme far-right ideology, widespread gun possession, and divisiveness across the national political landscape—especially on issues of race—suggest that the possibility of violence is not totally remote or unimaginable. In May 2023, the National Association for the Advancement of Colored People (NAACP) issued a travel warning for Florida, saying that Blacks should use extreme caution when traveling there due to the "openly hostile" environment endorsed by Republican governor Ron DeSantis and allied lawmakers. Anxiety about violence became a horrifying reality with the mass shooting in Jacksonville, Florida, in August 2023, resulting in the death of three Black bystanders at a local shop. The young, White, male killer was originally spotted driving into the grounds of Edward Walters University, a small private Historically Black Colleges and Universities (HBCU) campus, and putting on his tactical vest, gloves, and mask. It was later learned that he had a Glock handgun and an AR-15-style rifle decorated with a swastika inside his car. When approached by campus security, he sped off to then enter a nearby store, where he deliberately killed only Black shoppers. The university's president, Dr. A. Zachary Faison Jr., said, "He could have gone any place in the city, but he came to Florida's first HBCU first, and so I think you know, circumstantially, we can conclude that this is where he aimed to complete his horrid act."[12]

Certainly threats, and in some cases violence, toward scholars are extremely alarming, but they don't give the full picture. Higher education in the United States has been subject to the same "lawfare" tactics used by antidemocratic leaders to shore up their power base. Unlike direct violence, these practices are hard to monitor because they are diffuse, operate across various sectors, and are typically carried out under the banner of legitimate governance. Lawfare tactics include stacking education boards with far-right politicians and allied business associates, defunding university accreditation agencies, and ramming through state legislatures bills and policies to control curricula, academic employment, and college administrative processes. Lawfare tactics also include the use of lobbyists to promote policies and decision-making that limit university and college authority to self-govern. Together, these more insidious legal lines of attack aim to reduce university autonomy and bring into question scholarly expertise (see Kamola 2024).

Republican lawmakers and activists have also aggressively used lawfare tactics to target scholars who study disinformation and fake news and who question what MAGA Republicans call the "Big Lie" of the 2020 election that claims that victory was stolen from them. This line of attack inundates scholars with lawsuits, subpoenas, and demands for information, effectively tying them up in court. Noted Jamell Jaffer, the executive director of an institute at Columbia University that works to protect freedom of speech and a free press, "I think it is quite obviously a cynical—and I would say wildly partisan—attempt to chill research."[13]

At the federal level, lawfare tactics included two devasting opinions issued by the far-right supermajority 6–3 Supreme Court in June 2023. The first ruling, *Students for Fair Admissions v. President and Fellows of Harvard College,* took away a university's autonomy to use race-conscious admission processes.[14] Going forward, most colleges and universities will not take into consideration an applicant's racial and ethnic background for fear of being sued. Some analysts anticipate that the ruling will change what campus communities look like by drastically reducing the number of Black and Brown students attending college, as well as lowering their numbers in medical schools, law schools, business schools, and all sorts of graduate programs. What this case means is that in the name of promoting color blindness, which the Supreme Court falsely claimed is a constitutional principle, the Court effectively shored up systemic racism within higher education at the undergraduate, graduate, and faculty levels. In her dissenting opinion, Justice Ketanji Brown Jackson wrote, "Deeming race irrelevant in law does not make it so in life" (Harris 2023). Not surprisingly, the ruling was widely condemned by many social and racial justice groups as well as by the Democratic Party.

The second ruling by the Supreme Court, *Biden v. Nebraska*, denied student loan relief. The Democratic Party had seen this relief as essential to support young people who had made efforts to become educated but in the process had become overburdened with crippling amounts of debt (many issued by for-profit colleges working with unregulated, predatory loan companies such as Sallie Mae). The 6–3 court majority effectively punished those burdened by enormous school debts for trying to become better educated. Notably, this burden falls heaviest on women and students of color. The decision's refusal to provide any debt relief affirmed the anti-intellectualism and hostility of Republicans toward higher education. The ruling also reinforced the Republican Party's explicit racism and denigration of women, minorities, and migrants trying to improve their economic and social opportunities.

Whether the means employed are lawfare tactics or other physical, psychological, emotional, political, and economic modes of attack, what these actions make clear is a growing disrespect for higher education in general and academic freedom specifically. Denigrating the value of higher education as a public institution emerges as a common practice among antidemocratic regimes around the world. Comparisons show that repressive strategies operate in various ways in countries across national and substate contexts, reflecting a variety of legal, political, social, and religious circumstances and ideologies. What is similar across these various contexts, however, is the long-term objective of antidemocratic leaders around the world—namely, to denounce higher education and intellectual expertise, particularly targeting scholars' capacity to promote critical thinking that challenges the status quo and these antidemocratic leaders' authority to govern.

Policing College and University Communities

This book's title, *Policing Higher Education*, refers to the increasing surveillance and control over scholars' and students' freedom to think. Within almost all societies, the quest by those in power to control the minds of current and future generations, and by extension their capacities for political dissent, has a long and complex history. Over time, we see the state's use of education to promote ideology and control thinking in many forms and configurations. In the Euro-American context, some obvious examples are the Christian mission schools built to assimilate Indigenous youth in nineteenth- and twentieth-century British settler-colonial states (Churchill 2004; Minton 2019), the national restructuring of the modern US university in the early decades of the twentieth century (Barrow 1990), the push of racist eugenics research in Germany and the United States in the 1920s and 1930s (Crook 2002), the capitulation of students and intellectuals in Poland and elsewhere to Soviet propaganda (Milosz 1953), and the prosecution of US scholars associated with communism in the 1920s and later under McCarthyism in the 1950s (Schrecker 1986).

What is unique about these episodes is the way leaders sought to control and police thinking. Modes of policing change over time to reflect the political, economic, and social conditions at any given moment. In the 1960s and 1970s in the United States, actual police were brought to campus by university administrators to quell student activism and protest. As discussed in chapter 4, in this period, the National Guard and other law enforcement agencies were often mobilized to control campus life. This period of acute campus agitation was followed by decades of relative calm—at least on the surface. As the renowned historian of education Ellen Schrecker reminds us, behind the scenes, "hostile forces from outside the university moved in." She goes on, "Energized by the campus unrest, the [conservative] enemies of the liberal academy attacked the ideological and financial underpinnings" and in effect dismantled the "promise to extend the benefits of higher education to anyone able to profit from them" (Schrecker 2021:444). So began a decades-long covert assault on higher education and the freedom to think through corporatization, bureaucratization, and an encompassing audit culture that helped create an adjunct teaching sector (Schrecker 2010).

In contrast to the later decades of the twentieth century, in the twenty-first century the overt militarization of colleges and universities has again ramped up, and a police presence on university campuses has become mainstream. Often, the justification is offered that rising crime rates and shootings require more campus security—a rationale strongly supported by students' parents and many alarmed community groups. Today, armed campus police departments exist on the grounds of almost all large colleges. As discussed in chapter 5, the militarization of universities in the late 2010s and 2020s is part of a bigger trend by far-right leaders to clamp down on political dissent, evidenced by the introduction of anti-protest laws criminalizing public protests in the United States, Britain, Australia, and many other countries leaning toward antidemocratic extremism.

Below I describe two different modes of control that are less obvious than campus police in riot gear but today form the primary modes of surveillance and control. The first are policies and funding practices that are imposed by state and nonstate actors on colleges to curb academic freedom. The second, and much less discussed, mode of control is the self-censorship of scholars who live in fear of attack and choose to behave and work in ways that curtail the development of their ideas and critical thinking. Both modes of policing undermine the mission of universities to promote open learning and are crippling to thriving and engaged intellectual communities.

Policing the Academy in the Twenty-First Century

The dominant mode of policing is the actual monitoring of individuals by state and nonstate actors that seek to control what scholars can research, publish, and teach. These modes of policing may result in actual attacks and violence, leading to scholars and students being forced to flee. Attacks routinely occur in oppressive societies such as China, but as the SAR Freedom to Think Report states, "they also occur in more open, democratic, and stable societies, leaving no country immune from their threat. State and non-state actors, including armed militant and extremist groups, police and military forces, government authorities, off-campus groups, and even members of higher education communities, among others, carry out these attacks, which often result in deaths, injuries, deprivations of liberty, and the upending of scholars' and students' academic careers" (SAR 2020).

Mechanisms of control may include a police presence on campus and the use of force, rape, beatings, imprisonment, expulsion, and even death. But more often, less violent interference that impacts working conditions is involved, such as withholding funding for research, rewriting curricula, banning books and research agendas, and suspending or denying employment. Often, state leaders work with private business organizations and individual donors and philanthropists to control scholars whose research may impact them negatively (Mayer 2017). For instance, in the United States, the Koch family foundations, built on the vast wealth of the Koch family's business in petroleum production, have for decades interfered in universities by providing funding and behind-the-scenes censoring of research that does not match the Koch family's free-market libertarian ideology, as discussed further in chapter 5 (Wilson and Kamola 2021). As the historian Nancy MacLean has argued, the mission of the Koch family and its large network of conservatives in the finance, energy, and legal fields has always been "to save capitalism from democracy— permanently" (MacLean 2018). This mission is at its core incompatible with any aspiration for universities to promote democratic societies and a culture of inclusivity and equality.

The second form of policing involves preemptive self-censorship on the part of researchers, teachers, and students who may actively avoid topics that are deemed potentially controversial. In other words, actual bans in Republican-led states on taboo topics such as gender and sexuality, abortion rights, systemic racism, climate degradation, and anticapitalism also produce a chilling impact on all sorts of conversations beyond what is legally prohibited. Self-censorship reduces the likelihood of asking politically sensitive questions and hinders critical thinking and teaching. In a sense, laws prohibiting certain topics "discipline" the educator to not discuss a range of potentially sensitive issues (Foucault 1979). Self-censorship can also stifle a scholar's active research agenda.

In discussing self-censorship in Arab universities, Robert Quinn, the founding executive director of Scholars at Risk, notes that a few violent attacks on scholars or students create a wider climate of intimidation and are "efficient ways to maintain control over a society" (Quinn 2021). Alarmingly, Ai Weiwei, a Chinese artist banned from his own country for his controversial political art, argues that self-censorship can lead to the moral collapse of a society. According to Weiwei, "Wherever fear dominates, true happiness vanishes and individual willpower runs dry. Judgments become distorted and rationality itself begins to slip away. Group behavior can become wild, abnormal and violent."[15]

What makes these overt and covert forms of policing unique to the early decades of the twenty-first century is the rapid evolution of digital communications and AI that are creating new modes of surveillance and ways to undermine academic freedom. Today's policing of universities and colleges relies heavily on social media as a new policing technology. Understandably, scholars are anxious to avoid online surveillance, harassment, hate mail, and death threats from religious groups, conservative think tanks, far-right media outlets, activist groups, student groups, and outraged parents, quite apart from the possibility of being denied tenure or fired from their jobs by campus administrators or state lawyers. The power of social media and digital surveillance to chill research can be almost immediate. For example, in 2022, after Elon Musk took over Twitter, climate scientists were targeted within weeks. Ed Hawkins, professor of climate science at Reading University in the United Kingdom, said he experienced a huge increase in tweets from climate denier accounts, often citing conspiracy theories and discredited information.[16]

In other instances, activity on social media created toxic environments of cyberbullying directed at teachers. At the

University of Chicago, administrators refused to stop one student from harassing a professor who proposed to teach a class on whiteness. They had to basically admit that the university's declaration of free speech principles, the Kalven Report (1967)—often hailed as a guiding document for universities in the United States—was inadequate. As another student who wanted to take the class argued, this means that an antagonistic student, under cover of free speech, can "more or less intimidate and harass a professor, and sic your incredible following on TikTok and Twitter on them for the purpose of chilling speech."[17]

Across the United States, "sensationalized surveillance" is being orchestrated by far-right groups, such as Campus Reform and The College Fix, that employ a "freelance army of student correspondents" to make up stories about scholarly liberal bias that are then spread across social media platforms (McCarthy and Kamola 2022; Wilson and Kamola 2021). Radicalized students are motivated and financed by far-right organizations external to the campus to create sensational media stories that are then disseminated through conservative media outlets such as Fox and Breitbart (Binder and Kidder 2022:8). Faculty mentioned in the media often receive unpleasant emails and sometimes threats of violence and even death. Many self-censor their research and teaching so as to avoid future harassment. "The result is a distributed feedback loop whereby the surveillance apparatus pumps moralizing outrage into a right-wing media ecosystem, self-deputized vigilantes meet [sic] out their version of justice, and administrators are called upon to respond" (McCarthy and Kamola 2022:246).

Adding to scholars' fear and self-censorship is the far-right nonprofit group Turning Point USA, which hosts on its website a Professor Watchlist naming faculty who, the group claims, "discriminate against conservative students and advance leftist propaganda in the classroom." Turning Point USA, financed by Republicans and advised by people such as Barry Russell, former president and CEO of the Independent Petroleum Association of America, plays an increasingly dominant role in campus politics. According to Kerry Sinanan, an assistant professor of trans-Atlantic slavery at the University of Texas, San Antonio, this environment of fear has forced her to take a job outside the United States. She writes: "Anybody who thinks they can modify what they're doing and be safe is deeply mistaken, because authoritarianism is never about creating conditions for anybody to be safe. It's about making people feel insecure."[18]

The infiltration of campuses by external political forces using the "eyes and ears" of student vigilantes has become a relatively common practice in the United States and, increasingly, around the world. For instance, there are now Turning Point organizations in Canada and the United Kingdom. The impact of Turning Point and a growing list of similar surveillance activist groups has reached unprecedented levels with the use of social media platforms that amplify and spread the potential for online monitoring of scholars within and beyond national borders. To resist surveillance, the academic group Faculty First Responders monitors these extremist media organizations on its website and offers a range of resources to faculty who are harassed.[19] But this modest faculty-led group, like other faculty groups such as Academic Freedom Alliance, while highly commendable and courageous, is up against the enormous economic and political power of extremist transnational organizations and networks.

Structural Drivers of Academic Repression

John Douglass, in the edited volume *Neo-nationalism and Universities: Populists, Autocrats, and the Future of Higher Edu-

cation, provides a fascinating comparative analysis of the impacts of far-right leaders on universities across a range of countries including Britain, Poland, Hungary, China, Russia, Singapore, Hong Kong, and Brazil (Douglass 2021; see also Slaughter 2019). The volume emphasizes the extent of the "takeover" of universities by extremist political strongmen and the unfolding societal impacts that threaten principles of democracy. The volume does not, however, connect specific countries experiencing attacks on universities to larger economic, social, and political processes. I argue that, if we are to understand attacks on academic freedom as a global trend, it is essential to think beyond nationalist comparisons and explore what may be impacting all these countries concurrently, albeit in different ways. Notably, Michael Apple, a leading scholar of critical pedagogy, writes that "education cannot be understood without recognizing that nearly all educational policies and practices are strongly influenced by an increasingly integrated international economy that is subject to severe crises" (Apple 2010:1).

Today, higher education has become entangled within a global crisis in which free-market fundamentalism as the dominant economic framework is being seriously challenged (Mignolo 2023). Well before the coronavirus pandemic struck in early 2020, there were signs that the neoliberal economic model was in trouble, notably weakened by US trade wars with China in 2017. More recently, Russia's invasion of Ukraine in 2022 has also eroded the model. In addition, years of catastrophic environmental crises and regional droughts, floods, and famine have further challenged the sustainability of extractive capitalism and the world's reliance on burning fossil fuels, which climate scientists show is undeniably responsible for planetary warming. Together these events have contributed to a massive destabilization of supply chains and financial security. According to Indermit Gill, the World Bank's chief economist, "Nearly all the economic forces that powered progress and prosperity over the last three decades are fading."[20]

Massive instability in the global political economy has created unprecedented inequalities within and between nation-states. A 2023 Oxfam International report, *Survival of the Richest*, states, "During the pandemic and cost-of-living crisis since 2020, $26 trillion (63 percent) of all new wealth was captured by the richest 1 percent, while $16 trillion (37 percent) went to the rest of the world put together."[21] Notes Gabriela Bucher, executive director of Oxfam International, "While ordinary people are making daily sacrifices on essentials like food, the super-rich have outdone even their wildest dreams. Just two years in, this decade is shaping up to be the best yet for billionaires—a roaring '20s boom for the world's richest."[22] Tragically, a destabilized world economy in which billionaires make trillions also means that many millions of people—mostly living in the poorer countries of the global south—are experiencing unprecedented conditions of inequality, disenfranchisement, food insecurity, and disposability.

Significantly, while the economic future looks grim for masses of working and impoverished peoples, billionaires who have seen extraordinary increases in their wealth are now exerting enormous economic power on states, effectively influencing national politics. This is very evident in the technology sector with public battles pitched against and between Meta, Google, and Twitter (now X), but it is also happening behind the scenes in a range of sectors such as finance, energy, and defense. The result is unprecedented disparity between the world's "transnational capitalist class" and the rest of humanity, effectively breaking up the post–World War II international order and the "political organization of world capitalism" (Robinson 2023:231). Some scholars explain the current moment as one moving from unipolar globalism (established over 500 years of Western imperialism, justified through Eurocentric rationalism, and since the end of the Cold War explicitly led by the United States) toward global multipolarity and a recentering of global power toward regional alliances such as the BRICS countries (Brazil, Russia, India, China, and South Africa) (Mignolo 2023).

William Robinson, in his compelling book *The Global Police State*, describes the global political economy as "out-of-control" (Robinson 2020:6). As he explains, the destabilization of the global political economy is both the cause and the consequence of massive economic inequalities, in turn creating the conditions in which strongman autocrats appear attractive to so many people. And once in power, antidemocratic leaders (and the capitalist elites that bankroll their political careers) are deeply concerned about minimizing further disruptions to the global economy. Robinson argues that as many millions of poor and oppressed people take to the streets to demonstrate against social and political injustice and the lack of jobs and opportunities, the transnational capitalist class is forced "to impose increasingly coercive and repressive forms of rule" (Robinson 2020:5). New kinds of policing and social control then emerge, including mass incarceration, unregulated immigrant deportation centers, criminalization of poor and working classes, new systems of digital and technological surveillance, and new forms of capital-making warfare (Robinson 2020:3). As discussed in chapter 5, an escalation of anti-protest laws around the world has furthered these strategies of control as antidemocratic leaders try to stop people from assembling on the streets and protesting oppressive state policies.

I argue that the global assault on higher education and attacks on scholars and students should be understood in this wider context of "policing logics" that reflect global economic destabilization and realignments of political power. Since the 2000s in the United States, attacks on education and the "policing" of students predominantly occurred at the high school level in working-class and racially discriminated neighborhoods. This can be understood as an enduring legacy of Jim Crow segregation and the creation of a school-to-prison pipeline (Alexander 2012; Black 2016). Today, we are witnessing attacks on higher education that includes elite universities—both public and private—such as the University of Michigan, University of California, Harvard, MIT, and Columbia. Similar attacks on elite institutions and their relatively economically and racially privileged intellectual communities are happening around the world. In policing the ability of scholars to think, study and teach about power and political and economic oppression, these attacks in effect target entire populations. As Robinson reminds us, "Transnational capital has invaded the university and the educational system in every sense, from converting education into a for-profit activity and commissioning and appropriating research (often publicly funded) while simultaneously generating a major new source of financial speculation through student loans" (Robinson 2016:13). This context explains why antidemocratic governments are using heavy-handed policing to quell critical research and student protests that have erupted across campuses around the world, particularly in response to the Israel–Hamas war. In short, universities and colleges are being explicitly weaponized to serve authoritarian and corporate interests at both national and international levels.

For example, the prestigious Central European University came under aggressive attack by Hungary's authoritarian prime minister Viktor Orbán and was forced to move to Vienna in 2018 (Corbett and Gordon 2018). Relatedly, in Nicaragua under the dictatorship of President Daniel Ortega, six universities were forced to close; when they reopened, they had been entirely restaffed with scholars and administrators chosen by the government. In Brazil, the former authoritarian leader Jair Bolsonaro declared a ban on Paulo Freire's book *The Pedagogy of the Oppressed* and prosecuted any scholar referring to his critical writings (Knijnik 2021). In India, led by the far-right Hindu supremacist prime minister Narendra Modi, authorities unjustly detained and prosecuted scholars as "criminals" under anti-terrorism laws. And in Peru in early 2023, police raided the Universidad Nacional Mayor de San Marcos in Lima (the oldest university in the Americas), violently forcing students from their dormitories as part of a general attack on universities and a police crackdown on demonstrations against the far-right government. As noted by Salvador Herencia-Carrasco, a leading member of the Coalition for Academic Freedom in the Americas (CAFA), if this attack could happen in the presence of international journalists, one can only imagine what happens in rural universities out of sight of media attention.[23]

Controlling Curricula and Banning Books

Back in the United States, Republican governor DeSantis emulated overseas practices in Florida by essentially turning public education into a political arm of his government. DeSantis introduced a wave of legislation and regulatory controls aimed at limiting academic freedom and the ability of faculty to teach their own materials. Republican lawmakers and governors, along with many trustee boards stacked with political appointees, have instituted laws dismantling tenure, imposing political loyalty oaths, cutting university ties to accrediting organizations, defunding university projects, and seeking control over faculty hiring and firing. Book bans have also been widely imposed, censoring curricula in higher education as well as in secondary and primary schools. According to the American Library Association, the number of requests to ban books is the highest it has ever been, with attempts to censor 4,240 titles in 2023, a 65 per cent increase over the 2,571 titles targeted the year before. This increase reflects an unprecedented surge in book ban requests, which in the previous two decades saw an average of only 273 requests a year.[24] Revealingly, many of the books were about or were authored by people of color and LGBTQ+ individuals. Deborah Caldwell-Stone, director of the American Library Association's Office for Intellectual Freedom, said, "These attacks on our freedom to read should trouble every person who values liberty and our constitutional rights. To allow a group of people or any individual, no matter how powerful or loud, to become the decision-maker about what books we can read or whether libraries exist, is to place all of our rights and liberties in jeopardy."[25]

The seeming national crisis over books and what to think is driven by the far-right's intentional manufacturing of a moral panic. This explains DeSantis's attacks on public education and efforts to fuel mistrust about critical race theory (CRT) and "woke" faculty who are supposedly teaching students to be unpatriotic and hate White people. These strategies echo what Stuart Hall and colleagues famously analyzed in their book *Policing the Crisis* (1978), which examined the manufactured "moral panic" about supposedly "violent" and "lawless" Black youth in Britain in the 1970s. Led by Margaret Thatcher, leader of the conservative Tory party, this panic promoted an ideological "authoritarian consensus" on repressive policing practices targeting the working classes (Hall et al. 1978).

Today's manufactured moral panic about supposedly "socialist" and "liberal" professors and teachers has been very effective, especially in Republican-led states. A highly controversial example of DeSantis's attack on higher education occurred in January 2023. He overhauled the New College of Florida, known for its progressive curriculum and openness toward LGBTQ+ students, removing "six of the college's 13 trustees, replacing them with allies holding strongly conservative views. The new board then forced out the college's president, a career educator, and named Mr. DeSantis's former education commissioner, a career politician, as her replacement." Florida also introduced two laws, commonly called the "Stop Woke Act" and "Don't Say Gay Act," that prohibit classroom discussion about racism in US history as well as instruction related to sexual orientation or gender identity. As the school year began at New College in fall 2023, students were told that the gender studies department had been abolished and replaced with a new focus on finance and sports psychology—areas of study that are typically profiled as masculine. Moreover, more than a third of the faculty did not return to teach on the campus. Notes journalist Michelle Goldberg, "The dismantling of gender studies is striking because of how closely it follows a playbook for the ideological transformation of higher education pioneered in Hungary, which banned gender studies in 2018."[26]

Disturbingly, the argument used by state lawyers in defense of the "Stop Woke Act" is that college curriculum and instruction are "government speech" and not the speech of teachers, who are theoretically protected under the principles of academic freedom. These two laws have become the model for other Republican states with respect to implementing "educational gag orders." According to a report by the free expression group PEN America, titled *America's Censored Classrooms*, 36 US states introduced 137 gag order measures in 2022, all but one of them filed by Republican legislators (Johnson

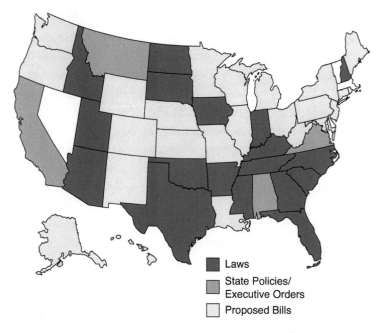

Figure 4. Educational gag orders in the United States, January 1, 2021–November 1, 2023. Reproduced with permission from PEN America. "America's Censored Classrooms 2023." https://pen.org/wp-content/uploads/2023/11/7-Educational-gag-orders-2023.png.

2022). Republican lawmakers introduced another 84 bills across the country by mid-2023 (figure 4). As noted by analysts at PEN America: "The early returns from the 2023 legislative sessions suggest that lawmakers' fervor to censor and ban content from educational institutions has not abated. Far from it. They have outdone one another in a race to the bottom, finding new, more extreme, and more conspiratorial ways to impose censorious government dictates on teaching and learning."[27]

Educators and students have put up widespread resistance to the "Stop Woke Act," resulting in it being put under a temporary injunction in March 2023. Legal challenges have also been mounted against anti-CRT laws. Despite these legal roadblocks, there is grave concern about the future of academic freedom in extremist Republican-led states. Commenting on events in Florida, Irene Mulvey, then president of the American Association of University Professors (AAUP), wrote that Florida's claim that curriculum should be considered "government speech" was wrong and that "government-mandated curriculum in higher education has no place in a democracy."[28] Also commenting on Florida, David Robinson, executive director of the Canadian Association of University Teachers (CAUT), wrote:

> It might be tempting for us in Canada to dismiss all of this as just another example of the messy and polarizing culture war waging in the US. But that would be a mistake. We are not entirely immune from the political assault on higher education we are seeing in Florida. While not as extreme, we have nevertheless witnessed an increasing tendency of our governments to meddle in the internal affairs of institutions.... So far, the students and academic staff in Florida have led the fight-back against the attacks on higher education. Administrators have either acquiesced or remained complicitly silent. There's an important lesson here for academics in Canada. When push comes to shove, we must be prepared to take the lead in defending the integrity of our institutions and of our work.[29]

Concluding Comments

It's about time for the wider public to appreciate what extremist leaders around the world already know—that attacking universities furthers their oppressive agendas and radical rule. The global lean toward antidemocracy is why protecting academic freedom is essential, even for those people who for various reasons can't or don't want to go to college. Academic freedom enables scholars to challenge powerful politicians and share new knowledge within societies and beyond the confines of national borders. Specifically, academic freedom enables people to learn from one another and to share new insights and understanding in the common interest of all societies, such as research on how to mitigate the accelerating climate crisis. Scholars who shine a light on how power operates in society enable students and the wider society to question antidemocratic state authority, push back against oppression, reclaim political accountability, and demand that governments rule for the majority and not the corrupt, elite few. That is precisely why far-right leaders want to control scholars and reduce university autonomy over their campus communities. As Ronald Daniels, president of Johns Hopkins University, noted, universities and colleges are targeted by far-right politicians because "these institutions are more intimately implicated in the enterprise of building and fostering liberal democracy than is typically acknowledged" (Daniels 2021:4).

In a material sense, attacks on academic freedom are both a cause and consequence of the global lean toward authoritarianism. Although typically overlooked, the assault on academic freedom joins other current crises not contained by national borders, such as climate degradation, mass migrations, pandemics, nuclearization, and transnational structural racism. In short, the assault on academic freedoms—including attacks on the right to question, the right to think independently, and the right to challenge the status quo—is one of the most pressing global challenges of our times.

Chapter Two

The Politics of Knowledge Production

Despite some people's claims that universities are politically neutral and so produce objective knowledge, the reality is that universities and colleges are and always have been political institutions—at least in the Euro-American academy. This is true in several ways:

- Universities are political because they are institutions of privilege and power (Mettler 2014; Stein 2022). Today in the United States, despite progress in terms of diversifying student bodies and to a lesser degree faculty demographics, elite universities remain largely accessible only to those from higher socioeconomic classes and backgrounds. Less elite four-year colleges and two-year community colleges have greater demographic and socioeconomic diversity. Still, just over half of all students attending college and graduate school in 2023 were middle-class and White.[1]

- Universities are political in that, particularly in colonial settings, they have historically been institutions of oppression over peoples that were colonized and marginalized, often forcing them to think and speak in the language of their oppressor (Ngũgĩ 1986; Spivak 1988; Wilder 2014). Today, legacies of colonialism and imperialism are deeply embedded within universities in the global north that produce, evaluate, disseminate, and dominate much of the knowledge production in the global south, in what the sociologist Raewyn Connell calls "the global economy of knowledge" (Connell 2019; Keim et al. 2014; Kiwan 2023).

- Universities are political in the sense that almost all universities—both public and private—receive some funding from the state and are functionally dependent on governments (and increasingly on wealthy donors and corporate sponsors) for their continuing survival.

- Within universities, there are always political struggles over access to funding and control of resources. These internal distributions determine what kind of knowledge is produced, which, in turn, has political implications beyond the university context. In the United States, the most privileged knowledge typically emerges out of science, technology, engineering, and mathematics (STEM) research and is heavily racialized (White), gendered (male), and status oriented (wealthiest student body).

In sum, universities are political institutions because politics determines what gets studied, who gets to do the study, who learns from those studies, and who gets to shape the social and political landscape beyond the university for future generations. The knowledge universities produce—be it in philosophy, medicine, history, physics, or media studies—is always political, even if scholars themselves do not think of their work in that way.

Many educators and commentators deny that universities are political institutions and argue that the university's primary function is to promote and disseminate new knowledge. The University of Chicago's Kalven Report (1967) appears to uphold this position, arguing that the university should remain neutral on political and social controversies. Although the report does not say that universities should never take a collective stand on a public issue, that interpretation is widely endorsed and has become a model for many universities and colleges. As stated in an American Association of University Professors document titled "Polarizing Times Demand Robust Academic Freedom," published in November 2023, however, the "academic community's central mission of education, research, and service [is] to the broader society and to the public good." In other words, universities don't just produce knowledge as an objective or apolitical enterprise. This is important because it means, as the AAUP statement goes on to say, that while "college and university leaders have no obligation to speak out on the most controversial issues of the day," it is "their duty is to protect the academic freedom, free speech, and associational rights of faculty and students to speak on all topics of public or political interest without fear of intimidation, retaliation, or punishment."[2] This means that a university president *does have an obligation* to speak publicly against external political interference in matters that typically are left for universities to decide on their own, such as what goes into course curricula; how faculty are hired, promoted, and fired; what research is given funding priority, and so on. These issues are appropriate for decisions by faculty-led shared governance committees—*not* boards of politically appointed trustees, wealthy donors dictating how their money is spent, or lobbyist groups working on behalf of political organizations, foundations, or corporate sectors. Against these inappropriate external influences, university leaders should be speaking out and working together as a united front against escalating political bullying and interference in campus life. Unfortunately, due to a range of factors including cowardice and inexperience, in practice this rarely happens.

Today, with a general absence of admirable university leadership, growing numbers of scholars and students are speaking out because they find that innovative and critical thinking has now been labeled—according to the far right—"divisive" and focused on "political and social controversies." Putting this differently, exploring and teaching evidence-based science and history are no longer associated with valid knowledge and teaching by the MAGA-led Republican Party. In the upside-down thinking of many conservatives, educating students about empirical facts (on enslavement, colonialism, climate crisis, evolution, reproduction, terrorism, nuclear warfare) is deemed an ideology of indoctrination and evidence of classroom bias. Facts—or more correctly discussions, debates, and reflections on the historical and contemporary significance of facts—have become weaponized in the ongoing cultural wars.

Under antidemocratic regimes, knowledge production is typically regarded by those in power as potentially politically risky, revolutionary, and dangerous to the status quo. Knowledge—be it new knowledge or old knowledge newly revealed—is carefully monitored, censored, and possibly even criminalized and prohibited. The goal is to create an unchallenged orthodoxy of ideas that coincide with those held by political leaders and to indoctrinate present and future generations with them. Jonathan Becker, vice-chancellor of the Open Society University Network, states that "the sad truth is that authoritarians are targeting higher education around the globe, be it in Russia or Hungary, the Philippines or Afghanistan, or now the United States. Leaders of these countries want a compliant and not an engaged citizenry. They see professors as hostile and students as a potential source of idealistic and, thus, fearless opposition." Becker goes on to say that this helps explain the economic arguments used to dismantle humanities and social science learning: "Taken together, the authoritarian assault on academic freedom and neoliberal attacks on 'impractical' subjects means that much of the academe is under assault, and the link between education and informed citizenship is discarded in the hope of forming a compliant population."[3]

In contrast, under democratic political regimes, knowledge production is based on evidence and intellectual expertise. Sometimes this process can be messy, with differences of opinion about how to interpret new evidence often creating arguments between scholars and schools of thought. And this is in fact the point—that ideas are constantly revised and rethought among highly trained experts in light of scientific breakthroughs, revelation of new evidence, and critical advances in theory and methods. In ideal conditions, academic freedom fosters engaged learning, enabling students and scholars to ask probing questions, learn from different perspectives and worldviews, question taken-for-granted assumptions, challenge bias and racism, and voice and disseminate their opinions in the public arena. Academic freedom also facilitates collaboration between scholars both nationally and transnationally (Kiwan 2023). Collaborative critical thinking, in turn, may promote new questions and ideas about social, political, and economic solutions to pressing issues and problems. Many scholars—in medicine, sociology, engineering, religious studies, and other fields—reflect deeply about their subject matter and how their work may improve society's functioning and create greater well-being for everyone.

Differences in attitudes about higher education on the part of democratic and antidemocratic regimes raise an important question. As political conflict escalates over what scholars can research, we should be asking, What is being overlooked or silenced in terms of knowledge production? It becomes clear that without the protections of academic freedom, scholars are prevented from developing new knowledge and sharing it with students and a wider public who have a right to know and debate about what experts think. The public, whose taxes help support universities, should be informed of advances in fields such as earth sciences, history, genetics, astrophysics, and literature. They should be aware that tobacco causes lung cancer, fluorocarbons create a hole in the ozone layer, human–animal interactions may result in pandemics, and modern-day sweatshops operate like plantation economies. The public also has a right to know of scientific breakthroughs such as new vaccines, new cures for cancer, new green energy production, new ways of producing food, and so on. And the public should know about past injustices and silenced histories that scholars can make meaningful as explanatory frameworks for today's ongoing social problems. Ideally, scholars should be funded and protected by the state, and in return, the state and citizens should benefit in all sorts of ways from their knowledge production.

Far-right politicians don't care about new knowledge producing social benefits for everyone. What they mostly fear is that academic freedom's pursuit of evidence-based facts will challenge their authority to govern. As Shalini Randeria—rector (university president) of the Central European University, who was forced to move from Budapest to Austria under Hungary's authoritarian regime—argues, "The backbone of a democracy is dissent, is argument, is critical thought. It's diversity, pluralism. If you want to stifle both pluralism and dissent, then you attack universities. As is the case with most of these authoritarian governments, if your idea is that higher education is about indoctrination and not education, then an autonomous university is a real thorn in your flesh."[4]

Antidemocratic leaders particularly fear that scholars will disseminate their evidence-based knowledge to the wider public, in turn inciting widespread political activism and opposition. This is the reason the authoritarian Chinese government under President Xi Jinping violently suppressed prodemocracy student groups in Hong Kong throughout 2019 and 2020. These groups were protesting the imposition of the National Security Law, which reduced people's civil and political rights. The protests were the largest ever seen in Hong Kong and threatened to spill over into the Chinese mainland. Violent conflict occurred over months and included police storming the Chinese University and Polytechnic University in November 2019. It is estimated that more than 10,000 people were arrested and that more than 4,000 of these were students, with 1,754 of them being under the age of 18. The protests effectively heralded the end of democracy and academic freedom in Hong Kong, creating a chilling effect on scholars and students in China and beyond to its diasporic communities in countries such as Britain, Canada, Sweden, Australia, and the United States (Thornton 2023).

Chinese oppression of students was dramatically underscored by the demolition of a sculpture commemorating democracy on the University of Hong Kong campus (figure 5). The 26-foot (8-meter) -tall *Pillar of Shame*, which depicted 50 torn and twisted bodies piled on top of one another, was made by Danish sculptor Jens Galschiot to memorialize the many lives lost during the bloody military crackdown on prodemocracy protesters in Beijing's Tiananmen Square on June 4, 1989. The sculpture had been at the university since 1997, the year China resumed control of Hong Kong when British colonial rule expired. At the time, China was keen to show the rest of the world that it supported democracy. Over the decades, however, China has gone from embracing democracy to criminalizing and outlawing it. And the Tiananmen Square massacre of 1989 remains a banned topic in China. In 2021, in a symbolic gesture, the *Pillar of Shame* sculpture was

Figure 5. Students cleaning *Pillar of Shame* by Danish sculptor Jens Galschiot. The sculpture was subsequently removed from the University of Hong Kong in 2021 in response to pro-democracy student demonstrations. Image by Studio Incendo. Wikimedia Commons. Licensed under the Creative Commons Attribution 2.0 Generic license. https://creativecommons.org/licenses/by/3.0/deed.en/.

removed by the Chinese government, despite protests by students and human rights activists. More recently in 2023, the Chinese University of Hong Kong fired the historian Rowena He after she published her book *Tiananmen Exiles: Voices of the Struggle for Democracy in China*. Chinese newspapers accused the author of using "academic freedom as an umbrella term to smear China and Hong Kong" and using "history as a political weapon to brainwash students."[5]

Academic Freedom and Human Rights

As I argued in the introduction, defending academic freedom should be understood as an ethical political practice that promotes social responsibility (Scott 1996). Academic freedom fosters independent thinking and liberation from mind control, enabling scholars and students to question what the state tells them and, if necessary, protest growing antidemocratic conditions. Academic freedom also enables scholars and students to communicate why they are protesting to others beyond the academy and helps educate the wider public. As the Hong Kong case illustrates, defending academic freedom is deeply connected to defending people's political rights—not as individuals but as members of just and diverse societies. These rights include the right to vote, receive a fair wage, have access to health care, drink clean water, protest corruption, and, ultimately, to live freely, whoever and wherever you are in the world.

In contrast to uprisings by students and faculty seeking to protect academic freedom in Hong Kong, Brazil, India, Hungary, and many other places around the world, the public response in the United States to attacks on higher education is largely indifference. While a few people working within universities—particularly faculty and students working in the humanities and social sciences—may be alarmed, most faculty are not. Certainly, with the ongoing crisis over the Israel–Hamas conflict, there was growing concern over what constitutes academic speech among some circles of scholars, students, administrators, and donors. This interest was heightened during the well-publicized hearing by Congress's House Committee on Education and Workforce, when representatives questioned university presidents from Harvard, the Massachusetts Institute of Technology (MIT), and the University of Pennsylvania (Penn) on December 5, 2023.[6] And concern was heightened still further by the more than 3,000 student protests and encampments supporting peace in Palestine that erupted on campuses across the country and around the world throughout 2024.

Beyond the world of academia, however, there is a general lack of public interest in political interference into university governance, research, and teaching. At the primary and high school levels, a good number of parents, librarians, board members, and school administrators have been very agitated by the massive Republican-led wave of book banning in primary and secondary schools, particularly of literature that engages race and LGBTQ+ issues. But when it comes to higher education, there is an overwhelming apathy among the public about what goes on in universities and colleges. Overall, prevailing anti-intellectualism has deadened people's imagination and ability to connect higher education with the defense of political and civil rights. As Henry Giroux reminds us, "The slow death of public and higher education does not augur well for democracy. Americans live in a historical moment that disavows critical thinking. Rather than being an object of critique, ignorance has become an organizing principle of politics, civil culture, and society itself" (Giroux 2018:169).

Against this gloomy backdrop of anti-intellectualism, I don't anticipate a great awakening among far-right extremists and their core supporters about the value of higher education.[7] But beyond the minority populist cult of Donald Trump and the MAGA Republican movement, for many millions of everyday people trying to understand what is really going on in society, it is vital to provide a clear argument about what academic freedom is and why it is so important. The public should know that the future of higher education is drastically changing. And the public should be reminded that universities must be defended and valued as vital spaces of public debate and places to think critically about the world and people's relationship to one another. Putting this differently, the protection of academic freedom is essential for everyone who wants to live in a just and fair society, even if you don't have a college background or your kids don't intend to go to college. This principle applies to those living in the United States as much as to those living in the Philippines, China, India, Hungary, Indonesia, Canada, Spain, Britain, South Africa, and Mexico.

Who Defines Academic Freedom?

As noted in the introduction, the concept of academic freedom—what some people call the freedom to think or freedom to learn—differs across countries and among scholarly communities that reflect the societies in which they work and teach. Henry Reichman argues in his book *Understanding Academic Freedom* (2021) that the meaning of academic freedom is complicated in practice and often depends on specific institutional, legal, and social circumstances. In theory, however, academic freedom is a simple idea. It is not reducible to a civil right like the freedom of expression, which in the United States is protected under the Constitution. Rather, academic freedom is more encompassing, in that it belongs to the whole academic profession to pursue inquiry and teach freely—"it functions ultimately as the collective freedom of the scholarly community to govern itself in the interest of serving the common good in a democratic society" (Reichman 2021:4).

Collective academic freedom includes the individual scholar's freedom to inquire, teach, and publish *and* institutional autonomy to protect that freedom. This definition was endorsed by the American Association of University Professors, first in 1915 and then again in its revised statement in 1940. Notably, a number of scholars involved in the 1940 statement had fled Hitler's attacks on universities in Nazi Germany to take up residency in the United States, including Albert Einstein, who joined the AAUP in 1935. As argued by Eva Cherniavsky, professor of American studies, the AAUP's original statement drew its inspiration from the nineteenth-century education reforms at the Humboldt University of Berlin (Cherniavsky 2021). Educators widely embraced the Humboldtian ideal of the university as advancing knowledge about the past and present (rather than simply providing training for specific jobs). Humboldt's concern to broadly educate the next generation to be engaged citizens and make well-informed and ethical decisions is a pedagogical model often associated with the liberal arts, but it exists in various formulations in many parts of the world.

Academic freedom as a collective professional right necessarily contains limits. A scholar cannot just teach or declare an opinion (i.e., "the world is flat"; "the moon is square"; "men are smarter than women"). Rather, research and teaching are regulated through professional standards and disciplinary norms that shape the university as a self-regulating scholarly community, in turn determining the limits of academic freedom. In other words, for the principle of academic freedom to apply, scholarly activities must be considered intellectually valid and fact-based by credentialed experts in the field in which a scholar works. This sounds simple, but in practice it is not always an easy formula to apply. Sometimes disciplinary norms may constrain critical thinking or create discriminatory environments for nonconforming scholars who are challenging established "knowledge" that may be bigoted or racist (Gabbert 2014; Saloojee 2014). Sometimes the autonomy of an academic community is conflated with a university's institutional autonomy, granting too much power to administrators to influence what gets taught and researched (Rabban 2014; Findlay 2014). Sometimes religious views inhibit academic freedom in faith-based colleges and universities (Baker 2014).

Joan Wallach Scott acknowledges in her excellent book *Knowledge, Power and Academic Freedom* (2019) that academic freedom is an aspirational concept that never can be fully implemented. It is universal as an ideal but assumes meaning only within specific historical circumstances and relations of power (Scott 2019:17). While academic freedom can be highly politicized, Scott argues that it is always an ethical practice that rests on two assumptions: (1) higher education produces public goods that benefit the wider society, and (2) the production of academic knowledge can happen only when scholars function as a self-regulating body that follows its own professional and intellectual norms (Scott 2019:7).

Scott's hesitation to precisely define academic freedom highlights that it is an organic and evolving concept, both dynamic in responding to changing political circumstances and fragile in its reliance on power relations between individuals, university institutions, and the state. This does not mean, however, that it is impossible to communicate the importance of academic freedom. On the contrary, if scholars want to continue to enjoy intellectual independence, they must step up and be prepared to define it in terms that make sense to themselves as well as to the wider public. Scholars must also be vigilant in nurturing the ethical principles of academic freedom that foster inclusion and equality and be ready to defend intellectual independence from political attack. Moreover, scholars in the global north need to learn from colonial histories of intellectual oppression and reflect on contemporary crackdowns facing universities in the global south. That what can happen over "there" can also happen "here" is a lesson that should never be forgotten. In short, all stakeholders in the educational process at all levels, including teachers, researchers, students, librarians, administrators, and wider publics, need to be involved in crafting a shared meaning of academic freedom. The privileged complacency that allows scholars to avoid thinking about academic freedom or making any attempt to define it—which is the norm in the Euro-American academy—is no longer acceptable.

Responsibility, Truth, Independence

Although the current moment presents unique challenges, there are lessons to be learned from past attacks on academic freedom. One of the most obvious historical examples that echoes today's rise of antidemocracy is the plight of scholars and universities under the catastrophic impacts of Nazi Germany as well as aligned fascist regimes in Spain and Italy in the 1920s and 1930s.

Albert Einstein was forced to flee Germany in 1933 to spend the rest of his life in the United States. In 1935, he joined the AAUP and was involved in revising its 1940 statement, which helped shape the concept of academic freedom that has largely prevailed in the United States ever since. Albert Einstein's story is a lesson in bravery, highlighting that academic freedom, perhaps above all else, is an ethical practice of social responsibility to pursue evidence-based facts about the world for the common good of society and its future generations (Einstein's story is also a lesson in the cowardice and racism of the American academy in the twentieth century). In pursuing his scientific theories, Einstein was forced to move numerous times to flee political interference in his groundbreaking research. Between 1915 and 1928, as director of the Kaiser Wilhelm Institute for Physics in Berlin, Einstein regularly lectured at Humboldt University and enjoyed an intellectual culture imbued with the Humboldtian concept of academic freedom.

While Einstein was traveling in the United States and spending time as a visitor at California Institute of Technology in 1933, Adolf Hitler came to power as chancellor of Germany. Within weeks, Hitler promulgated laws that excluded

Jews, socialists, and communists from holding positions at universities. Einstein's house in Berlin was raided, his bank account seized, and a bounty put on his head (Sayen 1985:17). Book banning and burnings of books written by Jewish and liberal authors also began, organized by radicalized students co-opted by Hitler youth programs and aided by university scholars who did not care, or dare, to protest (Neiman 2019). These events began a massive exodus of intellectuals and university staff from Germany to Britain, France, and the United States (Newman 2020) (figure 6).

Figure 6. On May 10, 1933, about 70,000 people gathered at the Opernplatz in Berlin, in front of Humboldt University. Students carried more than 20,000 books to the public square to be burned, including works by famous German authors. Photo by Georg Pahl. Image provided by Deutsches Bundesarchiv. Wikimedia Commons. Licensed under the Creative Commons Attribution-Share Alike 3.0 Germany license. https://creativecommons.org/licenses/by/3.0/deed.en.

Greatly distressed by the attack on higher education, Einstein's old friend, the leading German scientist Max Planck, approached Hitler regarding the breakup of the German scientific community. Hitler rebuffed Planck's concerns, declaring that he did not care. Despite this clear political message and the widespread crackdown on universities, however, Planck continued living and working in Germany. At that point, Einstein realized that many of his colleagues would ultimately buckle to the dictator and be forced to pursue the eugenically based Nazi science Hitler promoted (Sayen 1985). As a Jew and outspoken critic of Hitler, Einstein decided not to return to Germany and, after a short period in Belgium, took up a position at the Institute for Advanced Study in Princeton and became a US citizen.

In 1939, the year World War II broke out, Einstein informed US President Franklin D. Roosevelt in a letter about the potential of a new fission process that pointed to the production of the atomic bomb. Einstein was very concerned that Germany was intent on building nuclear weapons and that Hitler would not hesitate to inflict mass killings. Einstein was a self-declared pacifist and promoter of world peace. By drawing attention to Germany's nuclear program, however, he may have inadvertently pushed the United States to develop its own nuclear weaponry under the Manhattan Project.[8] Suspected of communist sympathies, Einstein was investigated by Republican Senator Joseph McCarthy; Einstein's phone was tapped and his mail opened (Jerome 2004; Jerome and Taylor 2005). As noted by historian Jamie Sayen, McCarthyism initially targeted scholars who were supposedly able to harm US interests, such as "atomic scientists and foreign policy specialists." One such scholar was J. Robert Oppenheimer, the so-called father of the atomic bomb, who was investigated for being a security risk in 1954. Sayen goes on to note that the label "communist" was quickly conflated "to mean anyone whose beliefs and behavior did not rigidly conform to 'Americanism.' Those who did not conform—individuals, scholars, public intellectuals, foreigners, political nonconformists—saw their constitutional guarantees of freedom, justice, and equality under the law suspended" (Sayen 1985:269). Adds Charisse Burden-Stelly in her remarkable book *Black Scare/Red Scare: Theorizing Capitalist Racism in the United States* (2023), the national crackdown on communists during the McCarthy era cannot be disentangled from national racism against Blacks. These connected targets of oppression were epitomized by people like W. E. B. Du Bois who, as a leading African American founder and member of the NAACP, worked with international anticapitalist movements such as the Industrial Workers of the World and eventually became a member of the Communist Party himself (Burden-Stelly 2023; see also Darian-Smith 2012).

Einstein came under McCarthy's scrutiny in part because he was suspected of communism and in part because he was a foreign Jewish physicist. Einstein's social views, however, also put him at odds with mainstream American values. Einstein was a profoundly ethical man and felt it his responsibility to openly use his intellectual fame to protest the criminalizing of homosexuality. Even more controversial were his public statements against racism and discrimination of African Americans. Einstein's views on this subject were expressed in earlier correspondence with W. E. B. Du Bois, who invited him to contribute to the NAACP's magazine *The Crisis* in 1931; Einstein responded with a short essay in German that Du Bois translated and published (Jerome and Taylor 2005:135–137).[9] Einstein was aware of the silencing of Black history and especially the cover-up of slavery within the US academy. In a lecture he gave in 1946 at Lincoln University, an HBCU and the

Figure 7. Albert Einstein teaching a physics class at Lincoln University, a historically Black university, in Pennsylvania in 1946. Reproduced with permission from the Temple University Libraries. John W. Mosley Photograph Collection, Charles L. Blockson Afro-American Collection.

first school in the United States to grant college degrees to African Americans, he denounced racial segregation, declaring, "The separation of the races is not a disease of colored people. It is a disease of white people. I do not intend to be quiet about it" (Jerome 2004) (figure 7).

For his controversial views, Einstein was interrogated by the McCarthy-led Permanent Subcommittee on Investigations of the Senate Committee on Government Operations. In a document recorded in the early 1950s, Einstein was asked questions on the value of academic freedom and the role of the intellectual in a democratic society. Because his answers are remarkably relevant today, they justify repeating.

What is the essential nature of academic freedom and why is it necessary for the pursuit of truth?

EINSTEIN: By academic freedom I understand the right to search for truth and to publish and teach what one holds to be true. This right implies also a duty: one must not conceal any part of what one has recognized to be true. It is evident that any restriction of academic freedom acts in such a way as to hamper the dissemination of knowledge among people and thereby impedes rational judgment and action.

What threats to academic freedom do you see at this time?

EINSTEIN: The threat to academic freedom in our time must be seen in the fact that, because of the alleged external danger to our country, freedom of teaching, mutual exchange of opinions and freedom of press and other media of communication are encroached upon or obstructed. This is done by creating a situation in which people feel their economic positions endangered. Consequently, more and more people avoid expressing their opinion freely, even in their private social life. This is a state of affairs which a democratic government cannot survive in the long run.

What in your opinion are the special obligations of an intellectual in a democratic society?

EINSTEIN: In principle, everybody is equally involved in defending the constitutional rights. The "intellectuals" in the widest sense of the word are, however, in a special position since they have, thanks to their special training, a particular strong influence on the formation of public opinion. This is the reason why those who are about to lead us toward an authoritarian government are particularly concerned with intimidating and muzzling that group. It is therefore, in the present situation, especially important for the intellectuals to do their duty. I see this duty in refusing to cooperate in any undertaking that violates the constitutional rights of the individual.[10]

It should give everyone pause that Einstein, who won the Nobel Prize in 1921 and enjoyed enormous fame as one of the world's greatest physicists, could then be subject to state censorship and violence under the Nazi regime and forced to flee. If he had stayed with his scientific colleagues in Germany, he undoubtedly would have been imprisoned and possibly sent to a concentration camp. Perhaps even more remarkable, however, is that seeking refuge in the United States had its own costs and challenges. In this supposedly "free" country, he wasn't persecuted so much for being a Jew, though there were many laws at the time limiting universities from hiring Jewish scholars (Leff 2019).[11] Rather, Einstein was subjected to political surveillance over his concern for racial equality, constitutional rights, anti-imperialism, and pacifism. His opinions were deemed potentially "traitorous" by Joseph McCarthy and the wider Republican Party. In our current post-truth age, when antidemocratic leaders openly denounce science and are unapologetically racist, homophobic, and sexist, Einstein's call to search for facts and disseminate truths about the past and present—despite risks of physical violence—is a powerful reminder of what is at stake in attacks on academic freedom.

Certainly, there are significant differences between the current moment and earlier periods of fascism and crackdowns on scholarly communities in the middle decades of the twentieth-century. As mentioned in chapter 1, the most obvious difference is how today's social media has created a completely new way to transfer extreme ideology and propaganda to millions of people—a mode of communication not imaginable only a few decades ago. This change has helped widen the concept of fascism beyond formal party politics and national regimes to encompass what Boaventura de Sousa Santos calls "societal fascism" (Santos 2001:186). Notably, societal fascism categorizes some human lives as more worthy than others, evoking other political theorists writing about "economies of death" that are intimately tied to racialized hierarchies of human value but not necessarily a formalized political ideology (Lopez and Gillespie 2015:179; Butler 2004; Mbembe 2019; Darian-Smith 2021).

Still, there are similarities between the past and more recent attacks on academic freedom, including how scholars should respond to far-right political interference in university education. Echoing Einstein, Noam Chomsky, amid the heady politics of the 1960s (described further in chapter 4), described "the responsibility of intellectuals to speak the truth and to expose lies." According to Chomsky:

> Intellectuals are in a position to expose the lies of governments, to analyze actions according to their causes and motives and often hidden intentions. In the Western world, at least, they have the power that comes from political liberty, from access to information and freedom of expression. For a privileged minority, Western democracy provides the leisure, the facilities, and the training to seek the truth lying hidden behind the veil of distortion and misrepresentation, ideology and class interest, through which the events of current history are presented to us. The responsibilities of intellectuals, then, are much deeper than ... the 'responsibility of people,' given the unique privileges that intellectuals enjoy. (Chomsky 1967; see Allott et al. 2019)

In the context of current attacks on higher education, many scholarly communities take their unique responsibilities very seriously, despite conditions of oppression and terror (Özkirimli

2017). For example, students and faculty demonstrated enormous bravery in participating in extensive protests across Turkey since 2015 in response to President Recep Erdoğan's actions in criminalizing scholars, appointing his own university leaders, and dismantling Turkey's higher education sector. These academic protests illustrate the collective strength needed from those inside and outside the university to fight back and resist repression. Against attacks on Boğaziçi University in 2021, an international solidarity movement was formed, with 2,340 academics from 50 countries signing a joint statement demanding academic freedom and university autonomy. Ultimately, however, such efforts could not prevent Erdoğan from appointing new administrators and effectively gutting the university, forcing many scholars to flee (Özdemir et al. 2019; Vatansever 2018, 2020; Doğan and Selenica 2022). According to Dr. Zeynep Gambetti, a professor of political theory at Boğaziçi University from 2000 to 2019, we must "rethink the role of intellectuals in dark times. The ivory tower has collapsed. We can no longer claim to be outside the political field.... Given the material and structural conditions of post-truth, constituting a new regime of truth, one that is inclusive and collective, calls for the labor of commoning" (Gambetti 2022:186).

The sentiment of "commoning" suggests the need to rethink democracy to better engage with and resist the global lean toward authoritarianism. If we take commoning seriously, we will need to develop a new conceptualization of democratic principles that expands upon the possessive individualism of Western liberalism to create relational and collective practices of inclusivity, equity, and justice for everyone. As argued by Silvia Federici, scholar and cofounder of the International Feminist Collective, what is important in commoning is not the sharing of material wealth but the sharing itself and the bonds of solidarity that it helps foster. She goes on, "No common is possible unless we refuse to base our life and our reproduction on the suffering of others, unless we refuse to see ourselves as separate from them. Indeed, if commoning has any meaning, it must be the production of ourselves as a common subject" (Federici 2019:110).

Academic Freedom versus Free Speech

Today in the United States, the idea of academic freedom is frequently conflated with the freedom of speech or expression. Robert Post, a former dean of Yale Law School who was involved in drafting the University of California's academic freedom policy, emphasizes that academic freedom and free speech are two fundamentally different ideas, however. Academic freedom is a collective right held by professional faculty members, whereas freedom of speech is an individual right protected under the Constitution's First Amendment (along with freedom of the press and freedom of assembly). According to Post, "here's the basic difference between academic freedom and the First Amendment: First Amendment rights are individual, but academic freedom applies to a discipline, meaning a community of inquiry. Knowledge is produced by a community of inquiry, and therefore the right of the discipline is not to be judged by those outside the discipline. The most basic point about academic freedom is that I, as a professor, can only be judged by my peers" (Post 2016, see also 2009).

Stating this differently, the university should *not* be considered a marketplace of ideas where people peddle their opinions, with the most popular, and often the most unsophisticated, ideas winning the day. Many on the far-right appeal to this "marketplace" narrative, which was introduced by the Supreme Court in *Keyishian v. Board of Regents* in 1967. Today, it is widely used to justify allowing far-right Republicans and their allies onto campuses and granting student audiences. The "marketplace of ideas" narrative tries to create equivalence between speech based on factual and professional expertise and speech that is ideological or propagandist. The university is not the same as the public square, however, and not all speech on campus is protected under the banner of academic freedom. According to sociolegal scholar Adam Sitze, there is a big difference between "*the pursuit of truth*, on the one hand, and the *unfettered exchange of ideas*, on the other" (Sitze 2017:599). Sitze continues, "The truth of the doctrine of the marketplace of ideas is that it excludes any truth except the laws of the marketplace itself" (Sitze 2017:597). Moreover, Joan Scott reminds us, "we can respect the rights of free speech without having to respect the ideas being uttered" (Scott 2019:121).

As argued by historians Richard Amesbury and Catherine O'Donnell in their article "Dear Administrators: Enough with the Free Speech Rhetoric!," allowing the marketplace of ideas concept "concedes too much to right-wing agendas."[12] It's not surprising that statements about the need to defend the concept have been issued by conservative organizations such as the Foundation for Individual Rights (FIRE). Such statements sound reasonable in their defense of "intellectual diversity" but in fact undermine the highly trained expertise of faculty and reduce academic speech to personal opinion. As discussed further in chapter 5, the narrative of the marketplace of ideas is a "well-funded political strategy" pushed by an extensive far-right network of donors, think tanks, and academic, political, media and judicial organizations such as the Heritage Foundation and the Koch family foundations (Wilson and Kamola 2021:ix,130–132). It "opens the door for the loudest, brashest, whitest, wealthiest, and most provocative voices on campus to remain disproportionately empowered," whether because of the threat of a lawsuit by an individual or the fear of being charged under new gag-order legislation now present in all Republican-led states (Wilson and Kamola 2021:153).

The distinction between academic freedom and free speech is important but in practice often creates confusion among scholars, students, and university and college administrators. And this confusion can be deliberately amplified and exploited for political purposes. For instance, in the post-truth political landscape of the United States, Republicans, and the extremist groups they support, both attack the principle of academic freedom and, at the same time, use it to argue that their lies are equivalent to scholarly knowledge and worthy of protection under the banner of academic freedom. This has been an effective strategy for furthering disinformation, including the lie that the 2020 election was stolen. And it is how Pennsylvania State University got itself into the predicament of letting Gavin McInnes, founded of the White supremacist Proud Boys, give a public talk on campus in October 2022. University administrators condemned the racist and misogynist views of the speaker; however, they also said that the campus was required to host the Proud Boys on free speech grounds. At the last minute, the event was canceled due to threats of violence as Proud Boy supporters used pepper spray on student protesters. The conservative student group that organized the event, Uncensored America, said it was sad about the cancellation, stating disingenuously, "We wanted people from all different political viewpoints to have a fun, entertaining, and peaceful evening" (Chappell 2022).

There is also confusion about academic freedom and the First Amendment among progressive scholars, though, unlike the confusion sowed by conservative groups, it is not intentionally misleading. For example, Stacy Hawkins, vice dean of Rutgers Law School, in her defense of marginalized student rights incorrectly argued that academic freedom emanates from the principles of the US Constitution's First Amendment.[13] Another area of confusion is whether academic freedom should be limited when someone—usually a student—argues they are harmed by ideas. As commentators have argued, however, the issue of relative harm should not apply so long as the ideas are presented for valid educational reasons and the presentation is not denigrating or disrespectful in any way. Apart from diluting the significance of academic freedom as a site of intellectual exploration, this line of argument aligns with arguments made by far-right Republicans who object to scholars teaching about the contemporary legacies of American slavery and racism because it upsets White students.

Confusion over the meaning of academic freedom was evident when Macalester College in Minneapolis held an exhibition of Iranian American artist Taravat Talepasand's work in January 2023. According to a biographical statement at the Law Warschaw Gallery, where the exhibition was held, Talepasand's art explores cultural and political taboos particularly against women. In a series of images titled *Blasphemy*, a veiled woman in one picture lifts her hijab to reveal skimpy underwear. The point of the images was to critique Iran's oppressive government and call for women to have autonomy over their own bodies. Some Muslim students protested against the pictures as being offensive and blasphemous, which was precisely the point. Arjun Guneratne, professor of anthropology at Macalester College, argues:

> Pain is what Iranian women who remove their veils and head coverings feel when they are beaten. Pain is caused every day to women and men in Iran, who are shot by the police when they demonstrate in the streets. Pain is what Iranians feel when they

are raped and tortured in the regime's prisons. But when people at Macalester are offended by a graphite drawing that depicts a partially nude woman in a niqāb, what is being caused is not pain, but offense. . . . If the only free speech you are prepared to tolerate is the speech that doesn't offend you, then effectively you don't believe in free speech. That seems to be the administration's position, framed in the language of "pain" and "care" as the reason to deny or to limit speech.[14]

In response to a student petition, Macalester College briefly closed the exhibition but then reopened it with warnings about content and frosted glass on some of the gallery windows. According to scholars Amna Khalid and Jeffrey Snyder:

We see three problems with this approach. First, it signals to students that they have an emergency brake they can pull whenever they feel harmed. Second, it deals a blow to faculty confidence when it comes to teaching sensitive content. Who wants to court controversy and risk their professional reputation when colleges are so quick to hit the pause button if students feel offended or hurt? Finally, it evades the question of what to do when a campus controversy results in conflicting claims of harm—which, as harm-claims become ever more incentivized by administrators, will surely happen more and more.[15]

A related event occurred in March 2023, when Judge Kyle Duncan, a Trump appointee, went to speak at Stanford Law School as the guest of the far-right Stanford Federalist Society. There the judge was booed by progressive students for his position against voting rights, same-sex marriage, and transgender rights. In an event that seemed staged for media dissemination, with Duncan entering the room taking photos and taping the event on his phone, students howled down the speaker while Duncan in turn stirred up the crowd with name-calling and mockery. Ultimately, Duncan claimed to be the victim of students who refused to let him give his prepared speech. As legal commentator David Lat argued about the event, "Members of Stanford FedSoc are entitled to invite Judge Duncan to campus, but they are not entitled to have him be well-received or to have their decision to invite him go unquestioned."[16] Two days later, the dean of the law school, Jenny Martinez, in a joint letter with Stanford's president, Marc Tessier-Lavigne, sent a letter of apology to Duncan. David Lat then summarized the fraught debate that pitted a guest speaker's harm against the harm caused by bigoted language directed at student protesters, writing that the dean "faces a predicament. . . . She's getting attacked by conservatives for being insufficiently protective of free speech (and insufficiently aggressive in punishing protesters), and she's getting attacked by progressives for being insufficiently protective of vulnerable members of the law school community. She's getting criticized by alumni for caving to the woke mob, and she's getting criticized by current students for caving to the forces of oppression."[17]

These university events—and there are many like them—create a slippery slope of confusion and ambiguity. The attempt to balance academic freedom against a student's personal sensitivities (as in the artist case) or conflating academic freedom with free speech (as in the Stanford Law School episode) opens up a space where one person's harm is pitted against another's. Both lines of argument diminish the importance of academic freedom as the keystone of the modern university's intellectual environment. Academic freedom is not about protecting the sensitivity of particular students or about allowing all speech the right to a campus audience. Civility, respect, and dignity should be maintained at all times; but, even so, not all students are going to like what they hear. And not all speech will pass the standards set by scholars who are experts in their field, publish in academic journals, and are members of professional associations. For instance, fascist speech should never be tolerated on campus, even if politicians use such speech in their public campaigning. And no student should be subjected to a speaker who argues that Blacks or women are intellectually inferior to White men—a statement that has no factual basis, scientific proof, or academic support.

As already mentioned, the university is ideally a place where scholars are free to research and teach, and universities maintain institutional autonomy so scholars and students can learn and think in new ways. But as the concept of scholarly freedom has become diminished in recent years, its meaning has become much narrower than the more holistic definition put forward by the AAUP in 1940. As Eva Cherniavsky has powerfully argued, this narrow approach is "a profound misinterpretation of what academic *freedom* most fundamentally represents. Academic freedom is not about the freedom of individual academics to say whatever they want—rather it defines the *collective freedom of the faculty* to set the norms of academic debate, free from interference by administrators, governing boards, or the state" (Cherniavsky 2021:9; author's italics).

Academic Freedom as Enabling Social Justice

I and others argue that we must recover the idea of academic freedom as both an individual and institutional right (Post 2016; Scott 2019; Cherniavsky 2021). I also argue, however, that we need to go one step further by reframing academic freedom as a collective right based on social responsibility and, by extension, enabling social justice. Significantly, this right relates to whole societies, not just scholars and students working in credentialed universities and colleges. This approach helps circumvent the argument of progressive scholars who attack academic freedom on the basis that it defends White privilege and racism—a claim that is justifiable but ultimately unhelpful in thinking about universities as one of the last remaining public institutions from which to study and critique systemic racism and structural inequalities. In other words, it is true that higher education has historically excluded marginalized voices and that it privileges White and wealthier students and faculty; but it is also true that universities offer a site to critique hegemonic knowledge production and shift higher education's orientation toward being "a crucible of transformative politics and pedagogy" (la paperson 2017:34). Putting it differently, the sociologist Raewyn Connel argues that "critical thought is necessary to research-based knowledge, and that can subvert hierarchy as brilliantly as any anarchist plot" (Connell 2019:111). And given the dominance of social media and its mode of truncated communication, the historian Ellen Schrecker adds the important observation that the academy is "the last remaining haven for reasoned dissent and the home of serious ideas that do not lend themselves to sound bites" (Schrecker 2010:233).

That a particular scholar may hold racist views—and claim academic freedom in defense of their scholarship—should not diminish the core principle of academic freedom, which is to conduct research and teaching according to professional standards and free from political interference. The end goal is to produce knowledge that contributes to the good of society by promoting innovative research, critical thinking, and inclusive teaching. So in taking a valid stance against higher education as an institution of White privilege and the ongoing production of racial, gender, and social inequalities, it is important to not throw the baby out with the bathwater (Bérubé and Ruth 2022; for a critique, see Snyder 2022). In these legitimate yet maddening conversations, I am reminded of the poetic wisdom of bell hooks and the final passage in her book *Teaching to Transgress*: "The academy is not paradise. But learning is a place where paradise can be created. The classroom, with all its limitations, remains a location of possibility. In that field of possibility we have the opportunity to labor for freedom, to demand of ourselves and our comrades, an openness of mind and heart that allows us to face reality even as we collectively imagine ways to move beyond boundaries, to transgress. This is education as the practice of freedom" (hooks 1994:207; see also Williamson-Lott 2018).

With today's global drift toward antidemocracy, I argue that academic freedom needs to become a more flexible and encompassing concept than has been historically envisaged within a modernist liberal paradigm. This requires, I suggest, two moves. First, academic freedom should be reinstated as both an individual and a collective scholarly right as articulated by the AAUP and documents such as the report *State of play of academic freedom in the EU Member States* (2023). Second, academic freedom should be conceptually broadened as a collective right held by entire populations within and beyond the academy. Academic freedom, then, goes from being an individual scholar's right that should be defended by the university and wider academy to being a human right collectively claimed and defended by society in the best interests of humanity. In other words, the subjects of academic freedom are the collective members of societies. This more-encompassing definition is better able to mobilize public dissent in response to oppressive state laws and policies, as well as to push back against decentralized attacks on scholars through aggressive social media campaigns and the insidious mechanisms of societal fascism. In short, attacks on academic freedom become everyone's problem.

In the context of higher education, the future I envision is one where research and learning communities are valued as self-determining professional units that are buffered by new lines of collaborative alliance within, across, and beyond university institutions. Holding these alliances together is a shared commitment to basic democratic principles such as social inclusivity, freedom to assemble and protest, participation in representative governance, and equal access to public health, education, and jobs. This vision suggests the need to build new networks of solidarity and connection among faculty and students (universities and colleges), learning communities (primary and secondary schools and libraries), and wider publics. When the authority of state governments is decentered, space is opened up for themes of liberation and independence to become more pronounced—just as they were among the pro-democracy student protesters violently attacked by riot police in the streets of Hong Kong throughout 2019.

A revisioning of academic freedom as a collective right delinked from oppressive nation-states is beginning to emerge in international legal documents such as the *Inter-American Principles on Academic Freedom and University Autonomy* (2021). This document expressly calls academic freedom an individual and collective human right, positing that knowledge must be "borderless" to fight against rising authoritarianism across the Americas (Snyder 2023; Darian-Smith 2023a). This innovative document and other national and international legal protections of academic freedom are further discussed in chapter 3.

Alongside law-based initiatives, several organizations and faculty research groups are promoting worldwide efforts to protect academic freedom by building collaborative networks of scholars and experts. For instance, the Network for Education and Academic Rights (NEAR) is a nongovernmental organization established in 2001 and sponsored by UNESCO. Based in London, NEAR works to protect academic rights and functions as a clearinghouse for information about attacks on scholars. Its members include Amnesty International, International PEN, and Human Rights Watch, and its partners include Scholars at Risk, the Arab Society for Academic Freedom, and the African Academic Freedom Network. An organization formed more recently is the Academy in Exile, which was established in Germany in 2017 and provides a space of collaboration for persecuted scholars. It has helped to fund fellowships and emergency stipends and to create arrangements for scholars at host institutions. Another notable group is the Global Observatory on Academic Freedom (GOAF), which was launched in 2021 with the support of the Open Society University Network (OSUN) and is now hosted by King's College London. GOAF connects scholars around the world interested in reconceptualizing academic freedom based on the "conviction that academic freedom is a necessary condition for universities to effectively pursue their duty of producing, transmitting and disseminating knowledge as a public good, locally and globally" (Popović et al. 2022). GOAF partners with a number of organizations helping scholars in need, such as the Research Network on Academic Freedom; Leiden University; Scholars at Risk; the International Association of Universities; the World University Service; and the Magna Charta Observatory, which was revived in 2020 in response to increasing far-right political interference in higher education. These are just a few of the many organizations emerging in response to global attacks on students and scholars.

Notably, I argue that academic freedom should not be conflated with any universalistic and predetermined notions of social justice based on essentialized identity politics, as some would argue. Rather, academic freedom allows scholars to analyze what social justice means to people and communities in their own terms. For instance, in the United States, social justice for the Inuit peoples resisting oil mining in Alaska may be conceived very differently from social justice for Venezuelan migrants arriving at the southern border or for small ranchers in upstate Oregon facing unprecedented drought caused by the climate emergency. Understanding what social justice looks like from the perspective of diverse communities—thus better understanding what futures they imagine and what social change may be most meaningful to them—is the kind of research that academic freedom can enable. This sort of inquiry is particularly important when thinking about the meaning of social justice in increasingly culturally pluralist and multiracial contexts that defy any singular definition of what social justice means and how to implement it (Shefner et al. 2014).

Relatedly, in addition to enabling social justice, there is an increasing recognition that academic freedom must also enable epistemic justice. Epistemic justice refers to the need to promote perspectives, worldviews, and different ways of knowing that are devalued within the Euro-American academy. The concept of epistemic justice is important for valuing and defending non-Western knowledge at a societal level, as well as defending underrepresented scholars and students, mostly from the global south, whose scholarly contributions are often overlooked. Historically, this underrepresentation included the exclusion of Indigenous and racialized minority perspectives, as poetically and tragically articulated in MariJo Moore's edited volume *Genocide of the Mind: New Native American Writing* (2003). More recently, however, it has included scholars and students within the dominant society who may be marginalized because of their national citizenship or precarious employment status. As noted by Milica Popović, director of the Global Observatory on Academic Freedom housed at the Yehuda Elkana Center for Higher Education in Vienna: "Epistemic positioning influences how the right to academic freedom is exercised by scholars both inside and outside of academia. Scholars who are marginalized, either because of an economic situation dictated by their non-tenured working conditions or their positionality (resulting from gender, ethnicity, citizenship status, language skills etc.), are often not considered *worthy* in the social and institutional struggle for academic freedom" (Popović 2022a; author's italics).

Another related term that has entered public discourse recently is "scholasticide." The term was first used by Karma Nabulsi, an Oxford professor and expert on the laws of war, to refer to the systematic attack on a society's education system as part of a wider campaign to wipe out a people's culture and traditional knowledge. Nabulsi used the term to describe what Israeli forces were doing in Palestine in 2009. Today the term has resurfaced in relation to the Israel–Hamas war that erupted in October 2023. Over the ensuing months, the war resulted in the complete destruction of the 11 universities in Gaza and left thousands of scholars and students dead or injured and 90,000 students unable to pursue their education. Palestinian historian Abdel Razzaq Takriti says that since the 2023 war began, Israel's scholasticide in Gaza has been "intensifying on an unprecedented scale." He goes on, "They're demolishing universities and schools intentionally. They bombarded and destroyed every single university. They're using schools as barracks and military stations." This is an effort to make Gaza an unhabitable territory, "by killing the person, but also killing the knowledge that they contain within them."[18]

Epistemic justice is a theme that is taken seriously in scholarly conversations about decolonizing the university and what this would mean in structural and material terms (Grosfoguel et al. 2016; Santos 2017). These conversations build on postcolonial and decolonial feminist scholarship and other critical approaches that for more than 40 years have called into question the violence of knowledge production in the Western academy (Spivak 1988; Shiva 1990). Some scholars have even labeled colonial and imperial violence toward the Other as "epistemicide" (Santos 2014; Grosfoguel 2013; Hall 2018). As argued by Claudia Brunner, "Epistemic violence is not external or alien to the academic realm. It is rooted in knowledge itself, in its genesis, formation, organization, and effectiveness" (quoted in Brunner 2021:204). How to promote the interrelated concepts of social justice and epistemic justice is an important conversation that is picked up in chapter 6 and examined in the context of revisioning public education against a backdrop of societal fascism, which demands that greater attention be given to the social dimensions of the freedom to think.

Concluding Comments

In the context of escalating attacks on academic freedom and the right to education, some legal and civil society organizations are thinking innovatively about new forms of democracy based in communities that are not bound by a centralized state apparatus. Specifically, groups such as Scholars at Risk, the Coalition for Academic Freedom (CAFA), and other organizations point to an emerging ethics of refuge and a politics of intellectual freedom that transcend national contexts yet are grounded within, and responsive to, the specificities of localized education institutions and working environments. Determining how to foster and develop such an ethics, how to convey its meaning to scholars and students, and how to communicate why it is needed to wider publics is part of the immense work ahead for those defending academic freedom.

These efforts raise a set of timely questions for a world experiencing the global rise of antidemocracy. Is it possible to disentangle academic freedom from antidemocratic and racially oppressive national contexts? In other words, could we reframe academic freedom to be a collective right of scholars and students delinked from national territories? How would this collective right be articulated, and could it be implemented and defended in international law? Perhaps more fundamentally, what constitutes the "common good" produced by academic freedom? Who benefits, and who is left out? And given the climate crisis, can we revision "commoning" to include people's relations to one another as well as to nonhuman environments? As Silvia Federici urges us, how can we "gain the capacity to recognize the world around us—nature, other people, the animal world—as a source of wealth and knowledge and not as a danger" (Federici 2019:77)?

These are not idle questions. Building a common political framework not grounded in competitive national interests is the imperative facing humankind as we contemplate an array of planetary crises, such as nuclear warfare, ecological collapse, and global famine and drought. Just how to do this remains well beyond the scope of this book. What is possible, however, is to rethink the future of higher education to ensure a commons of knowledge production that is ethical, responsible, and independent of extremist political control. Optimistically—and this is my profound hope—this commons will in turn foster creative political theory and new imaginaries of political participation across translocal and transnational contexts involving everyone as a common subject.

Chapter Three

Classrooms as Global Battlegrounds

In a powerful speech given to the Swedish Academy in March 2023, Arundhati Roy, renowned writer and human rights activist, described how thinking freely is now almost impossible in a world of political extremes, surveillance, and censorship. She said that people everywhere are experiencing

> the escalating policing of speech in ways that are very old, as well as very new, to the point where the air itself has turned into a sort of punitive heresy-hunting machine. We seem to be fast approaching what feels like intellectual gridlock. . . .
>
> In India, like in other countries, the weaponization of identity as a form of resistance has become the dominant response to the weaponization of identity as a form of oppression. Those who have historically been oppressed, enslaved, colonized, stereotyped, erased, unheard and unseen precisely *because* of our identities—our race, caste, ethnicity, gender or sexual preference—are now defiantly doubling down on those very identities to face off against that oppression.
>
> It is a powerful, explosive moment in history in which, enabled by social media, wild, incandescent anger is battering down old ideas, old patterns of behavior, entitled assumptions that have never been questioned, loaded words, and language that is coded with prejudice and bigotry. The intensity and suddenness of it has shocked a complacent world into re-thinking, re-imagining and trying to find a better way of doing and saying

things. Ironically, almost uncannily, this phenomenon, this fine-tuning, seems to be moving in step with our lurch into fascism.[1]

What Roy's speech underscores is that controlling the freedom to think is not limited to attacking scholars and students and policing university classrooms. Journalists, librarians, political activists, and public intellectuals are all under attack in antidemocratic societies. These people seek to tell the truth and push back against propaganda and tactical disinformation campaigns. This wider assault on journalists, writers, and dissidents is very important for highlighting the range of interconnected societal oppressions being implemented and practiced by far-right regimes and nonstate actors. The assaults also show the range of techniques used to restrict people's freedom to write and express their ideas.

PEN International, a worldwide organization that advocates on behalf of writers, monitors the growing number of persecutions in its annual case list. It notes, "In light of growing authoritarianism and conflict around the world, writers and artists increasingly face targeted persecution. PEN International's Case List 2023–2024 reveals that writers, journalists, and publishers across the globe are being subjected to arrests, detentions, and unjust imprisonments, often justified through vaguely defined offenses or fabricated criminal charges, following unfair trials."[2] In PEN's *Anthology Writers Under Siege,* harrowing accounts of imprisonment, assault, torture, rape, and death highlight the depravity and inhumanity of those in power over people daring to tell the truth and challenge authority (Popescu and Seymour-Jones 2007).

Scholars at Risk and Other Civil Society Organizations

Increasingly, harrowing tales are also being reported by scholars and students. These tales echo earlier accounts told by persecuted scholars caught up in the horrors of World Wars I and II. For instance, in Germany in the 1930s under Hitler, scientific research that was not in line with the National Socialist Party was outlawed and scholars were persecuted by the fascist regime. The UK Council for At-Risk Academics was established to offer safety to hundreds of German scholars fleeing their homelands in 1933. This organization and others such as the Philipp Schwartz Initiative and the International Institute for Education helped scholars escape Nazism and, in the process, promoted the value of democracy through the defense of academic freedom (Samuels 2019; Newman 2020). In the United States, the New School for Social Research set up the University in Exile for German scholars in New York City, also in 1933.[3]

Today, with the global lean toward authoritarianism, the persecution of scholars is escalating within and across countries and regions around the world. And with these greater numbers of attacks, the civil society response in the global north has expanded to include scholars from the global south. One of the more recent groups to bring attention to the global attack on researchers is the New University in Exile Consortium, which builds on the New School's historical tradition of providing refuge for persecuted scholars fleeing fascist Germany. Established in 2018 by its founding director Arien Mack, the Consortium includes universities and colleges in the United States, Canada, France, Germany, Ireland, Italy, Jordan, the Netherlands, Poland, South Africa, Spain, Sweden, Switzerland, and the United Kingdom. Each institution is committed to hosting endangered scholars as well as facilitating their participation in online weekly seminars that allow people from all over the world to share their experiences living in exile. Another important faculty-led group is International Solidarity for Academic Freedom in India (InSAF India), which is largely led by Indian scholars in diaspora. These scholars are deeply concerned about growing numbers of assassinations of scholars and canceling of lectures by academics critical of Prime Minister Narendra Modi's far-right Hindu nationalist government. InSAF provides a media platform for a range of organizations supporting scholars and hosts a webinar series titled "Academic Freedom in International Context."

Other large nonprofit organizations such as Scholars at Risk (SAR) (established 1999) and the Institute of International Education Scholar Rescue Fund (IIE-SRF) (established 2002) provide a model and inspiration for many emerging allies seeking to help oppressed scholars.[4] The Scholar Rescue Fund (which supports the Institute of International Education) grants fellowships to researchers fleeing persecution and is the latest iteration of many decades of work helping dislocated academics find refuge since the end of World War I. SAR is a much newer independent organization established by Robert Quinn, its founding executive director, and now based at New York University. SAR has rapidly grown since 1999 and now works with a network of 650 universities across 43 countries, organized into 16 national sections, and partners with 14 higher education networks. Together, these groups monitor attacks on scholars, provide counseling and aid, advocate for those who have been imprisoned, and in some cases facilitate temporary jobs in host countries. Typically, the scholars who are given SAR assistance come from conflict zones of war and civil unrest such as Afghanistan, Cameroon, Sudan, Syria, Yemen, Myanmar, Ethiopia, and more recently Ukraine and Gaza. Other scholars are fleeing regimes that have become dramatically more oppressive in recent years, such as China, Russia, Iran, Nicaragua, Nigeria, and Bahrain. Violations against scholars in these regions and states may include violent attacks, killings, student kidnappings, prosecution, wrongful imprisonment, and exile.

Lately there have been more calls for assistance from threatened scholars in what are thought of as democratic countries, including India, Indonesia, Philippines, Mexico, and the United States. In these countries, violations may involve physical violence but are more likely to be acts that undermine a scholar's academic freedom or impact the functioning of a scholarly institution. These acts are typically justified through new laws and policies put into place by far-right legislatures, university councils and boards, university administrators, and others. Such acts often include demotion, denial of tenure, dismissal or other professional penalties, systematic harassment and discrimination, replacement of university administrators, closing of universities, and destruction of campus facilities. In the case of the United States, such acts also include bomb threats sent by neofascist activists to Historically Black Colleges and Universities (HBCUs), intended to intimidate and disrupt academic activities.

Legal Protections of Academic Freedom

Scholars at Risk stands out from other aid organizations in that it also facilitates the production of new legal frameworks for defending academic freedom. Along with Aula Abierta, a Venezuelan academic freedom nongovernmental organization, and the Human Rights Clinic at the University of Ottawa, Canada, SAR helped draft the *Inter-American Principles on Academic Freedom and University Autonomy*, which was adopted by the Inter-American Commission on Human Rights (IACHR) in 2021. The document was drafted in the context of escalating antidemocracy across Latin America (and the United States) and the failure of state governments to protect scholarly communities. It was seen as necessary given the fundamental limitations of international human rights law in protecting academic freedom as a stand-alone, autonomous right.

Currently, academic freedom is legally recognized in international law only as a derivative of other rights, such as the right to freedom of expression, the right to education, and the right to culture and science enshrined in the Universal Declaration of Human Rights (1948, Articles 19 and 26) and the International Covenant on Economic, Social and Cultural Rights (CESCR) (1966, Articles 13 and 15). Because it is subsumed under these other rights, academic freedom lacks visibility, making it hard to monitor attacks and appreciate the scale and degree to which academic communities are vulnerable (Gomez Gamboa and Villalobos Fontalvo 2023:2–4). The *Inter-American Principles* reverses this derivative authority by making it clear "that academic freedom is an independent and interdependent human right, which enables the exercise of a series of other rights, including the right to freedom of expression, the right to education, the right to freedom of assembly, freedom of conscience, and freedom of association, among others" (Gomez and Villalobo Fontalvo 2023).

Significantly, the *Inter-American Principles* is an international law document produced by nonstate actors trying to circumnavigate autocratic national leaders (Darian-Smith 2023a). It is the result of an effort to resist antidemocracy and build cooperation among academic communities, activists, and civil society and human rights organizations across the Americas, in countries such as Brazil, Bolivia, Colombia, Mexico, Nicaragua, Venezuela, Canada, and the United States. The document provides a consistent set of guidelines to institutionalize academic freedom at a transnational and regional level. In the preamble, the *Inter-American Principles* explicitly outlines the need to define a concept of academic freedom that pushes back against rising attacks on teachers, students, and researchers, stating that academic freedom plays an essential role in "the fight against authoritarianism in the Americas"

(*Inter-American Principles* 2021:2). Overall, it is an innovative document setting up a new and encompassing framework that values academic freedom as an individual and collective enterprise critical to building inclusive and democratic societies and countering transnational antidemocracy.

The Coalition for Academic Freedom in the Americas (CAFA) is jointly led by SAR and the Human Rights Research and Education Center at the University of Ottawa. CAFA is a "network of universities, scholars, students and activists" headquartered at the Universidad de Monterrey, Mexico. Partnering with the Open Society Foundation and the Inter-American Commission on Human Rights, CAFA has established itself as a leading "hemispheric-wide" force in monitoring attacks on and disappearances of professors, teachers, and students, and producing public commentary on laws that violate the basic definition of academic freedom.[5]

SAR was also instrumental in helping forge the historic "Joint Statement on Academic Freedom" presented to the UN Human Rights Council on March 29, 2023. The Joint Statement was ultimately signed by 74 countries (including France, South Africa, and the United States), and underscores the global assault on academic freedom. According to the Joint Statement, "without freedom to teach and research, and without freedom to disseminate and debate the results of research, the achievement of the Sustainable Development Goals will be compromised. Without academic freedom, there is no safeguard against the manipulation of information or against the distortion of history. Regrettably, attacks on academic freedom are on the rise."[6] SAR's Robert Quinn responded, "We enthusiastically join the signatories' call for enhanced international cooperation toward strengthening the protection and promotion of academic freedom, and look forward to working with the UN, member states, and international stakeholders as they redouble their efforts in addressing this issue."[7] On July 11, 2023, SAR co-organized, with state sponsors from Uruguay, the European Union, Portugal, and France, a panel, "From Words to Action Implementing Academic Freedom under UN Human Rights Standards," which was a side event at the 53rd session of the UN Human Rights Council (UNHRC). Together, these efforts place SAR as an international leader in the fight against escalating attacks on scholars and universities.

Fleeing Persecution—Stories from the Frontlines

The national and international trends of persecution that SAR documents are not data points but actual lived experiences of scholars in exile. Appreciating threats to academic freedom as lived experiences is important to understanding the creeping insidiousness of societal fascism and its impacts on people who are reduced to living with oppression and threats of violence. It is important for all scholars who operate in relative safety to know about the plight of their academic colleagues in other parts of the world. Perhaps even more importantly, however, is that scholars hear directly from those under attack. Abstract notions of censorship and fear then become alive, humanizing victims and underscoring the emotional and physical short- and long-term consequences of attacks on individuals and broader academic communities.

What follows are stories from scholars threatened by state and nonstate actors in countries and regions experiencing conflict and war. Places such as Afghanistan and Yemen have long been sites of violence and civil war and are the locations for horrifying tales of scholars and students being persecuted by the Taliban and other extremist forces. Stories from scholars in more democratic countries highlight the lawfare strategies that antidemocratic leaders practice to put the "squeeze" on university communities in a variety of ways. Together, these stories highlight the distress that accompanies crackdowns on higher education, as well as the courage of everyday people forced into extraordinary circumstances.

The stories come from Afghanistan, Ethiopia, Hungary, Brazil, and Northern Ireland. A few of these narratives are transcripts of interviews conducted by Robert Quinn, founder of SAR and host of its *Free to Think* podcast series. According to the podcast website, the interviews "features conversation with interesting, thoughtful, and inspiring individuals whose research, teaching, or expression falls at the always sensitive intersection of power and ideas." The interviews present people "who have the courage to seek truth and speak truth, often at great risk."[8] These personal stories complement the *Free to Think* annual report published by SAR, bringing an immediacy to its worldwide reporting by connecting surveys and statistics with people's personal tales of bravery, hope, and deep sadness over the loss of colleagues and communities and in some cases their forced exile from families and homelands.

Afghanistan | Anonymous

I worked as a university professor in Kabul, Afghanistan for eight years. I was the dean of my department, and enjoyed working in an academic environment with the hardworking students of my country. Seeing my past students as graduate and doctoral students in the best universities in the world, and as high- ranking government and non-government employees, strongly motivated me to stay in my country and do my duty. With all my heart, I devoted myself to the education of students who I thought would play a very important role in the future of Afghanistan. In addition to facilitating knowledge production, I always tried to foster an environment that promoted insightfulness and awareness about the issues the country was facing. Open discussions were always a part of my classes and I had no qualms about talking about political issues and challenging the beliefs (religious and non-religious) of my students. Many times I was threatened by some of my students to not raise such discussions in my classes. But since I saw the great interest of most of the students in these issues, I did not take these threats very seriously.

But after some university professors were killed in Kabul and other provinces of Afghanistan in suicide and terrorist attacks, my concerns intensified. I felt extremely threatened when the Taliban came to power in August 2021. Then, my wife received an official threat letter from the Taliban due to her work with government and international projects, and was forced to resign from her job. When the Taliban entered Kabul, they threatened to harm me and my family and we could not leave the house for many days. At the end of August 2021, in the middle of the night, we left our house and all of our possessions and were evacuated to Europe. I am currently working as a visiting scholar at a university in Canada, and I would like to thank the great teams of SAR and IIE-SRF that helped me.[9]

Ethiopia | Anonymous

As a professor of law, I discussed the topic of human rights abuses and breaches of the laws of war in Tigray, a state in northern Ethiopia, during lectures of my December 2020 International Human Rights Law class. The discussions centered on claims of human rights breaches, including the targeting of civilians (murders, imprisonment), and the racial profiling of Tigrayans, which was also being covered by international news sources and human rights groups as a high profile topic at the time. The University administration accused me of acting against the federal government's actions in Tigray and sympathizing with the regional authority. Consequently, I was warned to stop referring to the situation in Tigray. This had the unintended consequence of self-censoring my lectures in subsequent classes. After I completed teaching the human rights course, I was not given any more teaching responsibilities for the semester that followed. As long as I was under monitoring and severe pressure, it was evident that I would not be able to continue teaching, and was gradually being removed from my academic position. Consequently, I was compelled to leave my position in February 2021. I then joined a think tank, where the harassment persisted. Unable to pursue my academic career, I fled the country and finished my postdoctoral research at an American university. Due to my risk of persecution, it was unsafe for me to return to Ethiopia. With the help of SAR, I was able to obtain a position at a university in the United States, where I continue to publish, and speak often at conferences and public events on human rights, the rule of law, and African studies. My research focuses on the increasing importance of, and threat to, supranational institutions including human right mechanisms and international courts. I will never forget the day I received the news from SAR that the university where I worked as a postdoc had agreed to host me. I am thankful and appreciative for the persistent effort that SAR made to help me. The constant hard work of SAR to help is not ordinary to find. Because of SAR, I am able to continue my research.[10]

Hungary | Rosa Schwartzburg

Rosa Schwartzburg wrote the following in response to the Hungarian government's assault on Central European University.[11]

The air forms a fog around my mouth as I watch my friends carry a coffin marked "Egyetem"—in English, "University"—across Parliament square. They march slowly, matching the dirge played by Rhythms of Resistance drums. When they set the coffin down, we encircle it, then bury it under soil and rocks, raking up the dirt with our hands. After a moment, one of our group digs a small hole in the soil-pile with his fingers and plants a seedling. We water the plant using a spare teakettle and join arms.

When I first joined the Szabad Egyetem (Free University), we were just a ragtag group of students from the Central European University (CEU) trying to keep our school from being kicked out of the country. By December 12, 2018, our small group had joined the 10,000 who came together in protest against the right-wing Fidesz party, led by the despot-populist Viktor Orbán. For a frigid week, we camped in front of Hungary's parliament to protest a regime that wanted to shut down our school, as well as a way of demonstrating the importance and resilience of education. Despite our organizing, on the first day of December, CEU announced that it would be moving to Vienna, Austria. After the announcement, we held our funeral for "Education." There, Hungarian students recited eulogies for their country, their youth, and for academic freedom in front of the most nationalistic space in all of Hungary.

Though we did not convince the Hungarian government to stop its senseless assault on CEU, Szabad Egyetem actually accomplished a much more important and sustainable achievement: We created a movement of students and free-thinkers dedicated to fighting against Orbán's despotic regime.

One of the first things I learned, as an outsider who just came to Hungary this year, is that it is not just CEU that is under attack from Fidesz but all Hungarian universities and academic institutions. The Corvinus University of Economics is being privatized; the country's textbook makers have all come under state control; the largest and best humanities university (called Eötvös Lorand University, or ELTE) in the country is being defunded; certain degrees (including my field, gender studies) have been banned; conferences on migration have been banned—and that is simply what has made it to press in the few Hungarian media outlets not controlled by strongmen of Orbán.

Though Orbán sought to stamp out dissent and free thought in Hungary, he only made us call out to one another in solidarity. We students of CEU were soon joined by Corvinus and ELTE students. Together we spent the occupation in a tent filled with leftist organizing discussions and strategy.

This happened despite the fact that modern Hungarians (particularly the younger generation) are generally reluctant to protest; the legacy of the '56 revolution—when after three weeks of protests against the Communist regime, Soviet tanks rolled in, killing and wounding thousands—and the subsequent decades of oppression still hang over the nation. Since the fall of Communism and the subsequent rise of Fidesz, there have been a handful of truly in-the-streets demonstrations—sporadic likely because of Fidesz's strategies of media manipulation and suppression of dissent.

During our occupation (and the weeks of organizing leading up to it) we did what students do best: We learned. We learned how to plan protests and marches. We learned how to set up tents in the freezing rain and how to plan an open university. And I certainly learned the most I'll likely ever know about Budapest municipal noise ordinances.

But most importantly, we learned solidarity. And it was this solidarity that carried us as Hungary plunged into what appears to be a moment of genuine and historic tumult. Protests broke out on December 12, when Orbán's administration forced two laws through parliament: a law giving the government power over the courts (seen as yet another step by Fidesz to establish autocracy) and the "Slavery Law," which allows employers to force their employees to work up to 400 hours overtime annually. Not only is this law unjust and burdensome to the already strained working class, Orbán and his party functionally ignored the entire democratic process by cutting off the microphones of opposition MPs while it was being debated in parliament. Hungarians across the country watched in rage—via Facebook Live or broadcast on one of the few independent media outlets—as Parliament descended into chaos, with opposition members blowing whistles and calling for radical action.

Outside, there were upwards of 10,000 people carrying flags and banners in Parliament Square, holding phones and smoke bombs aloft. Some were wearing yellow visibility vests—inspired by the *gilets jaunes* protests in France. Around me, people shouted *Fidesz afia!* and *Victator!* Police officers looked on in astonishment—particularly, I saw, when one demonstrator snatched a state-issued beanie off an officer's head. No one—not the police, not Orbán and Fidesz, not even the demonstrators themselves—expected this outburst of genuine, vocal dissent.

Perhaps these laws were simply the straws that broke the camel's back when it comes to the erosion of democracy in the post-Communist state. Or perhaps protesters were motivated by the workers' movement of the *gilets jaunes*—or perhaps by our small but vocal demonstration. It may simply be that movements are unwieldy and unpredictable, and December 12 was simply the day for it. But whatever the reason, we learned two new lessons.

First, these protests are serious, and they are violent. Police arrived quickly, appearing like bullet ants in their black body armor and glinting helmets as they circled the parliament building. Demonstrators trying to enter government buildings were beaten back by the police; as people rushed the door, the officers swung at their ribs with riot batons, often resulting in a sickening crack. Many of us were pepper-sprayed repeatedly, and a fellow student at CEU was arrested and jailed.

And as the state grows more violent, so do the protests. Demonstrators throw wine bottles at police. Jobbik, a far-right party with a sizeable extremist wing, swarm the marches with their flags and welding torches. As I walk home from the protests one night through the winding streets of Pest, a young Hungarian friend tells me: "We need things to change—we need people to get out in the streets." The winter cold envelops us both, and he adds: "I really believe that things will not change in Hungary without some bloodshed."

Acknowledging possible violence was one lesson. But the second was that the greatest weapon those in this movement have is solidarity and the capacity to learn from one another.

A key reason these protests have been sustainable is because they are built on alliances between labor unions and student groups. During the Szabad Egyetem occupation, our group hosted a group of Hungarian union leaders. It was at this event, hosted in a leaky tent, that the labor representatives and student leaders first collaborated. While students have the idealism and energy to organize on the ground, labor unions often have the skill and more substantial ties to community networks. Unions can teach students about strikes and negotiating with the frustrating Hungarian political parties, while students can push and critique in new ways. We can learn from each other.

And simply put: We are stronger together. On December 16, the protests increased from 10,000 to 15,000. The streets are alive with chants; from all across central Budapest you hear *Solidaritás!* (Solidarity!) ringing out. And across Hungary villages and cities other than the capital are protesting as well; for the first time since the fall of Communism in 1989, all 19 counties of Hungary are planning a massive action on January 19.

But more important, I would argue, is what is happening after the protests, in people's homes, in bars, and in classrooms afterhours. Now organizers from across Hungary are meeting and planning and exchanging ideas—organizers who never would have interacted if these protests hand not begun in the first place.

Where Orbán tried to crush dissent, the people responded by organizing, sharing, and learning from one another. Like the seedling on our coffin, this revolt cannot merely be buried; through any amount of soil, it will only grow stronger and stronger as it pushes up toward the light.

Brazil | Robert Quinn Talks with Camila Nobrega and Débora Medeiros

Description of Episode: Robert Quinn in conversation with Camila Nobrega, a Brazilian journalist, fellow at the Alice Salomon Hochschule, and PhD candidate in the political science department at the Free University of Berlin, and Dr. Débora Medeiros, a researcher at the Institute for Media and Communication Studies and researcher with the Collaborative Research Center Affective Societies, also at the Free University. They discuss threats to academic freedom in Brazil, including pressures on researchers working on socio-environmental conflicts and with intersectional communities, all within the context of a governmental "weaponization" of higher education as a means of advancing an authoritarian agenda.

> ROBERT—So there is pressure on research communities, and funding challenges and maybe hiring challenges, but does it go beyond that, does it ever go to physical or other kinds of threat?
>
> CAMILA—Yes it does, and I take the example of Brazil. . . . There are some cases of censorship and also specific cases of direct threats. For example, there is one researcher who works on pesticides, and she had to leave the country because her research was showing that many pesticides being used in Brazil are prohibited in the European Union. A lot of economic interests try to [stop this research]. She was able to speak out.

ROBERT—Why did she have to leave the country? Did she come under pressure?

CAMILA—Yes, she received a lot of direct threats from different sources, and she didn't have the support to continue to continue her research. But she is still doing it with support from peers and research groups but now outside the country.

ROBERT—Débora, is there a larger context here? What is the general situation for academic freedom in Brazil?

DÉBORA—Yes absolutely there has been an escalation of the threats since 2016. . . . It started with austerity policies to all public services in Brazil that is still going on with Bolsonaro who weaponizes austerity. So instead of just cutting funds generally for federal universities in general which are the largest institutions in Brazil, the funding is now cut in certain disciplines and institutes, so Bolsonaro really weaponized the austerity policy from his predecessor to really control ideologically what is going on in universities. So, we have this escalation going on at the federal level since 2016.

ROBERT—You say certain disciplines and certain institutes, but are there specific topic areas that are under heightened pressure?

DÉBORA—In addition to social environmental research coming under greater censorship (as mentioned by Camila) we have people studying gender issues in gender departments, and people studying safety and public policies about security, for example the police, they are under threats. You also have people in the humanities and social sciences, they are much more in focus and . . . marginalized in terms of knowledge production. They are subject to budget cuts and by

attempts to influence who can be president of the
university ... because Bolsonaro really tries to put
people who are loyal to his ideology into positions of
leading federal universities.

ROBERT—We have seen some of these dynamics in other
countries recently, combat or dispute over appointments of rectors by the executive in Turkey, Hong
Kong, and we have also seen the marginalization of
certain disciplines or departments, particularly gender
studies in countries in Africa and Eastern Europe, and
certain topics such as Critical Race Theory in the United
States. Débora, what do you think is the motivation
behind these efforts and why try to marginalize?

DÉBORA—I think there are various levels of motivation.
You have at the federal level efforts to push a conservative view of the world, so knowledge that is produced
that contradicts the policies of the government ... they
don't want to hear this kind of information circulating.
But at the state level, and even internally within
institutions, you have conservative actors and paramilitary structures. We had a killing of a student inside a
university, and it's very likely there were paramilitary as
campus security, which is illegal of course, but he was
killed because he was vocal about this. So, you have
actors that are encouraged and empowered by federal
policies at the local level, and who persecute their peers
or members of the academic community. There is
definitely a conservative backlash that is going on in
Brazil right now.

ROBERT—Where would you like your research on
academic freedom and social environmental conflict to
go? What would you like people to know about what
you are discovering?

CAMILA—Basically when we talk about academic freedom, we usually don't see it in different dimensions or intersectionalities. When we talk about gender or sexual orientation or race, it is not the same for every researcher even within the same context, and it really depends. For example, in Brazil now there are some Indigenous peoples who are going to universities and doing their own research about their own peoples, and they find different kinds of institutionalized racism. This is one topic we should go deeper into to understand academic freedom with its different layers. Universities are still usually places of elitism, composed of middle-class white peoples, and we still see a lot of sexism in universities. Its super rare to see Indigenous researchers even in a country such as Brazil which has more than 100 languages and thousands of different peoples. So, this is what I would like to understand behind the social conflicts and what they show; not just the conflicts as problems but what kind of visions of the world are under dispute. How are people impacted, and what kinds of risks are faced by those from different backgrounds?

ROBERT—That is really helpful to me because over the years we have lots of conversations about intersectionality but usually in the context of discrimination, and not directly anchored to the concept of academic freedom so that's a really interesting and important point and I thank you for that. . . . Débora, is there a final thought you would like to share with our listeners about concerns about academic freedom or otherwise right now?

DÉBORA—Thank you for asking that. I think it is important to highlight that Brazilian universities have been at the forefront of academic innovation for a long time. We have a great number of excellent researchers working in Brazilian institutions and they are under attack and emigrating because they don't have the logistical conditions and are being placed under threat from ideological actors. They are leaving the country, and it is important to reflect on what this does to science. They are very competent researchers, and they are enriching the countries they are arriving at. For the ones who remain and try to keep working under very difficult conditions, I think it is important for those working in institutions in the global north to provide support in forms of cooperation. A lot of people already work with partners inside Brazil, but it's important to know that cooperations are decisive right now to really strengthen scholars who need to be visible abroad, and to have partners that back them up. Those with partners in Brazil should be aware of the difficulties—it's a duty to really be there for them. They aren't just providing the data but are competent partners in their research.

ROBERT—Thank you, Débora, for reminding us of that duty to be there with our partners as equal partners, and for reminding us that Brazilian higher education is very rich and strong, and as you said a leading sector.... I like your message that if we in the community can stay in solidarity and stay partners, we can ride this out. Camila, what about you? Are there any final thoughts you would like to share about your research or about academic freedom concerns generally?

CAMILA—I think it is super important what Débora just said, to build equal partnerships and to understand that political contexts can change a lot. I think the case of

Brazil is emblematic of Latin America and that researchers are facing a very hard time. But despite this, researchers are working and producing new data on academic freedom. It is a very difficult but important time to increase international networks and collaborations.

ROBERT—Terrific and thank you, Camila, and thank you, Débora, both very much for sharing your work and experiences and everything you are doing.[12]

Northern Ireland | Robert Quinn talks with Colin Harvey

Description of Episode: Robert Quinn talks with Colin Harvey, a Professor of Human Rights Law and former Head of the School of Law, Queen's University, Belfast, about what UN experts described as a "smear campaign" against him for his work debating the possibility of new constitutional arrangements for the island of Ireland after Brexit. An expert on human rights and constitutional law and former Commissioner of the Northern Ireland Human Rights Commission, Harvey references growing up during the "conflict," achievements under the Good Friday Agreement, and how these are threatened by Brexit. Harvey sees the pressures on him as part of a larger struggle against human rights and democratic values going on around the world and says that academics have a responsibility to robustly defend those values, despite the risks.

ROBERT—In the last six months or so your name has been brought up in the print media, social media, even by some politicians if I am not mistaken. And you have been compared to Nazis and paramilitaries and I think one journalist suggested you should be voted off the island. What's this recent notoriety all about?

COLIN—It means going back a number of years, to the work I and others have been doing in a post Brexit context. Maybe to explain that to your audience—in 2016 the UK voted to leave the European Union but interestingly Northern Ireland voted to remain, so it was essentially removed from the European Union against the wishes of the majority of its people. Which is quite a big deal here ... Brexit has essentially taken one part of the island out of the EU and one part remains in the EU, so for many people it is a practical and symbolic repartition of the island once again. ... I have found myself caught up in all of that in terms of those bigger constitutional questions, and that has made me a bit of a target primarily for those who would like to maintain the union with Britain and perhaps don't want that conversation to be happening at all. ... And I have been the target of traditional news media but also social media where I found myself a target particularly in Loyalists [British] media circles. I have found myself been called the most remarkable things. ... To be candid by targeting me, they are intending to send a message to others. ... I have found myself at the center of a whirlwind really.

ROBERT—How has that social media denigration affected you and your work?

COLIN—I have been involved in public life for years, but I have never experienced anything like this, even during the earlier conflict. It has been a very intense and difficult time, and I have ploughed on since I don't want to be derailed, but it is also intensely difficult. ... To be honest it is unsettling and unnerving, and you're at the same time trying to do your day job of teaching and researching and get on with it.

ROBERT—So we have this labelling or othering—have you ever felt your position as a professor at your institution was at risk?

COLIN—Yes, I have. . . . there has been reassurance and an enormous amount of support and solidarity, but to be candid you do worry that your university may say this guy isn't worth all this hassle, you know. That's always on your mind.

ROBERT—Have you ever felt physically threatened or that anyone that is close to you would be at risk?

COLIN—Belfast is a small place, and even if nobody has issued an express death threat against you, when you are consistently labelled people may believe that. They don't see you as an academic, or as a civic actor. Some of the language about me is that I am part of some weird conspiracy trying to take over.

ROBERT—In a recent statement the UN rapporteurs and experts on freedom of speech . . . called what you are experiencing a "smear campaign" and denounced baseless claims against you and warned that attacks against academics can not only have dire consequences for the academic community but for the country. How do you feel about that statement? Was it helpful?

COLIN—I really appreciated that statement and all the expressions of support and solidarity, Rob.

ROBERT—What you are describing reminds me of what we are seeing all around the world and reminds me that one of the things I have seen in this work is that violence isn't the primary tool of oppression. Rather it is isolation and pressures, whispers, and insinuations or outright accusations that cut the ties between people and isolate the person they are trying to silence. And sometimes that creates the space where it is easier for violence to happen, but often it's just to create that isolation and the psychological impact on the individual in the middle of it. Is that right?

COLIN—Rob, that's a very interesting way of putting it. Ultimately as I have said before people are trying to send a message through me because they want me to stop and the conversation to stop.... I am a former head of Queens law school and served in relatively prominent positions in public life, but my professional life has been transformed since I started this conversation. Suddenly I am an inconvenient person to have on a project.... People like me have had a virtual target painted on my back

ROBERT—Do you ever want to say, enough is enough, I have done my part, and sort of step away and work on something else?

COLIN—No! and I'll tell you one of the reasons that's concerning me.... There are arguments and forces that are emerging across Europe and the wider world that scare and worry me. There are voices and echoes of the past that are emerging around authoritarianism and around Jews and challenges to basic democratic rule of law rights and values that we sometimes take for granted. There is a real struggle over human rights going on around the world and we need to robustly defend some of those values. The viciousness on new platforms and media and the repetitive and aggressive antidemocratic voices that are gaining a foothold around the world—that can't win, that can't prevail. I am involved in human rights and equality, and I work on constitutional law because I fundamentally believe in all the values that underpin all those concepts around human dignity and human rights.... Speaking in a

European context at the moment, that [conversation] can't just be in academic articles. You've got to engage disinformation and let me be very honest, basic lies, and that has to be challenged by academics and others.... I just want to end with this ... I haven't stepped into this space accidentally, and what I've done I have done consciously and deliberately because I feel I have a responsibility as an academic embedded in this society, that we are essentially here to serve and do what I have done.

ROBERT—Thanks very much for sharing your time and your story and for reminding us that there is a responsibility that comes with the role of being a scholar in society, and that includes a responsibility to each other and be in solidarity.[13]

Living with Exile

Increasingly, scholars and students are forced to live in exile, separated from their families and homelands. Others stay behind—amid anxiety and insecurity—and live with exile as a constant potential. In the book *Academics in Exile: Networks, Knowledge Exchange and New Forms of Internationalization*, authors talk about scholars experiencing "inner exile," which involves self-censorship about politically sensitive topics, and contrast this form of intellectual flight with "physical exile" and leaving to avoid the threat of violence (Axyonova et al. 2022:12). They also point out that even when a person is fortunate to be able to leave and avoid harm, most exiles struggle with ongoing visa issues, border controls, and the hardship of adapting to new social and academic environments. Many do not have secure jobs, and most displaced scholars are essentially invisible to their new colleagues, who often see them as risky to talk to or temporarily employed and so irrelevant to their own careers. So even for scholars and students who are lucky enough to be free from immediate oppression, the long-term mental distress and social isolation can be heartbreaking.

Years ago, Edward Said commented on the "crippling sorrow" of exile, and his words continue to resonate with many today:

> Exile is strangely compelling to think about but terrible to experience. It is the unhealable rift forced between a human being and a native place, between the self and its true home: its essential sadness can never be surmounted. And while it is true that literature and history contain heroic, romantic, glorious, even triumphant episodes in an exile's life, these are no more than efforts to overcome the crippling sorrow of estrangement. The achievements of exile are permanently undermined by the loss of something left behind for ever. (Said 2000:137)

Apart from the incredible distress of being a scholar in exile, Said turned to the positive contributions of emigrants in the development of Western modernity. Among other things, Said stressed the power of exiles to question dominant European cultural ideas by juxtaposing them with their own. This in turn promotes critical thinking and opens opportunities for intellectual growth and innovation (Said 1996). For Said, the process of talking with marginalized others and looking at the world through their gaze—as if the entire world is a foreign place—enables new forms of knowledge to be produced and alternative futures to be imagined (Barbour 2007).

Another, more contemporary scholar who links intellectuals in exile with bigger historical forces is Asli Vatansever, a sociologist of precariat academic labor. As part of the group Academics for Peace, she was forced to flee Turkey under its "illiberal" democracy in 2017 and, along with many other Turkish scholars, ended up living and working in Germany.[14] She talks movingly about her own experiences of exile as "purgatory" in her book *At the Margins of Academia: Exile Precariousness and Subjectivity*. According to Vatansever:

> To be in exile means to live with a specter—the specter of your future and your past, and the specters of all that you had acquired to carefully build your precious "self." Or, more honestly: To be in exile means that you have become a specter yourself and you keep haunting your present and your future. After all, exile is a haunted castle, in which everything spooks around, and at the end you don't even know whether it is all a nightmare or you have become a nightmare yourself. (Vatansever 2020:162)

Whereas Edward Said focused on the role played by exiles in the Western academy against the backdrop of colonialism and displacement, Vatansever analyzes how a neoliberal global economy both commodified knowledge and created conditions of labor precarity that are amplified by today's lean toward authoritarianism (figure 8). In the twenty-first century, this interrelated set of conditions has caused a wave of scholars to be dislocated within and between countries around the world. Writes Vatansever: "The Turkish state's war against dissident scholars should be viewed as a part of an overall anti-intellectualist restructuration. As such, it is strongly related to the political economy of neoliberal populism which aims at killing two birds with one stone: Undermining the rational and critical agency by refuting scientific thought, while in the meantime precarizing and, thus, politically and socially weakening the skilled/intellectual labor force via deregulatory market mechanisms" (Vatansever 2020:1–2).

In the United States, scholars and students may not be forced to leave their country. They may, however, decide to

Figure 8. Faculty in the snow, protesting in silence. Boğaziçi University, Turkey, January 2021. Photo by Can Candan.

migrate internally to work in universities and colleges not subject to the book bans, censored curricula, loyalty oaths, and gag orders now prevalent in Republican-led states. While the pain of leaving may not be as extreme as it is for those who are forced to flee their homelands, it can still be very disruptive and distressing. For those scholars who stay behind, migrations of colleagues can also take a toll. Apart from self-censorship, a sense of abandonment and insecurity may prevail. The decision to stay or leave is typically agonizing for everyone.

The internal movement of scholars from far-right to more progressive states within the United States is already happening. Analysts note that at the start of the 2023–2024 academic year, many faculty and teaching positions have opened up in Florida, which is experiencing a significant "brain drain" and a loss of 20–30 percent of faculty members at some colleges. The exodus of faculty is directly connected to Governor Ron DeSantis's aggressive attack on scholars' academic freedom.

For instance, at the New College of Florida, DeSantis overhauled the board of trustees, which then quickly sacked the college president, head librarian, and director of diversity programs, as well denying tenure to five faculty members. Liz Leininger, an associate professor of neuroscience who joined New College in 2017, said she began looking for an "exit strategy" as soon as she found out about the board of trustee replacements. Fortunately, she found another excellent academic position and did not have to give up her career. Said Leininger, "All of the legislation surrounding higher education in Florida is chilling and terrifying. . . . Imagine scientists who are studying climate change, imagine an executive branch that denies climate change—they could use these laws to intimidate or dismiss those scientists."[15] Like other faculty concerned about being subpoenaed, Leininger was forced to use personal email and encrypted text messages, given that there was "very much a policing of ideas."[16] In a personal conversation I had with Leininger about leaving New College, she was clearly distressed about saying goodbye to students and colleagues but in the end understandably found it necessary.[17]

The economic precarity of scholars and its impacts are discussed in greater depth in chapter 4. This chapter is focused more on the personal toll that precarity exacts and the emotional pain of losing a sense of agency and being forced to flee in order to think critically about one's place in society and current world events. The stories by scholars from around the world function as a wake-up call about what is now unfolding in the United States. As one Turkish scholar said: "I cannot bring myself to define myself as exiled, but I guess we are in exile. I mean, since we cannot go back, right? But I guess I have [a] problem with admitting it. It was something that I read in books about, never thought it could happen to me, but apparently it could. I guess we are in exile" (Vatansever 2020:106).

The stories of scholars who have had to flee family, friends, and their entire former lives—with many never able to return—are truly heartbreaking. In their new "homes," scholars often have to learn local languages, navigate different academic cultures, reposition partners and kids in new schools and jobs, and at times combat depression and mental health issues as they come to terms with a completely new way of life. Often, their scholarship is ignored or overlooked, and many are burdened with precarious futures that may mean giving up entire academic careers. All the while they are often reminded that they should feel grateful for being at their host institutions. Stories of scholars in exile remind us that as faculty in the United States increasingly work with scholars fleeing persecution overseas, as well as with scholars recently arrived from other parts of the country, it is vital that all of us in the academy be more knowledgeable, supportive, and empathetic to their needs in rebuilding scholarly and social communities. This effort may include thinking together about the changing relationship of academia and the state, as well as the changing conception of academic work under conditions of antidemocracy and precarity (Vatansever 2018; see also Burlyuk and Rahbari 2023).

What follows are two excerpts from scholars in exile. The first was written by Cheikh Kone, a student who fled the Ivory Coast after writing against government corruption in 2000. He hid on a container ship that eventually landed him on the western coast of Australia. There he was put into indefinite detention in one of Australia's notorious immigration camps, which have been condemned by the United Nations for their extreme violation of human rights (notably, under the former

Republican George W. Bush administration, the United States modeled its immigration centers and immigration policies on the Australian system and received similar condemnation from human rights agencies). Cheikh Kone was eventually released, with the help of PEN International advocating on his behalf. His experience echoes that of many students and scholars similarly swept up in political turmoil and fleeing persecution, only to be victimized again by harsh immigration policies in the receiving country in which they land.

The second excerpt was written about Salim, a scholar from Syria who was "rescued" by the New University in Exile Consortium in 2018. It is a powerful story that highlights the pain and loneliness of being forced into exile and indefinite refuge, possibly never to see family and friends again. The account also emphasizes, however, the incredible bravery of people having to face extreme challenges, often needing to learn new languages and navigate a sense of being irrelevant to their new colleagues. Salim's story echoes the sentiment of Asli Vatansever, who writes about the need to form a communal transnational scholarly community delinked from actual academic institutions. As she writes, this "alternative, nomadic intellectual subjectivity" can be thought of as a form of resistance to precarity and institutional abandonment under authoritarianism (Vatansever 2020:110–111).

Ivory Coast | Cheikh Kone

> I was brought up in a country without democracy, like so many in the world. But like so many in the world democracy was what I believed in. As a student protesting against one-party rule in that country, the Ivory Coast, democracy seemed the way of a brighter, better future. It was my own belief in democracy that led me to criticize my government. . . .

I fled first across the border into Ghana, travelling by road but hidden. From Ghana I made my way to Togo and then on into Benin. There I was put on a container ship I hoped would take me to Europe, but which instead deposited me in South Africa.

After spending the longest six weeks of my life in a South African port scraping a living, I stowed away in another freighter without knowing where it was bound. After eight days and nine nights without food or water, my companion from Sierra Leone and I were discovered in the engine room by the sailors. We feared for our lives, but the Italian sailors looked after us well and told us that the vessel was headed for Belgium and that in three days we would be in Brussels.... The following morning the vessel docked in Freemantle [Australia].

I was put in a van and driven for about twenty minutes. The vehicle stopped in front of a huge steel gate: on the side of it a sign read "Immigration Reception and Processing Centre." The entrance to the Centre looked like the gates of a prison. Confused, I asked one of the officers with me if were being detained. He said, "No." Then the gate opened and the van entered. As I got out of the van my first impression was that the place seemed like a jail despite the officer's words. All I could see was an endless barbed-wire fence. I was handed over to another office and led away.

Inside the Centre they searched my arms, my legs, my groin, roughly. Then they put me in a small room with cameras for several hours. I was now convinced that I had been jailed and that I was a prisoner of Australia, a place that I had always thought so friendly.... When night fell I was transferred to another building. I was to spend the next two weeks there. To use the toilet I had to wait for hours; I was not allowed to use a phone, to watch television or even to use a pen. I was only allowed outside into the fresh air for one hour every twenty-four....

A week later I was interviewed by the immigration office. This interview was even worse. He questioned everything I said and constantly put me down. "So you think you are intelligent?" he demanded. I said again and again that I had rights, that this is not the way people should be treated. He told me these so-called rights would be my downfall in this process. When at last this torture ended, I was taken to an open compound where I was left with many others and a multitude of nationalities. A week later I was refused refugee status.

I spent another two and a half years in the Centre. We were treated like children, every aspect of our lives controlled. First they gave us identification numbers. Suddenly I was no longer Cheikh Kone but NBP451. Every morning at 6 a.m. they woke us and made us line up for a head count before breakfast.... If the officers could not find a particular person, everybody had to stay where they were, as if we were playing a game of "freeze" with no moving whatsoever. Gates were locked, all cameras were checked, officers were on alert watching anyone who moved until the missing number was found. These lockdowns could last three to six hours; children were expected to stand still and if a mealtime coincided with the lockdown it was postponed.

But it was the nights that were the worst. Before I was sent there I only had nightmares while I slept; there we had nightmares while awake. The screaming and yelling was constant and never seemed to stop. People would run by in the corridors, their footsteps so loud you could not shut them out and the officers' radios never seemed to stop, no matter how far away they were from the rooms. Over time I saw inmates mutilating themselves and sewing their lips together. I saw one man attempt suicide by climbing a tree and jumping head first out of it.... There was so much pain—suicide attempts, constant crying, shouting, the rules, the unpredictable lockdowns—that even now, three years later, sitting in my rented unit with a regular job and my girlfriend on her way home from work, I find it hard to type. Just thinking about it brings back such horrible memories, so much hurt that as I type the tears are coming, the hope I hung on to disappearing when I remember seeing people I had befriended doing what I would never imagine human beings capable of. I can't write any more, it hurts too much but I refuse to let me heart be hardened by it and so I make myself let it go....

Between adolescence and adulthood a political ideal called democracy caught my attention. Amidst the mosaic of ideas that offered themselves I quickly became an advocate of this ideal, believing in its strengths. After spending almost three years in an immigration detention centre in a so-called democratic country, I don't know what to believe any more.[18]

Syria | Salim

Melissa Fay Greene, a professor of writing and a two-time National Book Award finalist, writes movingly about a student called Salim who was forced to flee his Syrian homeland and begin a new life as a medical student in New York City. Melissa writes about the New University in Exile Consortium, which was set up in 2018 (discussed earlier). The Consortium hosts in-person and virtual meetings for scholars who have been forced to leave repressive regimes and who are dealing with the realities of their new host countries and institutions.

Salim's story is horrifying but not especially unusual for many Syrians. Salim, while participating in March 2011 in a peaceful pro-democracy street demonstration inspired by the Arab Spring, witnessed widespread violence and beatings of protesters and the arrest of hundreds. As a paramedic, he rushed to a hospital to help deal with the many civilians who required urgent medical care. Over the following weeks, with other medical coworkers, he was able to set up underground makeshift care centers. One day after visiting one of these centers, he was arrested and held in a cell with twenty-five other prisoners, then interrogated and tortured over 115 days. Upon release, he was conscripted into the Syrian military, the very forces that had oppressed him so violently and cruelly. So he left for the United States.

About Salim and other scholars forced to flee repressive regimes, families, and homelands, Melissa writes:

> Now they try to cobble together new lives in the lands offering them sanctuary, without knowing whether to plan for a couple of years or for decades. Everyone longs to go home, where they have left behind loved ones, colleagues, and political allies, but the current regimes know their names and faces. Many have struggled with immigration paperwork, unsure when their visas will expire. For most, that depends on their work situation, but few have job security.

His university was a Consortium member, so Salim was invited to participate. The simple act of telling his story at his first meeting was a turning point. The group was moved by his suffering, and they understood it. He began to feel less alone. Earlier in the evening, Salim had observed: "Being in prison and being in exile, in both places, there is that sense that you don't exist. It's not that you're not important, it's that you don't exist. It's like you are being kicked out of history." That sense of historical erasure, shared by many in the group, is a grave sign about the state of the world. Indeed, 2022 marks the 16th consecutive year of democracy in retreat, according to a recent report from Freedom House, a human rights watchdog, "shifting the international balance in favor of tyranny." Democracies are shaken by illiberal forces within their borders. Authoritarian states support one another—Iran and Russia underwrite the Syrian government; Russia and China support Venezuela. President Trump was a fan of Brazil's Jair Bolsonaro and of Hungary's Viktor Orbán.

Salim sees the New University in Exile as an act of resistance against these terrifying trends. "The Consortium tells us to open up to each other and try to make something out of this time, to continue the work we were doing before," he says. "I think the Consortium is actually helping us stay within history."[19]

Concluding Comments

This chapter discussed monitoring agencies, such as Scholars at Risk, that are working on behalf of faculty and students fleeing oppression, harassment, and threats of political persecution. These various organizations, as well as university groups set up to receive scholars in exile, have created a network of support and solidarity to help targeted scholars and advocate on their behalf. These groups are also trying to establish more robust international legal frameworks that speak to a growing transnational intellectual community. Clearly, their work needs to be supported and further expanded to meet the rising crisis of scholars and students in need.

The harrowing tales of scholars in exile help humanize the global attack on academic freedom, underscoring scholars' personal fear and bravery as well as their attempts to regain a sense of self and dignity and agency amid incredible insecurity. These tales show scholars facing life-changing circumstances and remind us of the social injustices involved when attacks are made on academic freedom. Such injustices are amplified by the emotional, psychological, and cultural tolls exacted from people, in addition to the economic precarity and political disenfranchisement they face, when forced to leave their jobs and homes. Perhaps most importantly, these stories need to serve as a wake-up call to us all. In the coming years, more and more scholars and students are likely to experience similar social injustices both in the United States and overseas.

On reflection, it seems incredible that we are facing a global attack on academic freedom, given the hope and optimism around the societal benefits of public higher education that emerged in the 1950s and 1960s. How have scholars and students who supposedly represented the nation's hopes for the post–World War II generation now come to be considered by far-right politicians and their core populist supporters as "enemies of the people"? The next chapter explores the shifts within higher education in the second half of the twentieth century that set up the political, social, and economic conditions that form the backdrop to today's general undermining of higher education and specific targeting of scholars' freedom to think and ask probing questions.

Chapter 4

Higher Education and Democratic Dreams

Today's aggressive assault by the far right on scholars and students did not just appear out of nowhere. While it is important to recognize the unique political and material conditions that frame the assault on higher education in the early decades of the twenty-first century, it is also important to see that these more recent developments are linked to the highly contested history of public higher education since the 1960s. Historically, many people in the United States considered universities and colleges a public good, but there has always been tension over the purpose and objectives of higher education. Should knowledge and teaching be for expanding national prestige and developing security and technology expertise? Or should knowledge and teaching be for furthering democracy, building an inclusive society, and helping to foster class and social mobility?

The chapter begins with a description of higher education in the United States in the post–World War II era, as it opened up under the GI Bill to millions of students who previously had not imagined going to college. These efforts toward reimagining higher education as a driver of democratization were heavily influenced by the turbulent racial politics of the civil rights movement of the 1950s and 1960s, which reverberated across Europe and other countries in the global north, as well as the post–World War II anticolonial movements in the global south that pushed for control of universities free from Western curricula, racism, and governmental oversight.

The optimism about public higher education as a "democratizing" project included opening campuses to a more diverse student body that included students of color and women. In the United States, higher education saw significant achievements with the emergence of interdisciplinary programs such as African American studies, women's studies, and ethnic studies, as well as the federal enforcement of Title IX, which required universities and colleges to accept women students. Between 1961 and 1970, 200 new public universities were built across the United States as well as in Australia, India, France, West Germany, and Britain. What connected these institutions across international borders was a "utopian" belief on the part of scholars, administrators, and government leaders that higher education would help build more democratic societies (Pellew and Taylor 2021). This belief reflected an enormous public investment in educating a postwar generation through developing national knowledge capacities and prestige on an international level. It also reflected a postwar shift in economic power and realignment of the world's political order away from Britian and wider Europe toward the United States.

These achievements came at a cost, however. As widespread student agitation picked up in the mid to late 1960s, chiefly in protest of the US war in Vietnam and the military draft, there was heavy police presence on campuses, and student clashes with the National Guard became common in the United States. Concurrently, universities around the world were met with a conservative backlash that sought to rein in "radical" students and their antiwar stance as well as their push toward social justice and inclusive knowledge production. Throughout the 1970s and 1980s, governments began to explicitly use universities for national scientific and economic purposes, and there was a worldwide swing toward thinking about the university as an instrument of the state. As national governments increasingly dictated the kind of research to be funded, there was also an incremental chipping away of academic freedom and university autonomy. Universities' dependency on state governments that had oversight over them made higher education increasingly susceptible to political interference.

Overall, this chapter narrates the move in public higher education since the 1960s. As universities became slowly but steadily more inclusive in terms of student demographics and political aspirations, they were subject to a conservative backlash. Universities became more dependent on state funds and government oversight and explicitly turned into an instrumental arm of the state (Schrum 2019). Part of this process was the corporatization and management of universities and colleges by bureaucratic agencies and audit surveillance throughout the 1980s and 1990s. This shift in higher education's purpose is important for understanding today's far-right attacks on scholars and students who are again rising up and demanding—in ways that echo student protests of the 1960s—that higher education be committed to principles of social justice and diverse multiracial worldviews. These demands are more applicable than ever before in a world facing unprecedented levels of inequality and poverty, unfolding climate crises, and escalating cultural diversity driven by the mass movement of millions of people fleeing conflict, political insecurity, and environmental degradation.

Utopian Universities

In the wake of World War II, reflecting the country's postwar economic boom, public higher education became a top priority in the United States. Congress passed the GI Bill in 1944, providing tuition and living expenses to millions of war veterans returning from fighting in Europe and the Pacific (Altschuler and Blumin 2009). The GI Bill was intended to make higher education available to many previously denied such opportunities because of their lower socioeconomic status and class backgrounds. Efforts to create a more equitable society were echoed in the report *Higher Education for American Democracy*, issued by the President's Commission on Higher Education in 1947.[1] Despite these policy aspirations, however, the higher education industry's focus on providing for veterans favored men, who far outnumbered the women who served in the armed forces in World War II. Moreover, according to the historian Hilary Herbold, the promise of the GI Bill was largely unfilled for Black veterans, who lived mainly in Southern states that were still deeply segregated under Jim Crow laws. These veterans often could not afford to leave home, and even if they did apply to college, they found it very difficult to overcome the racial discrimination of admission boards (Herbold 1994; Stein 2022).

For the many thousands of White men who could benefit from the GI Bill, there was a large movement by veterans and their families westward to take advantage of cheap housing and embrace the mythical American dream. Often overlooked, however, is that this expanding higher education sector and the development of land-grant universities came at a huge cost. Echoing the reliance of earlier private universities such as Harvard, Yale, Princeton, and Georgetown on slave labor and financial profits from selling slaves (Wilder 2014; Blight 2024), land-grant universities relied on the forced removal of Native Americans from reservations and homelands. Land-grant universities were part of a wider strategy of settler colonialism that built on the Spanish mission system and resulted in large-scale violence, dispossession, and ultimately genocide of many Indigenous peoples across the middle and Western regions of the United States (Madely 2017; Adams 2020; Lee and Ahtone 2020; Stein 2022).

The process of stripping First Nations of their lands began in the early days of colonialism during the seventeenth and eighteenth centuries. The scale of land dispossession expanded enormously in the nineteenth century, and under the Morrill Act (1862), land appropriation was legalized to build federal "land-grant" colleges. The Morrill Act amounted to what historian Margaret Nash calls a "state-sponsored system of Native dispossession" (Nash 2019:437).[2] The Morrill Act was accompanied by a suite of federal laws such as the Homestead Act (1862) and the Hatch Act (1887) that were designed to encourage settlement of westward-moving populations. Overall, the United States privatized more than a billion acres of land, with about 11 million acres allotted to land-grant universities (Platt 2023:28). These new institutions of higher education were intended to instruct growing populations primarily in the fields of agriculture, science, and engineering. For instance, Texas A&M originally opened in 1876 as the Agricultural and Mechanical College of Texas. Notably, these new universities did not educate Indigenous youth, who were sent to off-reservation boarding schools, such as the Carlisle Indian Industrial School in Pennsylvania, which were established in 1879 to assimilate—through violent conditions that often led to death—young Native Americans into modern, "civilized" Western society (Churchill 2004; Moore 2003; Minton 2019; Adams 2020).[3]

The Morrill Act enabled the building of the University of California, Berkeley, the first university in what would become the University of California's 10-campus system. With the university motto *fiat lux* (Latin for let "there be light"), the vision of a more inclusive educational system was infused with the ideology of manifest destiny, with the aim of bringing learning and civilization to a wilderness occupied by bears, wolves, and "savage" Native peoples (Platt 2023:150).

The University of California land-grant system rapidly expanded in the late 1950s. Fields and ranches were quite literally taken over by the University of California, and university buildings began appearing on the predominantly agricultural landscape. UC Davis, UC Riverside, UC Santa Barbara, UC Santa Cruz, and UC Irvine sprung up across Southern California. Notably, UC Irvine was seen as an experiment in expanding the land-grant university campus from one focused on agriculture to a campus dedicated to interdisciplinary social sciences where models of administration, management, and policy would be developed and taught (Schrum 2019:189–213). This shift in focus reflected the post–World War II public optimism about the promise of public higher education and ushered in a new era that regarded the university as "a problem-solving instrument" that could provide solutions for challenges of modern society such as urban planning, economic development, and national defense (Schrum 2019:213).

The campus building craze epitomized a flourishing higher education industry driven by the dramatic rise in the number of children—often called "boomers"—born after the war, between 1946 and 1964. California's population alone went from 7 million in 1940 to 16 million by 1960. With the rapid expansion of universities and state and community colleges throughout the 1960s and 1970s, opportunities gradually spread to women and students from a range of ethnic and socioeconomic backgrounds. Native Americans were still largely excluded, however (Hutcheson et al. 2011). This opening up of educational opportunities also reflected a diversifying population, with the numbers of Latinx and Chicanx students remaining small but steadily rising.

Yet against this more inclusive vision of higher education, conservative forces were gathering. William Buckley, a student at Yale University, helped mobilize right-leaning student groups and wrote a controversial book in 1951 titled *God and Man at Yale: The Superstitions of Academic Freedom*. In it, he denounced what he claimed was anticapitalist and anti-Christian "collectivist" thinking being taught on his campus, though his real target was the progressive effort to democratize higher education (Buckley 1951; Shepherd 2023). The book was well received within a rising conservative movement that Buckley would go on to help establish, but the book also received criticism. Wrote McGeorge Bundy, a leading Harvard scholar at the time, "The book winds up with a violent attack on the whole concept of academic freedom. It is in keeping with the rest of the volume that Mr. Buckley does not seem to know what academic freedom is" (Bundy 1951).[4]

Buckley's belittling of academic freedom and his overall anti-intellectual conservative position resonated with Cold War geopolitical tensions. Within higher education, there was deep suspicion of any faculty member with communist affiliations, and during the mid to late 1940s, fears escalated that communism was being taught in classrooms and that universities were becoming breeding grounds of indoctrination (Schrecker 1986). US Senator Joseph McCarthy chaired the Permanent Subcommittee on Investigations of the Senate Committee on Government Operations, and he was emblematic of a campaign against "disloyalty" that included investigating journalists, Hollywood figures, and unionists as well as scholars deemed to be teaching "unpatriotic" curriculum and thought to have connections with Communist Party and Soviet networks.

McCarthyism spearheaded a much wider set of repressive measures implemented by local university presidents and administrators, trustee boards, city boards, and state legislators (Schrecker 1986). There was general consensus that association with the Communist Party disqualified teachers intellectually and professionally. Many academics thought that when their colleagues were investigated and chose not to answer by using their constitutional Fifth Amendment rights, they brought shame on their institutions and threatened the increasing dependency of universities and colleges on federal funding (Schrecker 1986:320). Overall, both public and private universities were quick to fire or not rehire any professor associated with communism. It is estimated that about 600 educators at all levels lost their jobs. The chilling effect on intellectual thinking through self-censorship was more widespread, however, and "though not quantifiable, this may have been the greatest tragedy of McCarthyism's effect on academia" (Aby 2009:122).

Emerging Student Activism

Against these repressive measures, students started to mobilize and resist. Students for a Democratic Society (SDS) was established in 1960 and over the ensuing decade grew to include 30,000 supporters and 300 campus chapters. Student protests erupted across many campuses objecting to McCarthyism's political interference in academic freedom and students' free speech, as well as the increasingly brutal Vietnam War, which threatened male students with the prospect of being drafted. At the UC Berkeley campus, students organized by the Free Speech Movement demonstrated throughout 1964. Despite the administration's efforts to shut down the movement and seek assistance from the Federal Bureau of Investigation (FBI) (Platt 2023:187), students occupied Sproul Hall and held public demonstrations. These acts resulted in the arrest of 800 students on December 4, 1964, leading to mass student strikes. Significantly, in an emergency meeting, the faculty academic senate met and voted 824–115 to endorse the students' demand that the university not restrict the content of speech on campus. According to those present, students wept with relief as the faculty emerged to widespread student applause.

Robert Cohen, historian and graduate of UC Berkeley, writes, "The Free Speech Movement was the first revolt of the 1960s to bring to a college campus the mass civil disobedience tactics pioneered in the civil rights movement. Those tactics, most notably the sit-in, would give students unprecedented leverage to make demands on university administrators, setting the stage for mass student protests against the Vietnam War" (Cohen 2009:1). These tactics appeared across the higher education landscape, at HBCUs, small liberal arts colleges, and large public and private universities (Kendi 2012; see also Ferguson 2017). In many southern states, both Black and White student activists were monitored by the FBI and local police intelligence units, called "Red Squads," that tried to silence their opposition to racial discrimination (Michel 2024). Notably, as argued by historian Joy Ann Williamson-Lott, Black student agitation over racial bias and denials of academic freedom in higher education played an important—and often overlooked—role in the greater Black Freedom struggle against Jim Crow that resulted in the passing of the Civil Rights Act of 1964 and the Voting Rights Act of 1965 (Williamson-Lott 2018, 2024).

In addition to the racial turmoil within the United States that was playing out in university campus politics, what was happening in universities across the global south also deeply influenced US student activism. In the post–World War II era, students and scholars in Africa, South Asia, and Central and South America were demanding the end of colonial rule. They sought to establish their own universities and academic curricula free from the constraints of colonial oversight and political interference (Ngũgĩ 1986; Alatas 2000; Federici, Caffentzis and Alidon 2000; Mamdani 2007; Al-Bulushi 2023). These groups explicitly linked academic freedom with human rights, liberation, and the building of new independent nations.[5]

Despite widespread challenges, some formerly colonial-controlled universities began to "open up" to nonwhite students. Often these moves were met with political retaliation. For example, when the Nationalist Party regime took control in South Africa in 1948, universities that had allowed some Black students into their medical schools were increasingly threatened. In response, academic leaders at the University of the Witwatersrand, Johannesburg (Wits), and the University of Cape Town (UCT) condemned attempts to segregate the student body according to race with the intention of creating a university apartheid system. Notably, these leaders turned to the concept of academic freedom as a way of making their argument against external political interference.[6] Despite the public outcry among university leaders and worldwide sanctions against the Afrikaner government, however, the racist state apparatus was institutionalized across South Africa's universities. Tensions between universities and the national government steadily increased throughout the 1960s and 1970s, erupting in the Soweto student uprising in 1976, when many young people were killed by police and thousands more injured. Neville Alexander, who spent 10 years imprisoned alongside Nelson Mandela, described the uprising:

> The struggle of students for better conditions in schools, colleges, and universities was seen to be inseparable from the struggle for liberation (i.e., the struggle for democratic rights for all) and eventually from the struggle for class emancipation. And, as these things go, once this link has been established in the consciousness of the new generation and in the concrete fact of thousands of Soweto students fleeing into neighboring territo-

ries to find refuge in the guerrilla training camps of the African National Congress and Pan Africanist Congress ... the Freirian idea of education for liberation came to express precisely the dialectical shift that had, quite unintentionally, been brought to the surface by the volleys of rifle fire that drowned in blood one of the most heroic episodes in the history of our people. (Alexander 1992:26–27)

Political theorist Isaac Kamola argues that anticolonialism throughout the 1960s reverberated across the global north, rupturing Euro-American imperialist sensibilities. In what Kamola calls "The Long '68," he argues that what is typically understood as a mass organization of student and labor unrest primarily involving US and European countries in 1968 was in fact deeply influenced by anticolonial struggles that had been building for a decade across the global south (Kamola 2019a). These struggles were particularly evident in Africa, which between 1957 and 1968 experienced an extraordinarily rapid independence movement that left 40 countries free from European colonial rule. Kamola goes on: "A more temporally and spatially expansive understanding of these protests makes it possible to appreciate the profound role African anticolonialism played in the long '68, locating student protests—whether in Paris, Berkeley, Mexico, Kampal, Dakar, Tunis, Dar es Salaam, or elsewhere—as common struggles not only over the formation of a world capitalist system but also over the emergence of a 'world university system' ... that brought the non-Western world to the forefront" (Kamola 2019a:305, 307).

In the United States, at San Francisco State University, student strikes broke out in 1968, led by a coalition of student groups calling themselves the Third World Liberation Front (TWLF). The group deliberately used the term "Third World" to refer to the nonaligned regions of Asia, Africa, and Latin

America and the oppressed peoples of the world, connecting the group's US-based experiences of racial discrimination under Jim Crow with the fight for independence and freedom by peoples oppressed under Western colonialism and systems of racial apartheid.[7] Students demanded recognition of women's rights and gay and lesbian rights and specifically demanded the establishment of a Third World studies curriculum that would build a "New World Consciousness" recognizing the unique intellectual contributions of minority scholars, mainly from the so-called Third World (Africa, Asia, Oceania, Latin America, Caribbean) but also from the First World (the capitalist West) and the Second World (the socialist East) (Okihiro 2016:16). As explained in the TWLF's demands to administrators, "Third World peoples must have the power to develop and control their own education... with the specific need to control the hiring, firing, and tenure of faculty members."[8]

The strikes went on for months and were met with armed troops; many students were arrested and injured, and some professors lost their jobs. Penny Nakatsu, a student leader who joined the coalition, explained, "The power of the state was trying to literally beat down the strike and strikers.... It was literally a practiced, orchestrated, military movement" (quoted in Ehsanipour 2020, figure 9). By the end of 1968, a faculty senate committee agreed to the formation of a Black Studies program and the possibility of an ethnic studies program, which was established as the College of Ethnic Studies the following year. However, as Asian American scholar Gary Okihiro has powerfully argued, in that "post-1968 version of ethnic studies, patriarchal nationalism eclipsed Third World consciousness and solidarity" (Okihiro 2016:31). Tragically, a Third World Studies curriculum based in world history and transnational analysis, and demanding the self-determination

Figure 9. Police officers in riot gear, marching in formation. San Francisco State College strike, December 11, 1968. Photo by Terry Schmitt. Courtesy of University Archives, J. Paul Leonard Library, San Francisco State University.

of all oppressed peoples across national divides, would never be fully realized.

While some US student protesters invoked Third World anticolonialism, other student groups were profoundly influenced by civil rights movements at home and overseas, resulting in surging antiwar unrest in France and Britain, across Europe, and in other parts of the world. The year 1968 saw mass public demonstrations that involved police on the streets, clouds of tear gas, and state violence against demonstrators. In Czechoslovakia's Prague Spring uprising, students marched against the Soviet takeover before being violently put down by military forces. In Amsterdam, students marched against the

Vietnam War and the horrors of the Tet Offensive that killed 1,500 Americans and showed the world that the US-led war was at a stalemate. In Australia, antiwar protests were frequent, with scores of students and union members arrested in Melbourne and Sydney in demonstrations against the National Service scheme, which forced conscription on men over 18 years.[9] In Paris, a small group of students took over a room at the Paris University at Nanterre to protest class and race discrimination and state-controlled funding of university resources. Student conflicts escalated over some months, and protests were joined by trade unionists and participants in New Left movements. In May 1968, 11 million workers joined students in the streets to take part in wildcat strikes protesting a range of issues including state militarization, US imperialism, and capitalist exploitation of people and natural environments.

War, Whiteness, Women, Waste

Throughout 1968 and into 1969, thousands of students across the United States protested a range of issues such as the Vietnam War, racial and gender discrimination, and the unregulated pollution and degradation of the natural environment. By 1970, 240 universities had staged demonstrations against President Nixon's expansion of the Vietnam War into Cambodia. Many of these demonstrators also rejected political interference by the Central Intelligence Agency (CIA) and the Department of Defense in university research, teaching, and administration.[10] According to the anthropologist Richard Price, the growing national security state sought a wide range of scholars, including engineers, physicists, anthropologists, historians, and sociologists, to study countries considered enemies, as well as potential client states that formed the territorial battlegrounds of the Cold War. Academics were vital to "produce and maintain the hardware and ideology needed to sustain decades of competition against the Soviets" (Price 2011:39–40; see also Price 2004). As public knowledge grew about the CIA's interference on campuses, however, students started to demand the removal of defense-funded programs and research centers. By 1966, the CIA was aware of its waning popularity, and by 1968, the agency had recorded 77 anti-CIA campus protests (Price 2011:45; Zwerling 2011; Chomsky 1997).

Student tensions concerning issues of racism also exploded with the assassination of Martin Luther King Jr. in April 1968. In the immediate aftermath of the assassination, Columbia University students protested the administration's racist policies, and three school officials were held hostage for a day. Riots broke out on other campuses as well as across 100 cities in anguish over the killing of MLK. Washington, DC, became engulfed in public demonstrations with the Poor People's March, which sought to renew antipoverty efforts and establish an economic bill of rights for predominantly Black communities— an effort pushed by MLK's Poor People's Campaign. In the summer of 1968, the nation's capital saw the setting up of Resurrection City on the Mall, which included an encampment of 3,000 tents housing 5,000 protesters for more than a month.

On a related but different front of inequality, the women's rights movement, often called the women's liberation movement, also picked up momentum during the 1960s. Originally motivated by French feminist Simone de Beauvoir's bestselling book *The Second Sex (Le Deuxième Sexe)*, published in 1949, second-wave feminism was revitalized with Betty Friedan's *The Feminist Mystique*, published in 1963. Friedan wrote about society's entrapment of women in bored and unfilled lives of domesticity and spoke to concerns among women students that their voices were dismissed, even by progressive New Left movements. Calls for women's studies departments in many colleges and universities helped galvanize what was a diverse and conflicted women's liberation movement, divided over issues of abortion, racial inclusion, and such demands as the abolition of Miss America pageants. As noted by bell hooks, an emerging Black feminist scholar at the time, this movement, while relatively progressive, was very much a White feminist movement that still clung to racial biases marginalizing women of color (hooks 1994; Salper 2011).

Further aiding women's liberation was the introduction of the birth control pill in 1960, championed for years by Margaret Sanger, president of the Planned Parenthood Federation of America. The birth control pill was an enormous success, and within three years, 2.3 million American women were using the contraceptive. It was not until 1972 that unmarried women were given widespread access to the pill, however, reflecting prevailing patriarchal and sexist attitudes at the time. By the early 1970s, real progress for women's rights was being made: Congress in 1972 passed Title IX of the Higher Education Act, which prohibited educational programs from discriminating based on sex. All-male schools were forced to open their doors to women students. Another extraordinary victory for general equality was the Supreme Court ruling in *Roe v. Wade* in 1973, granting women rights to bodily autonomy, abortion, and access to reproductive care. This ruling, in combination with wider access to the pill, enabled many young women to pursue higher education and enter the labor force for the first time, liberating a whole generation from traditional domestic gender roles. Indicating the growing global power of women during the 1970s were changes in laws across numerous countries that allowed women autonomy over their own bodies and the right to have an abortion (United Kingdom 1967; Canada 1969; United States, Tunisia, and Denmark 1973; Austria 1974; France and Sweden 1975; New Zealand 1977; Italy 1978).

Adding to the wave of social protests that took place throughout the 1960s and exploded in 1969 was the issue of environmentalism. This dimension of student agitation at the time is often overlooked, but it played a central role in building an emerging national environmental movement. Rachel Carson's book *Silent Spring* (1962) fostered growing awareness of the damaging impacts of air and water pollution, and the US government responded by passing the Endangered Species Preservation Act (1966) and the Clean Air Act (1967). A major oil spill that erupted in Santa Barbara in January 1969, however, really galvanized the green movement. At the time, it was the worst spill in the country's history, contaminating beaches and killing many birds and fish along a 75-mile coastline. Gaylord Nelson, a Democratic senator from Wisconsin, promoted student teach-ins on the environment in the wake of the oil spill, modeled on earlier antiwar teach-ins against US imperialism overseas (figure 10). Remarkably, a year later, 20 million Americans demonstrated across the country in support of better regulation over pollution and toxic waste on the first Earth Day, June 22, 1970. Earth Day helped spark worldwide activism and the emergence of green political parties in Germany, Australia, New Zealand, Switzerland, and Britain, as well as the United States.

Conservative Backlash

Demands by students and activists for civil and political rights, including protection of the environment, were met with a widespread backlash by the Republican Party (Schrecker 2021). Students calling for academic freedom and state noninterference on university and college campuses provided Republicans with the justification to target university administrators in efforts to quell wider social unrest. This backlash against higher education was epitomized by the sacking of Clark Kerr

Figure 10. Police move in behind a student teach-in blocking the entrance to the Santa Barbara wharf on the first anniversary of the Santa Barbara oil spill on January 29, 1970, Santa Barbara, California. Photo by Bruce Cox. Reproduced with permission of *Los Angeles Times* via Getty Images.

(president of the Regents of the University of California) by Republican Ronald Reagan (then-governor of California) for not being tough enough on students in 1967. Reagan was dealing with state budgetary deficits; taking advantage of the public's financial anxiety, he declared that taxpayers' money should not be "subsidizing intellectual curiosity" and "intellectual luxuries" but should be spent on training students for jobs (Reeves 2010). As noted by commentator Dan Berrett, Reagan's public announcement in February 1967 was the day the purpose of college changed in the United States (Berrett 2015).

As campus tensions mounted throughout 1967 and 1968, Reagan became more aggressive, realizing that attacking student protests would win him support from the rising conservative movement. He likened students to Hitler's Brownshirts and said faculty were turning university campuses into "staging areas for insurrection" (De Groot 1996:116). Claiming that California was in a state of war, the governor argued that "the only thing that can win in campus guerilla war is . . . you eliminate them by firing the faculty members and expelling the students" (De Groot 1996:117–118). Reagan crudely and revealingly also appealed to racism, claiming that "Negroes" had attacked a university dean "with switchblades at his throat" (De Groot 1996:115). Reagan's open attack on universities stoked public fear and "moral panic," leading to calls for a tough law-and-order campaign that helped Richard Nixon get elected to US presidency a year later, in 1968 (Cohen 1972:28; see also Hall 1978).

The Republican law-and-order mantra fueled widespread student antiwar strikes throughout 1969 and 1970 that saw the National Guard called to many campuses. Among numerous instances of police violence and student conflict were the protests that broke out at UC Berkeley in what came to be called the People's Park incident on May 15, 1969. As armed police stormed the demonstrators, one person was shot and later died; 128 people were admitted to the hospital. That evening, Governor Reagan sent in an enormous force of 2,700 national guardsmen, who for two weeks patrolled the streets amid tear gas and barricades (figure 11). Other incidents included the burning by students of the Bank of America—which was seen as a symbol of the establishment—at UC Santa Barbara in February 1970.

Among the highly charged and violent demonstrations of this time, the deadliest event occurred in May 1970 at Kent State University, when 28 national guardsmen opened fire on unarmed students, some of them protesting the expansion of

Figure 11. National Guard troops confront protesters at People's Park in UC Berkeley, 1969. Photograph by Ted Streshinsky. Courtesy of the Streshinsky Family. Reproduced with permission of Getty Images.

the war into Cambodia. Sixty-seven shots were fired, killing four students and injuring another nine (figure 12). Ten days later, two Black students also protesting the invasion of Cambodia were killed by police at Jackson State University in Mississippi; however, this episode of violence is rarely remembered. Kent State's horrific events were immortalized by singer-songwriter Neil Young, who, immediately upon seeing images of killed students in *Life* magazine, wrote the protest song "Ohio." The song was quickly recorded by the band Crosby, Stills, Nash, and Young and became an instant hit. The song criticized President Richard Nixon for sending in the National Guard and killing students who were protesting the killing of innocent civilians in Cambodia. *The Report of the President's Commission on Campus Unrest* concluded

Figure 12. Surviving Kent State shooting victim Alan Canfora, waving a flag before the Ohio National Guard, as pictured in the May 15, 1970, issue of *Life* magazine. Photo by student John Filo. Wikimedia Commons. Public domain.

that the shootings were "unnecessary, unwarranted, and inexcusable." Nixon denounced these findings, however, and went on to be reelected to the US presidency in 1972; in Ohio, he won the vote by a sweeping margin of 21 percentage points.

The End of Utopian Universities

The utopian promise of public higher education that flourished in many global north countries throughout the 1960s came to an abrupt halt by the 1970s, as governments in the

United States, Britain, Australia, West Germany and France, among others, came to see higher education as in need of being reined in and tightly managed (Pellew and Taylor 2021). Many of these governments thought that students and faculty had become too radicalized and that their demands for progressive pedagogies that included diverse multiracial worldviews and student participation had gone too far. In the United States, notes historian Ellen Schrecker, "higher education would never again enjoy the near-universal respect and financial support of the American people."[11]

The conservative backlash against higher education sought to impose two intertwined agendas to further respective national interests. The first agenda sought to curb the increasing numbers of minority students who were attending public university and gaining professional and political power. The second agenda was more internationally facing and revolved around making Western countries, led by the United States, dominant in terms of political, military, and economic power. Forging a focused research and teaching program in higher education served both purposes for the elite socioeconomic classes in many countries of the global north.

Agenda 1: Blocking Minority Students in Higher Education

In the United States, many middle-class White people linked campus disruptions to the civil rights movement and its antiracist demands for better housing, jobs, and health care for Blacks, Latinx, Chicanx, and Indigenous communities. In short, they blamed students of color for the widespread agitation on college campuses during the 1960s and early 1970s that had led to international disruptions and national embarrassment.[12] The Republican backlash under President Richard Nixon was predominantly directed at African American, Latinx, and Asian American students. In other Western countries, this conservative agenda mainly focused on students who had migrated from former colonies in Africa, South Asia, and the Americas. For instance, in Britain, students of South Asian descendant from India, Pakistan, and Sri Lanka were targeted, while in France students who came from North Africa and in particular Algiers and Morocco were targeted.

The Republican backlash against minority students manifested in reduced federal funding to support public education at all levels. Despite the desegregation decision in *Brown v. Board of Education* (1954), defunding involved redrawing primary and secondary school districts to favor White suburban schools over urban schools that served many Black and immigrant students. Defunding was largely justified through arguments for urban renewal that reversed New Deal policies supporting the poor and cleared inner-city "slums" and urban decay for redevelopment (Stoesz 1992). Other Republican strategies included reducing support for bilingual education, dropping summer school and adult education classes, and imposing informal segregation policies linked to transport accessibility and entrance testing. At the college level, tuition fees were introduced in California under Reagan that "recast the students as investors in themselves" and ushered in a new corporate vision of public higher education as a service provider that spread across the entire country (Feldblum 2023).

Relatedly, the Republican agenda against minorities also included an attack on women's political and civil rights. The feminist movements of the 1960s and 1970s were mobilized in part because women now had access to birth control and could better manage their career decisions, including pursuit of higher education. Throughout the 1980s and 1990s, Republicans and particularly conservative Christians were concerned about growing numbers of women in the workforce and their impact on male power and traditional patriarchal values. This deep worry about gender equity launched a behind-the-scenes campaign to overturn *Roe v. Wade* (1973). Decades later in 2023, after President Trump stacked the Supreme Court with a far-right 6–3 judicial majority, victory for the patriarchal extremists was finally secured. *Roe v. Wade* was overturned, and a fifty-year history of women having rights to reproductive autonomy and thus greater access to higher education and equal job opportunities was reversed. To date, of the many countries that legalized abortion around the world in the 1960s and 1970s, only the United States has revoked this core human right for women.

Agenda 2: Promoting Defense and Economic Interests Through Higher Education

The second conservative agenda was to use higher education to push national defense and economic interests. This strategy moved away from the pursuit of knowledge for the common good toward an "instrumental" approach that was driven by what was considered a priority for the nation. Against the backdrop of the Cold War, many countries increased spending on science and military technology that would improve their national security and defense capabilities (Pellew and Taylor 2021). The United States led on this front, developing federally funded granting agencies such as the Department of Defense (established 1947) and the National Science Foundation (established 1950), which then contracted elite universities that had the faculty expertise and resources necessary for "Big Science." As the historian John Thelin notes, the wartime Manhattan Project at the University of Chicago was a good model for this kind of state–university scientific enterprise (Thelin 2019:259, 272; see also Saltman and Gabbard 2011).

While some elite universities, such as Stanford, Caltech, and MIT, flourished under the new system, other elite universities, including Harvard and Yale, had to adjust to relying on federal funding to support large-scale applied research projects (Harris 2023).

One consequence of this emerging dependency of research on federal funding was that the government's role in shaping what, why, and how learning occurred in the classroom became less ambiguous. In other words, embedded relations between the higher education community and the federal government were less deniable. Federal control over revenue streams meant that "an external federal agency had the power to alter campus governance and institutional mission, including essential tenets of academic freedom" (Thelin 2019:274; Newfield 2021:264).

In addition to serving scientific and defense interests, universities were also instrumental in furthering national economies through free-market ideology or what is often referred to as neoliberalism. This radical economic ideology opposed Keynesian economics, which had supported the New Deal and government employment programs during the Great Depression after the stock market crash of 1929. Neoliberals, in contrast to Keynesians, argued in favor of less government oversight and of deregulation of industry, banking, and economic development (Oreskes and Conway 2023). Neoliberal logic was promoted by mainstream Euro-American neoliberal economists influenced by the teachings of people such as Friedrich A. Hayek, Milton Friedman, and James M. Buchanan, each of whom received the Nobel Prize for economics in 1974, 1976, and 1986, respectively. These economists and their business allies helped establish a vast international network of think tanks, conservative foundations, and private institutes to help push the neoliberal agenda around the world

(Mirowski and Plehwe 2009; Slobodian 2018). Although neoliberal ideology has shifted over time, a constant element is the submission of politics to economic metrics and markets (Peck 2010:xii-xiii; Chomsky 1999). This required banks, financiers, and businesses to transform government priorities so that they served corporate interests rather than citizens' needs. Relatedly, neoliberalism also opposed the principles and practices of democracy that seek to limit the power of markets to freely exploit human and nonhuman resources. Notes the political theorist Wendy Brown, "Throttling democracy was fundamental, not incidental, to the broader neoliberal program" (Brown 2019:61–62).[13]

In an extraordinary memo sent to leading US business leaders in 1971, lawyer and future Supreme Court Justice Lewis F. Powell Jr. laid out a blueprint for ensuring the survival of the "free enterprise system" against state regulation and taxation (Powell 1971). The memo beseeched corporate leaders to join the fight against "extremists on the left" who challenged the profit-making logic of capitalism. Specifically, he put the primary blame on university intellectuals and called for the defunding of higher education. At the same time, he called on the national Chamber of Commerce to establish its own "staff of highly qualified scholars in the social sciences who do believe in the [enterprise] system." These scholars were to publish, speak on campuses, and vet textbooks "especially in economics, political science and sociology" (MacLean 2018; Mayer 2017; Schrecker 2021:450–451). Ellen Schrecker notes that conservative foundations created "a shadow academy":

> They [foundations] endowed professorships, supported free-market economics departments, and developed programs that pushed the virtues of free enterprise at dozens of universities. Brand-name colleges got their share, but so too did lower-tier

regional institutions like Middle Tennessee State University and Virginia's George Mason University. Funders sought out promising conservative students, subsidizing their publications and political organizations and sponsoring their future careers. By the 1980s, these efforts had created a chorus of seemingly respectable voices delivering a devastating critique of the traditional university.[14]

As already mentioned in chapter 1 and picked up again in chapter 5, taking over the production of research and curriculum in higher education was essential in furthering the conservative economic agenda. This was reflected in the rising number of economics departments and business schools and the new field of law and economics that sprung up on many campuses and that by 1991 had established its own professional association. The rapid shift in higher education toward economics and business is evidenced by student's bachelor's degrees in the United States: in 1965, 43 percent of students earned BA degrees in letters and sciences; by 1980, about 25 percent of degrees were in letters and sciences, and business had become the most popular major (Berrett 2015). To this day, market-oriented economics and business degrees remain the most sought-after college majors, involving approximately one-quarter of all undergraduate students.

Throughout the 1970s, 1980s, and 1990s, neoliberal logics helped justify the United States' neocolonial aspirations to open new overseas markets and take advantage of cheap labor and natural resources in the global south. These aspirations were dramatically demonstrated with the 1973 US-led coup in Chile, which overthrew the democratically elected administration of President Salvador Allende, leader of the Unidad Popular government. Allende proved to be a political and economic threat: after coming to office in 1970, his government began pushing back against United States and European companies that had controlled Chile's natural resources (predominantly oil, gas, and minerals) for many years. This angered the US and British governments, which backed a miliary coup against Allende led by General Augusto Pinochet (Kornbluh 2003). Notably, economists trained by Milton Friedman at the University of Chicago—the "Chicago Boys"—helped establish a neoliberal constitution and usher in a pro-business "economic revolution."

Friedman visited Pinochet in March 1975 to present plans for an austerity strategy that deliberately gutted social services and education and decimated the working classes. Attacking universities, burning books, and closing social science departments (for supposedly indoctrinating students) happened quickly in Chile (figure 13). By the end of 1975, more than 24,000 faculty, students, and staff had been expelled; many were sent to prison (Ben-Ghiat 2020:75). For 17 years Pinochet led a brutal authoritarian dictatorship, decimating democratic institutions; imprisoning, torturing, and disappearing thousands of political activists and intellectuals; and sending 200,000 people into exile.

Notably, what happened in Chile was part of "Operation Condor," a regional covert Cold War operation led largely by the United States from the mid-1970s into the early 1980s (McSherry 2005). In the name of fighting communism, Operation Condor joined together eight far-right military dictatorships in Argentina, Chile, Uruguay, Bolivia, Paraguay, Brazil, Peru, and Ecuador into a coordinated terrorist network that brutally attacked intellectuals, students, and activists across the continent. This brutal regional attack paved the way for the opening of economic markets and the exploitation of cheap labor and natural resources by the US and Europe.

Figure 13. Book burning in Santiago, Chile, September 1973. Wikimedia Commons. Public domain.

Chile's dictatorship under Pinochet influenced the thinking of Prime Minister Margaret Thatcher in Britain and President Ronald Reagan in the United States, among many other political leaders. Over subsequent decades, neoliberal ideology slowly became embedded within an international economic system that today largely operates behind the scenes and is opaque to most people. This system is financially controlled by the World Bank and the International Monetary Fund

(IMF), administered and managed by the World Trade Organization (WTO), and facilitated by a densely woven system of international law, transnational legal networks, global law firms, and public–private trading agreements (Hickel 2018). The system is also furthered through a complex web of tax havens and secretive financial dealings, including offshore trusts and shell companies, that shields massive accumulations of private and corporate wealth from regulatory scrutiny.

Market Logics and Reshaping Higher Education

Global financial institutions serving corporate capitalism had a significant impact on higher education around the world throughout the 1980s and 1990s (Giroux 2014). The World Bank and the IMF aggressively pushed a neoliberal educational agenda on global south countries seeking structural adjustment loans to help stimulate economic recovery. As a result, western foreign intervention into national systems of higher education became more pronounced in Asia, Latin America, the Caribbean, and Africa. According to the coordinators of the Committee for Academic Freedom in Africa, this led to the African educational system entering a "historic crisis": "All funds to public education were cut; many teachers and other academic staff were retrenched, and wages were frozen. As a result, in a few years, the existence of what had been one of the main conquests of the anticolonial struggle—the development of an African educational system—was seriously undermined" (Federici et al. 2000:xi; see also Mamdani 2007; Mamdani and Diouf 1995). Scholars Edward Carvalho and David Downing write that these financial institutions "made the privatizing, vocationalizing, and instrumentalizing of education part of the conditions that borrowing nations must implement in order to receive desperately needed loans for essential human services." Carvalho and Downing also note that, as a result, "around the world, public access to and control over many fundamental resources, from water supply to higher education, have been shrinking alarmingly" (Carvalho and Downing 2010:7).

The academy in the United States was not immune from global market forces. Together, the World Bank, MIT's Center for International Studies, and the Harvard Business School played a major role in promoting the concept of "globalization" and the idea of a single global market led by the United States and Europe (Borstelmann 2012: chap. 3, 4; Harris 2023). As argued by Isaac Kamola in his important book *Making the World Global: US Universities and the Production of the Global Imaginary*, market ideology was increasingly embraced by academic institutions and their financial networks during the 1990s (Kamola 2019b). Charlie Eaton, in his book *Bankers in the Ivory Tower: The Troubling Rise of Financiers in U.S. Higher Education*, adds that higher education became—at least for some elite financiers—a very lucrative business opportunity (Eaton 2022). Shiela Slaughter and Gary Rhoades arguably present the most impactful scholarship theorizing the marketization of higher education in the United States in their book *Academic Capitalism and the New Economy: Markets, State, and Higher Education* (2004). This book set in motion a large body of scholarship analyzing the many ways market logics permeated higher education and converted universities and colleges into corporate institutions (Slaughter and Leslie 1997; Newfield 2008; Saltman and Gabbard 2011; Cantwell and Kauppinen 2014).

The market takeover of higher education was one consequence of the emerging hegemonic dominance of neoliberalism under Reagan's presidency, 1981–1989, and Thatcher's leadership as prime minister, 1979–1990. These two major world leaders helped usher in the triumphalism of Western laissez-faire capitalism with the fall of the Soviet Union in 1991. In the United States, this process was aided by the Council for National Policy (CNP), which was established in 1981 during Reagan's first year in office. The CNP coordinated planning among powerful Republican figures, media entrepreneurs, donors, and evangelicals for long-term strategies to promote their collective interests. The CNP was "a little-known club of a few hundred of the most powerful conservatives in the country," meeting three times a year in secrecy.[15] Anne Nelson in her book *Shadow Network: Media, Money and the Secret Hub of the Radical Right* explains that the CNP sought to take over the Republican Party as well as to undermine sectors that challenged fundamentalist Protestant values. "These included public schools that taught evolution, universities that taught climate science, and businesses that supported equal rights for the LGBTQ community" (Nelson 2019:49). The CNP participated in a stealthy orchestration of antidemocracy that has been building over decades, with part of that strategy being the planned attack on progressive public education (Giroux 2014).

Cornel West, a leading Black philosopher, activist, and public intellectual, affirms that a stealthy undermining of democracy has taken place through the conservative takeover of public higher education. According to West:

> It's true that in the '60s you had these ivory tower institutions that were far removed from the realities of everyday life. And it was primarily pressure from the left that gave visibility to these issues, with the struggle against white supremacy, male supremacy, struggles against American imperialism in Vietnam, and so forth. But under the Reagan years, you actually then had right-wing social movements and right-wing organizations penetrating the academy in such a powerful way—learning their lessons

from the left, but using them for right-wing purposes, with their independent networks of think tanks and various foundations, and so forth and so on. (interview with West, Carvalho 2010:271)

Policing Universities Through Corporatism and Precarity

The global rise of free-market economics and political conservatism during the 1980s and 1990s was accompanied by new modes of policing academic freedom. Unlike the strategies used in numerous countries in the global south, however, in the United States new policing strategies over higher education were mostly nonviolent. What was experienced was a transition away from overt police presence on university and college campuses—as when the National Guard was deployed on the San Francisco State, UC Berkeley, and Kent State campuses in the 1960s—toward more insidious modes of political and economic control over lines of inquiry and teaching (Schrum 2019). American studies scholar Christopher Newfield argues in his book *Unmaking the Public University: The Forty-Year Assault on the Middle Class* (2008) that in the name of corporatization, privatization, and austerity measures, a coalition of conservative business, government, and academic groups intentionally gutted higher education to dismantle its democratizing goals and impacts. This involved a range of strategies such as defunding certain departments and disciplines (mainly in the humanities), restructuring grant distributions, and creating a mindset in which students were viewed and viewed themselves as paying customers.

Most obviously, control over public access to higher education was achieved by raising tuition for postsecondary education (Goldrick-Rab 2017). This limited higher education to wealthier, whiter students who could more readily afford rising annual costs and caused widespread outrage and distress among students. Inspired by the Occupy Wall Street demonstrations that erupted in 2011, students erected tents on the UC Berkeley campus in protest of tuition hikes. When students refused to remove the tents, police moved in; a video shows police beating students and one faculty member with batons on November 9, 2011. About a week later, at the UC Davis campus, tensions mounted as more tents were set up by students and police asked for their removal. On November 18, 2011, in an image that went viral, a police officer nonchalantly walked down a line of sitting students shooting pepper spray into their faces in an effort to dispel the crowd (figure 14). As noted by political theorist Farah Godrej, policing student protest within the University of California is often "deeply disproportionate to its peaceful character" and often reverts to criminalizing student behavior through a rhetoric of impending violence and the use of laws to prosecute and intimidate (Godrej 2014:128; see also Nocella et al. 2010; Nocella and Gabbard 2013).

Alongside the dramatic rise in tuition, universities and colleges increasingly came to rely on bankers and loan agencies to finance their institutions as state funding and student enrollments declined. Since the 1990s, elite universities have steadily invested in high-yielding hedge funds, particularly those managed by alumni, to grow their endowments. Private-equity firms and a largely unregulated financial industry have taken advantage of these institutional weaknesses, pushing further into university management of and investment in university housing, banking, and health and food services. As explained by sociologist Charlie Eaton, "Private equity looks for rent-seeking opportunities. These can occur in higher education and elsewhere when there are increased public subsidies or potential monopolies to exploit. The private-equity invasion of university housing and online-degree pro-

Figure 14. Officer Lieutenant John Pike, of the UC Davis police, pepper-spraying seated students on November 18, 2011. Photos by Louise Macabitas, UC Davis student. Licensed under the Attribution-NonCommercial-ShareAlike 2.0 Generic license. https://creativecommons.org/licenses/by/3.0/deed.en.

gram management fits with these strategies."[16] The growing dependence of universities on private capital has diluted faculty governance and has also made the institutions increasingly vulnerable to political interference. This university dependency on external funding has been consolidating over decades and has embedded private-sector and business-friendly priorities into scholarly research, learning, and student life (Schrecker 2010).

New modes of policing also involved creating cumbersome bureaucratic processes of state oversight and accreditation and an "audit culture" of surveillance that impacted many practices in higher education. For instance, universities in Britain, Australia, New Zealand, and across Europe have for some decades dealt with state-imposed "performance indicators" that in effect regulate, quantify, and discipline academic thought (Shore 2008; Halffman and Radder 2015; Kimber and Ehrich 2015; Shore and Wright 2015). Somewhat ironically and very tellingly, even business schools that promote an accounting mindset are now concerned that the prevailing audit culture undermines their pro-business training and the wider purpose of higher education to promote innovative thinking (Huzzard et al. 2017).

Audit Culture

Audit culture refers to the managerial system that has permeated the Euro-American academy and many colleges and universities around the world. Audit culture involves various ways of accounting, measuring, and rewarding certain types of "quality" knowledge production over other intellectual work that may be regarded as lacking impact or performance. What counts as quality work is typically determined by its commercial value, as measured by patents and intellectual property rights over inventions and technological and scientific innovations. Given the dominance of free-market logics, it is not surprising that intellectual work in less directly applied areas (often associated with the humanities) is considered "soft" and increasingly irrelevant, while STEM research is "hard" and receives the majority of state support and university funding.[17]

Within audit culture, "there is a focus on branding, marketing and management speak such as performance, student evaluations of teaching, work-integrated learning, creative industries, world-standard research and quality audits" (Kimber and Ehrich 2015:88). This focus promotes the "publish or perish" mantra, which is demoralizing, anxiety-producing, and exhausting, pitting individual scholars against one another as they compete for funds, teaching relief, and various types of resources. Writes Peter Fleming in his funny yet very serious book *Dark Academia: How Universities Die*, "It is lamentable that even scholars who are ardent critics of the neoliberal university still rejoice when their Google Scholar Citation Score increases and would seemingly run over their next of kin in a small jeep if it meant getting published in a 'top' journal" (Fleming 2021:5). Notes Liz Morrish, who resigned from her faculty position in the United Kingdom due to intolerable working conditions:

> There are also emerging threats to academic freedom in the form of slippage between the audit and disciplinary functions of performance management. Until recently, I had spent my entire career without having encountered a single colleague undergoing disciplinary action or performance improvement monitoring. Now, recourse to these procedures has become almost commonplace in some universities. It is not clear what results managers expect to emerge from a system that torments staff [faculty] with unattainable targets, constant surveillance, constant audit and the knowledge that any dip in "performance" may result in their con-

tracts being terminated.... It is obvious that there can be no self-determination or academic freedom within a working environment that is censorious and authoritarian, regardless of how many times "empowerment" features in the [university] strategic plan. (Morrish 2017)

One of the most insidious ways academic freedom and critical thinking are policed is through the use of audit culture to justify journal rankings. Typically, scholarly journals are assessed by an impact factor that is then translated into a numbering system and citation index, which can be applied to an individual scholar in merit reviews. Universities may have different performance equations in different countries, but across the board this system is favored by administrators, who can quickly assess the relative status of a candidate without having to read or engage with their work. Scholarship is reduced to an accounting system. Not surprisingly, many faculty target their publications for top-ranked journals, and some even try to "game" the system (Wilsdon et al. 2015). As analysts have noted, however, "the focus of such performance indexes present a shift towards industrial measurements of productivity that do not involve serious consideration of intellectual quality" (Tourish et al. 2017). Nor does such a system promote new thinking or provocative questions that may not be well received by high-impact journals. In short, conventional thinking that produces "safe" and incremental research is rewarded, while critical and innovative thinking that challenges the status quo may be punished. For some scholars, particularly in STEM areas, this may not be an issue. For other scholars and particularly for those doing qualitative humanistic research, however, the audit assessment system is coercive in policing what research and teaching "count" from the perspective of administrators.

Compounding the problem is the way audit mechanisms and performance indicators determine university and college rankings. Rankings were originally established to assure taxpayers and governments that public moneys were being spent effectively. Now, however, they have taken on enormous significance in a highly competitive higher education market. Some rankings, such as *US News and World Report*'s Best Colleges Rankings, sort institutions within one country or according to a specific discipline. Others—such as *Times Higher Education*'s World University Rankings, the QS World University Rankings, and Shanghai Jioa Tong University's Academic Ranking of World Universities—rank universities worldwide. Rankings not only help students decide which campus to apply to but can also shape policy decision-making within university administrations as well as state educational policy concerning the distribution of financial resources.[18]

For individual scholars, the audit culture system functions at multiple levels and in diverse ways to police their research and teaching. At the most basic level, if universities and colleges have low rankings and can't attract new students, budget deficits may force administrators to lay off faculty. Even scholars who have job security, however, are consciously and unconsciously corralled into doing certain kinds of research that can be published in high-impact journals and satisfy externally mandated performance indicators. In many ways, audit culture has heightened scholars' surveillance, accountability, and self-disciplining in a way that a few decades ago was unimaginable. This reality is noted in research showing that "these new regimes of accountability," justified in terms of efficiency and transparency, have opened universities up to greater state scrutiny and intervention (Shore and Wright 2015:425–426; Shore and Wright 2024:119–138; Spooner 2023). And with rising antidemocracy, political intervention via a justifiable audit culture is escalating, further undermining scholarly agency and academic freedom.[19]

Precarious and Adjunct Labor Force

Relatedly, the corporatization of universities has created a precarious labor force of adjunct and contract-based lecturers vulnerable to lack of union representation and susceptible to the whims of university administrators. Liz Morrish's observations about the intrusiveness of university management, noted earlier, highlight the ways an audit culture monitors scholars and teachers and the dramatic change in how colleges are being run. This change is marked by rising numbers of very well-paid managers and executives and the steady decline of tenured faculty and researchers on long-term employment contracts. "Now nearly 75 percent of the instruction at colleges and universities is in the hands of exploited and insecure, but highly trained and often devoted, faculty members who lack the time and resources to give students the attention they need."[20] As teaching quality has been reduced, administrators have gained more power over the hiring and firing of faculty and also more power to undermine working conditions by breaking up student and faculty unions and diluting or dissolving faculty-led university governance.

An increasingly "insecure" academic labor force is more easily controlled by university presidents, provosts, and deans. Unable to collectively mobilize and fight back, many scholars and teachers are overwhelmed by a system that runs on their precarity and economic insecurity. Qualified people are forced into adjunct teaching roles and unpredictable living conditions. Typically, these short-term contracts offer low wages, no health benefits, and no access to professional development opportunities. Notably, occupational precarity disproportionately impacts early-career scholars, women scholars, and scholars of color who are often already marginalized within the academy (O'Keefe and Courtois 2019; Ivancheva et al. 2019; Reyes 2022). Some commentators argue that this causes "epistemic injustices" and that greater attention needs to be paid to the working conditions of universities and colleges where scholars work and teach (Popović 2022a). According to Milica Popović, "academic freedom is not merely an issue which can be solved with strategic goals and policies: it begins with the very conditions under which academics work. While there are variations in the way staff are treated in different disciplines, such epistemic injustices spill over into academic injustices within academic communities themselves" (Popović 2022b).

A system based on labor precarity impacts everyone, not just those who are forced to lead lives of economic uncertainty and second-class status. Universities and colleges function as mini worlds, reflecting, performing, and reinforcing wider social values and priorities. In addition to diminishing alternative perspectives and worldviews, academic precarity has another consequence: it models for everyone within the institution a certain set of social relations and presents it as acceptable. As Vijay Prashad writes in an essay titled "Oppressive Pedagogy: Some Reflections on Campus Democracy," students are taught a certain way of being in the world that is inequitable and problematic:

> Indeed, the campus is no longer an "ivory tower" or a "city on the hill." It more closely resembles that other major culture-creating institution, the US Corporation. Income inequality (between the president and the janitor) is stark, but this is only the most vulgar instance of the convergence of academic and corporate cultures. The assault on campus unions that try to provide a living wage for the workers, on graduate student unions that try

to get a wage for indentured teachers, on adjuncts who enjoy no security of tenure, *teach* our students that the corporate free market culture is acceptable and that it is rational. (Prashad 2009:179; author's italics)

Concluding Comments

Between the 1960s and the 1990s, public higher education shifted in terms of its democratic aspirations and primary goals. In the United States as in many other countries, particularly in the global north, colleges and universities shifted from trying to serve the best interests of citizens to being instrumentally useful as part of the Cold War security apparatus that included the opening up of new economic markets in Latin America, Asia, Middle East, and Africa. Reflecting these shifting objectives and priorities, the value of academic freedom as a spearhead for developing critical research and building more inclusive academic communities was diminished as well.

This transition is evident in the way academic freedom has been policed over the decades. The 1960s and 1970s saw a heavy police and military presence on campus that resulted at times in physical violence toward students and faculty. This explicit form of policing, with pepper spray, tasers, and guns, then gradually gave way to insidious modes of control over college campuses through defunding public education and privatizing and corporatizing university administration. This shift was most clearly manifested in a system of audit management and an escalation of precarious working conditions for teaching staff increasingly composed of adjunct and contract-based educators in the 1980s and 1990s.

As discussed in the next chapter, the political and administrative goals of public higher education in the United States have again shifted in the twenty-first century in the wake of 9/11, looming climate catastrophe, and more recent challenges to free-market fundamentalism. Today, the weaponizing of universities has become an explicit strategy of far-right politics, and the re-militarizing of campus life has assumed new significance. In recent years, Republicans have whipped up populist outrage against critical race theory as well as instruction on LGBTQ+ issues and have implemented wide-ranging laws that police curricula and teaching. Corporate interests—both national and international—have also stepped up their external interference in campus life through philanthropic funding of research that often promotes neoliberal ideology and extractive capitalism. A notable example is the funding of centers supporting nonrenewable energy development, which devalue climate science and the catastrophic impacts of planetary warming. In the context of further reductions in state funding for public education, wealthy donors and entitled alumni have also played an outsize role in determining what gets researched and taught in universities and colleges around the country. Classrooms have once again become political, economic, and ideological battlegrounds, and students and faculty are facing a heavy police presence on several fronts. Policing includes the threat of physical violence but also works through more discrete modes of surveillance, self-censorship, and harassment on social media, with consequences including suspension, expulsion, demotion, salary reduction, and job loss.

Chapter 5

Weaponizing Universities in the Twenty-First Century

In the first decade of the twenty-first century, in the years immediately following 9/11, higher education in the United States was used to bolster a national security state leading the global war on terror. Any scholar or student critical of US imperialism and US-led wars in Iraq and Afghanistan was vulnerable to reproach by fellow faculty and administrators. Censorship was particularly directed at scholars who were vocal about the fabricated story of weapons of mass destruction that justified the United States and its allies in invading Iraq and inflicting torture, death, and massive devastation on civilian populations overseas. Throughout the decade there was much academic discussion about the weaponization and transformation of higher education to serve national security interests (Schueller and Dawson 2009; Carvalho and Downing 2010; González 2014). These conversations began to decline, however, as the war on terror dragged on; attention drifted to the 2010 Arab Spring, when protests erupted against oppressive state governance in the Middle East, and to the Occupy Wall Street Movement in 2011, protesting a global political economy that favored corporations over the well-being of ordinary people.

In the second decade of the twenty-first century, particularly with Trump's presidency in 2016, new tensions emerged that dramatically destabilized the global political economy and, in a sense, eclipsed the focus on the war on terror. Trade wars with China, rising antidemocracy at home and abroad, a global pandemic, the Black Lives Matter and #MeToo movements, logistical breaks in supply chains, battles over social media monopolies, Russia's invasion of Ukraine and the Israel–Hamas war, all against a backdrop of increasingly catastrophic weather events, have changed and divided the national landscape. And with the rise of new conflicts and crises, different enemies entered the spotlight. These included old Cold War foes such as China and Russia, as well as new, previously unimagined adversaries such as the COVID-19 virus and a planet whose warming is out of control. Militarily, politically, economically, socially, and environmentally, the early years of the 2020s looked very different from the early years of the 2000s for people living in North America.

As discussed in chapter 1, one of the main structural drivers of today's wave of academic repression is the worldwide challenge to free-market fundamentalism. Today, more and more people are questioning neoliberal ideology and extractive capitalism, whose negative impacts have created a world of massive economic inequality and social injustice over many decades. Throughout the postcolonial era of the 1950s, '60s and '70s, people living in the global south loudly challenged the continued Western neocolonial exploitation of their cheap labor and natural resources that created suffering in their countries. Now, however, the mechanisms of exploitation have explicitly materialized within the rich countries of the global north. In short, it is becoming increasingly impossible to ignore the material conditions that have created unprecedented concentrations of wealth and mass inequality within and across all countries and regions of the world. This inequality is marked not just by falling levels of health, education, and job opportunities, but also by new modes of inequality linked to a rapidly unfolding ecological crisis and related conflicts over natural resources. Catastrophic floods, fires, heat waves, and rising oceans are all markers of a new world order and foreshadow massive realignments of geopolitical power (Latour 2017; Ghosh 2017). This sense of extreme instability is noted in a United Nations report released in July 2023, *A New Agenda for Peace*. In its opening comments, the report states that the world is at a crossroads: "We are now at an inflection point. The post–cold war period is over. A transition is under way to a new global order. While its contours remain to be defined, leaders around the world have referred to multipolarity as one of its defining traits. In this moment of transition, power dynamics have become increasingly fragmented as new poles of influence emerge, new economic blocs form and axes of contestation are redefined" (United Nations 2023:3).

The idea of global power realignments is very disturbing to many, especially to multinational corporations anxious to defend the status quo and their extraordinary economic profits. For big corporations—particularly those in the energy and finance sectors—there is a mounting urgency to preserve the false promise of trickle-down-economics (Oreskes and Conway 2023). Many of these capitalists are aggressively working with antidemocratic politicians, ushering in a political landscape that is increasingly authoritarian in the servicing of corporate interests. Some of these corporate giants, however, are also working behind the scenes to control the production of knowledge. They are concerned that scientific expertise may reveal to the wider public the vast devastation to humans and environments that their "profits over people logic" has enabled. This suggests that the politics of knowledge production explored in chapter 2 has assumed exceptional intensity in the current moment. Relatedly, it also suggests that reframing academic freedom as an enabler of social responsibility to wider societies is now more important than ever before.

Weaponizing Universities in the 2020s

Today, what we are seeing around the world is that universities are being weaponized by the far right. In the United States, Republican leaders are not using war rhetoric about "evil" dark-skinned enemies to rally the country against another nation, as was the case with President George W. Bush in the aftermath of 9/11. Today, in contrast, Republicans are targeting opponents supposedly lurking at home among us; teachers and scholars have become "the enemy of the people." These extremist politicians have effectively sowed disinformation to create a new moral panic about public education and its challenge to traditional gender roles, Christian values, and White nationalist narratives of the country's history. Echoing the censorship of intellectuals under McCarthyism in the 1940s and 1950s, today's antidemocratic leaders are obsessed with faculty loyalty oaths, claims of classroom indoctrination, book bans, and curriculum revisions. The result of the moral panic is that public education—at all levels—is a hot-button issue in Republican Party strategy and political speeches.

The culture wars, and their racist, sexist, and religious undertones, have played a major role in stoking public resentment against scholars and teachers. As discussed further in this chapter, the deliberate mobilization of White Christian nationalist outrage against critical race theory (CRT) illustrates the effectiveness of Republican strategies to shut down teaching about the enduring legacies of slavery, racial discrimination, and White supremacy. Moreover, according to the Nobel Prize–winning economist Paul Krugman and other analysts, Republicans have now extended the culture wars to include climate change as part of their renewed efforts to attack scientific expertise more generally (Hoffman 2015; Wilson and Kamola 2021; Abel 2024).[1] The fierce denigration of science was explicit in the far-right antivaccination movement during the COVID-19 pandemic, and arguably that anti-intellectual agitation has now been redirected to focus (again) on climate science.

All of this seems correct, but it's important to note that the culture wars also function as a loud distraction from what is really going on in terms of a destabilized multipolar international order. I argue, as have others, that despite all the moralistic talk against "woke" progressives, the central battlefront is not about social issues but rather the economy. In many ways the current attack on universities and colleges is a continuation—albeit much more explicit and aggressive—of the conservative attack on public education that has been waged for more than fifty years (Newfield 2008). Following this argument, the primary objective of today's Republican war on higher education is straightforward: to maintain political power and extraordinary profit margins while stopping any challenges to the status quo prompted by research, teaching, and campus activism. In other words, the primary goal is not to govern the country according to a set of traditional conservative values but to retain exclusive power and control over the economy.

Denying Scientific Expertise, Expanding Extractive Capitalism

As this book was being written, scientists told us that 2023 was the hottest year on record and the hottest in 120,000 years of planetary history. Canada burned for months, turning skies in the United States to toxic orange. In July, four continents were under extreme heat warnings as temperatures soared, sending millions of people underground and many more millions into starvation across drought-afflicted East Africa. Scientists told us that deadly heat waves are the result of a human-caused climate crisis resulting from burning natural resources, specifically nonrenewable fossil fuels, which cause most of the greenhouse gas emissions that warm the planet. The global scientific community argues that to mitigate ecological collapse, humans, especially those in wealthy countries who consume the majority of the earth's oil and gas, must stop burning fossil fuels and stop extractive capitalism.

Against this material reality, Republican-led states such as Texas, which is the biggest producer of oil and gas in the United States, seek to limit research on the negative impacts of greenhouse gas emissions and stop teaching on the climate crisis in classrooms. For instance, in May 2023, Ohio's Republican legislature passed Senate Bill 83, which bans university courses that raise "controversial beliefs or policies" and explicitly lists climate change as a controversial topic that cannot be discussed (along with abortion, electoral voting, and LGBTQ+ issues). This political interference in the classroom effectively makes teachers who discuss the climate crisis vulnerable to punishment and dismissal. Bans on campus discussion of what students are actually experiencing in their daily lives—extreme heat, difficulty breathing, inability to attend class because of wildfires or floods—underscore the absurdity and desperation of these lawfare tactics by the far right. These bans also point to the degree ordinary people are willing to submit to political extremism and acquiesce to self-evident distortions of the truth.

Decades of Climate Science Denialism

Distressingly, the ecological catastrophe unfolding before us has been predicted by climate scientists since the 1980s. Against mounting scientific consensus that climate change is caused by greenhouse gas emissions, oil and mining corporations took extreme measures to deny this knowledge for decades. For instance, as early as 1981, an expert with Exxon admitted in an internal memo to his colleagues that carbon dioxide emissions were linked to global warming. Despite that information, Exxon participated in a widespread climate science denial campaign and spent more than $30 million on lobbyists, think tanks, and researchers to promote climate science skepticism. In 1988, the climatologist James Hansen put the US Congress and the general population on notice that greenhouse gases were building up and effectively warming the atmosphere.[2] This was internationally confirmed with the founding of the Intergovernmental Panel on Climate Change (IPCC) that same year.

In response to scientific evidence, the energy sector went on high alert and established the Global Climate Coalition in 1989 to lead media campaigns intended to stop the regulation of greenhouse gas pollution. The coalition brought together a broad spectrum of Big Oil companies and energy-sector lobbyists to sow disinformation and skepticism about climate change to ensure continued deregulation and maximum profit margins (Hoggan 2009; Oreskes and Conway 2010; Freese 2020). From the late 1980s and into the 1990s, this disinformation campaign was in full swing, creating confusion about climate science findings and attacking the legitimacy of climate scientists. Although the campaign started in the United States, by the mid-1990s it had filtered out to other countries such as Britain, Australia, and Canada.

Conservative politicians and industry networks heavily promoted nonacademic testimony as expert evidence, arguing that there was no scientific basis for climate change claims (Dunlap and Jacques 2013). Tellingly, the small number of atmospheric scientists openly skeptical of climate change received compensation from oil and gas companies. For instance, Willie Soon of the Harvard-Smithsonian Center for

Astrophysics was paid more than $1 million by ExxonMobil, the American Petroleum Institute, and Koch Industries to dispute scientific evidence about the impact of human-generated greenhouse gases (Worth 2021:130).[3] According to the French philosopher Bruno Latour, with mounting evidence on climate change and a finite limit to the planet's resources, political and economic extremists had to come to terms with a new reality that threatened their power and profits. Hence company executives, such as those at ExxonMobil, had to constantly proclaim that an ecological threat didn't exist. As Latour evocatively stated, *"they had to stop pretending, even in their dreams, to share the earth with the rest of the world"* (Latour 2017:19).

One reason Big Oil's disinformation campaign was successful was that corporations were able to control the public narrative. Professional skeptics financed by conservative think tanks were given overblown coverage in mainstream mass media. Editors and journalists, particularly those working for Fox News and other news outlets owned by media mogul Rupert Murdoch, were often pressured into covering certain stories (Wolff 2010). The result was that "reporting on climate in the United States became *biased* toward skeptics and deniers" (Oreskes and Conway 210:214). This bias was also evident in Australia, where Murdoch's company, News Corp, controlled—and continues to control—many news outlets. Murdoch announced his retirement and the handing over of his media empire to his son Lachlan in September 2023, but that doesn't mean it will stop pumping out sensational, self-righteous, and grievance-driven news that is deeply skeptical of the mounting climate crisis. The cumulative result is that, for decades, climate science has been denounced by conservative politicians who are supported by corporations and economists pushing a profit-driven agenda reinforced by far-right global print and social media companies such as Murdoch's News Corp.

Climate Denialism Today

Today, disinformation about climate change is being widely and deliberately spread through social media. Adding to this largely unregulated social media onslaught is a wave of conspiracy theories arguing that planetary warming isn't real, and even if it is, it does not result from people burning fossil fuels. According to journalist George Monbiot, "Climate science denial, which had almost vanished a few years ago, has now returned with a vengeance. Environmental scientists and campaigners are bombarded with claims that they are stooges, shills, communists, murderers and pedophiles."[4] Conspiracy theories against climate science are often backed by political lobbyists for fossil fuel companies, underscoring what I call a "deadly global alliance" between antidemocratic politicians and oil and gas corporations that greatly benefit from the antienvironmental policies and widespread deregulation that have become a signature feature of far-right politics worldwide (Darian-Smith 2022, 2023b, 2023c).

Trump's campaign to be reelected president in 2024 made explicit this connection between authoritarianism and the oil and energy mining sector. In contrast to earlier years when the collusion between corrupt politicians and multinational corporations was often hidden behind closed doors, now there is no mistaking their "partnership." In July 2023, Trump announced that if elected to a second presidential term, he would consolidate his power by eliminating an independent Justice Department and take full leadership of all federal administrative agencies. This announcement effectively outlined how the US constitutional republic would be replaced by an authoritarian state.[5] Then a month later, in August 2023,

Trump endorsed a sweeping plan set out by the Heritage Foundation called Project 2025 that detailed how Republicans would dismantle existing laws that seek to reduce planetary warming.[6] "The plan calls for shredding regulations to curb greenhouse gas pollution from cars, oil and gas wells and power plants, dismantling almost every clean energy program in the federal government and boosting the production of fossil fuels."[7] The plan also seeks to reverse a scientific report issued by the Environmental Protection Agency in 2009 that links carbon dioxide emissions to public health endangerment.

In effect, the MAGA-driven Republican Party has signaled to the energy and finance sectors that if Trump is returned to power, they will be granted unfettered authority to continue to extract fossil fuels and make extraordinary profits—even though unanimous climate science shows these activities are accelerating ecological collapse. The blatantly destructive greed of Republicans and mining corporations is mind-blowing. Perhaps even more mind-blowing is the willingness of millions of Americans, who are struggling with financial and health precarity that is amplified by unprecedented catastrophic floods, hurricanes, wildfires, and heat, to support the candidate associated with Project 2025.

Miseducating Students

Not surprisingly, the global attack by energy and finance sectors on climate science also plays out in higher education policies regarding environmental education. As already mentioned, in the United States, the Republican Party has a long history of denying the climate crisis, even though researchers have known about the disastrous impacts of oil and gas mining and the resulting greenhouse gas emissions since the 1980s. But Republicans have not always been climate science deniers (Turner and Isenberg 2018; Gamper-Rabindran

2022:470–474). As discussed in chapter 4, student activism in the wake of the Santa Barbara oil spill in 1969 helped galvanize public opinion about the devasting impacts of industrial pollution and global warming. A year later, the first Earth Day brought 20 million Americans—at the time 10 percent of the entire population—to the streets to protest and demand change for the "common good" on April 22, 1970. According to the Earth Day Network, "thousands of colleges and universities organized protests against the deterioration of the environment and there were massive coast-to-coast rallies in cities, towns, and communities.... Earth Day 1970 achieved a rare political alignment, enlisting support from Republicans and Democrats, rich and poor.... The first Earth Day led to the creation of the United States Environmental Protection Agency [EPA] and the Passage of the Clean Air, Clean Water, and Endangered Species Act."[8]

Prompted by public concerns, in 1970, Congress passed the National Environmental Education Act, which created an Office of Environmental Education (OEE). The act reflected a new perspective on the interconnection between human health and environmental degradation, and the OEE helped design "lesson plans and teacher guidebooks and influenced the inclusion of environmental issues in science textbooks" (Spring 2018:501). However, the act was funded only until 1975 and then repealed in 1981 after Republican Ronald Reagan became US president. This was the same year, it should be remembered, that an expert with ExxonMobil admitted in an internal memo to his colleagues that carbon dioxide emissions were linked to planetary warming.

Against the undercutting of climate science by the Global Climate Coalition, a new National Environmental Education Act was passed in 1990. The act was remarkable for recognizing that "there is growing evidence of international environmental problems, such as global warming, ocean pollution, and declines in species diversity, and that these problems pose serious threats to human health and the environment on a global scale." It noted that "efforts to inform and educate the public concerning... environmental problems are not adequate." To address the problem, section 10 of the act established a foundation to help coordinate agencies and higher education activities for the following purposes: "to extend the contribution of environmental education and training to meet critical environmental protection needs, both in this country and internationally; to facilitate the cooperation, coordination, and contribution of public and private resources to create an environmentally advanced educational system; and to foster an open and effective partnership among Federal, State, and local government, business, industry, academic institutions, community based environmental groups, and international organizations."[9]

Scholars at the time were jubilant about this bipartisan "renewal of commitment" regarding environmental issues in the early 1990s (Marcinkowski 1991). Enthusiasm was reflected in a surge of scholarship in the earth sciences as well as in the social sciences exploring environmental racism. This body of scholarship was important for examining the disproportionate impacts of industrial pollution on Black urban communities as well as Indigenous groups whose reservations were often used as dumping grounds for radioactive toxic waste (i.e., Bullard 2000). This enthusiasm for analyzing environmental issues in higher education was short-lived, however. Funding dwindled, and the implementation of education programming diminished throughout the mid to late 1990s, especially when Republican George W. Bush became president in 2001. Then, in the wake of 9/11, the country suddenly turned to the external threat of global terrorism and concern for research and teaching about environmental degradation dramatically declined.

Today in the United States, the absence of environmental education at all levels of public education is staggering. A recent study showed that college textbooks in biology have decreased their coverage about climate impacts since the 2010s, and coverage of climate solutions has decreased by 80 percent in recent decades. Professor Jennifer Landin, one of the researchers involved in the study, argues that this leaves students with a sense "that nothing can be done, which is both wildly misleading and contributes to a sense of fatalism regarding climate change."[10] Adds Katie Worth, a journalist who has written a very revealing book titled *Miseducation: How Climate Change Is Taught in America*, the vast majority of science classes in high schools and colleges use textbooks that downplay climate science and suggest that the outcomes of planetary warming are debatable. For instance, one book states that climate change may cause harm but could also be a good thing for farmers who now have a longer growing season and can grow crops in regions that were previously too cold (Worth 2021:81). Adding to the misinformation problem, three companies produce textbooks for most of the country, and they modify their textbooks according to the dominant political views in each of the 50 states (Worth 2021:93). This means, Worth argues, that "ideology trickles from elected officials through educational departments and into classrooms. Accurate information about climate change thus becomes the purview of children living in liberal states, while children living in conservative states are frequently provided fodder for denial" (Worth 2021:103).

At colleges and universities, an absence of instruction about the climate crisis is exacerbated by the interference of conservative philanthropic organizations in academic research and campus life; for example, companies such as ExxonMobil, BP, Shell, and Chevron fund bogus academic research. A report from the nonprofit group Data for Progress estimated that these giant energy companies donated or pledged $677 million to 27 universities between 2010 and 2020 (Table 1). Notable is the extraordinary amount of $154 million going to UC Berkeley, underscoring its "foundational and ongoing reliance for a large part of its budget on private funding," despite its brand of being "one of the world's greatest public universities" dedicated to issues of social justice (Platt 2023:196). Also notable is the $57 million going to Stanford University where its new Doerr School of Sustainability has come under scrutiny for rolling out a research agenda around carbon capture—a procedure that has not been scientifically proven and distracts from the issue of regulating greenhouse gas emissions in the first place. Stanford's internal documents show that this

Table 1. Top 10 universities receiving fossil fuel funding, 2010–2020

University	Donations
University of California, Berkeley	$154 million
University of Illinois	$108
George Mason	$64
Stanford	$57
University of Texas, Austin	$45
MIT	$40
Princeton	$36
Rice	$28
Texas A&M	$26
Harvard	$21

Source: Data taken from Data for Progress, "Accountable Allies: The Undue Influence of Fossil Fuel Money in Academia," March 1, 2023. https://www.dataforprogress.org/memos/accountable-allies-the-undue-influence-of-fossil-fuel-money-in-academia.

agenda was shaped during behind-the-scenes meetings with Big Oil corporations as well as Bank of America that is a leading financier of the fossil fuel sector.[11]

One of the leading players influencing academic research to avoid investigating the negative impacts of planetary warming is Koch Industries, the second largest privately held multinational corporation in the United States. Koch Industries' fortune is based on refining crude oil and the distribution of fossil fuels, chemicals, and minerals, among other investments, making Charles Koch one of the richest people in the world. The Koch family foundations are the charitable arm of the corporation and support a vast network of think tanks, academic centers, student groups, policy lobbyists, and media outlets. As Ralph Wilson and Isaac Kamola write in their riveting but disturbing book *Free Speech and Koch Money: Manufacturing a Campus Culture War*, the Koch network is

> a well-funded ideological and political machinery that seeks nothing less than social transformation. To this end, the Koch network has long devoted considerable energy and resources to gaining footholds within the university, and thereby changing the ideas that are produced, taught, researched, and published therein. The resulting network of academic centers and think tanks reproduces an ideology that coheres around the language of "individual freedom" and "Western civilization," while denying the existence of actual material and historical legacies of racial, gendered, and class-based exclusions, marginalizations, and violence. Instead, this libertarian ideology holds that possible outcomes only follow from individuals maximizing utility within the freedom of immaculately self-regulating markets. The intellectual, ideological, and political infrastructure created by the Koch network seeks to remake the United States, and the world, in the image of this hardline libertarian worldview. Doing

so, however, requires fundamentally remaking institutions of higher education, which have been a prominent source of intellectual criticism of the Koch network's preferred libertarian fantasy. (Wilson and Kamola 2021:vii; see also Mayer 2017; MacLean 2018)

In recent years, the Koch family foundations have stepped up their donations to higher education, investing in academic departments and centers. Many of these units are modeled on the Institute for Humane Studies at George Mason University, which claims to promote "intellectual discovery and human flourishing."[12] Between 1998 and 2019, the Institute for Humane Studies was overseen by Charles Koch, who pushed free-market fundamentalism and governmental deregulation in various areas, including industrial pollution and greenhouse gas emissions. During this period, the Institute received more than $52 million dollars from wealthy donors including the Koch family foundations (Wilson and Kamola 2021:117).

The Institute for Humane Studies is one of many academic centers and departments that receive funding from far-right political donors. "In 2016, 259 universities received a combined total of more than $50 million from the Koch foundations alone, with 59 campuses receiving more than $100,000. In 2019 the Koch foundations contributed a total of $123 million to academic institutions, up $23.9 million from the previous year." Between 2008 and 2017, the Charles Koch Foundation gave more than 70 percent of its charitable donations to colleges and universities, amounting to a massive $235 million dollars (Wilson and Kamola 2021:116–117).

Tellingly, in many of its donor contracts to universities the Charles Koch Foundation stipulated control over faculty appointments and stated that moneys would be withdrawn if scholarship didn't promote free-market enterprise. Institutions such as Florida State University, Utah State University, West Virginia University, and Clemson University in South Carolina have all been consumed by controversy over corporate sponsors' meddling in the universities' internal processes. The American Association of University Professors has voiced concern over political interference in higher education for years, and former AAUP president Cary Nelson publicly stated that Charles Koch's interventions violated academic freedom.[13]

I experienced firsthand the insidious policing of research and self-censorship when I was invited to give a public talk at the University of Pittsburgh in early 2023. The talk was on my new book *Global Burning: Rising Antidemocracy and the Climate Crisis*, in which I discuss the antienvironmental policies of far-right governments, including the former Trump administration. The talk was well received. Afterward, however, I was approached by students and faculty who told me how brave I was for saying what I did, which took me completely by surprise. My work has been called a lot of things—both good and bad—but never brave! In later private conversations over coffee, I learned that the campus had accepted a Charles Koch Foundation gift of $4.2 million to set up a new Center for Governance and Markets in Pitt's Graduate School of Public and International Affairs in 2019. In the years following the gift's acceptance, some students and faculty felt pressured to silence any criticism of free-market capitalism and its negative impacts on the environment. In hushed tones, one faculty member told me that a good number of senior scholars had taken early retirement or left for other jobs where they would have greater autonomy over the direction of their scholarship.[14]

Awareness is increasing within US higher education of political interference by megawealthy donors, alumni, and private foundations in university research and teaching (McGoey 2016; Kimball and Iler 2023). This interference is very apparent in top-tier research universities—both public and private. That doesn't mean that the thousands of non-elite teaching-based colleges are not impacted, however. For instance, take the influence of the far-right media outlet Prager University Foundation, known as PragerU. This is not an accredited university but rather an advocacy media outlet cofounded by conservative talk show host Dennis Praeger in 2009. The outlet produces short videos and entertainment—what it calls "edutainment"—targeting kids and young adults. This material promotes climate science denialism, likens climate science activists such as Greta Thunberg to Nazis, and says slavery is not really a problem. Its website states that it is "the world's leading conservative non-profit, focused on changing minds through the creative use of digital media." A powerful fundraiser, PragerU received at least $8 million from evangelical oil and gas billionaires Farris and Dan Wilks over the years and about $200 million between 2018 and 2022 from Republican donors. Notably, the "edutainment" for students is featured in educational curriculum in Texas, Florida, and other Republican-led states.[15]

Resisting Political Interference, Divesting from Fossil Fuels

As political interference in research and teaching mounts, students and faculty are mobilizing to protest the pressures of Big Oil money and its impact on academic freedom.[16] Some students formed the UnKoch My Campus group, which focuses expressly on Koch's interference in higher education. Other groups, such as faculty and students at Harvard University, called for action that resulted in the campus divesting its $42 billion endowment from the fossil fuel industry in 2021. This major divestment followed other campuses that had divested, including the University of California's 10-campus system.[17] A year later, in 2022, Harvard students coordinated demonstrations around the world with students at George Washington University, Tufts, Dartmouth, the University of Cambridge, Imperial College London, and the University of Toronto in Canada. These student groups called for universities to reject funding from Big Oil and for campus administrators to address their conflicts of interest and step down from holding board positions or consulting for energy corporations. These efforts were facilitated by the Fossil Free Research Coalition, "an organization that supports the international movement of students and faculty working to expose and dismantle fossil fuel industry's toxic influence on higher education, especially concerning climate-related research."[18]

Despite increasing resistance by student groups to external political influence over university life, however, it is difficult to fully grasp the scale of the problem or how to fight against it. Putting this differently, for universities to divest from fossil fuels addresses only one front of a widespread attack on climate science. And beyond classrooms, across a large sector of the US population and especially among older generations who have been brought up on biased school textbooks, skepticism about climate research remains deep. So, while climate skepticism exists in other countries, today the United States is the only "advanced" society in the world where a significant proportion of citizens still believe that the climate crisis is a hoax or unrelated to human activity. The deliberate disinformation campaigns and conspiracy theories promoted by the far right exacerbate this widespread ignorance. According to Jennie King, who is a leading expert on climate denialism at the Institute of Strategic Dialogue, an international watchdog group on political extremism, "denialism is making a real comeback, but in a way that is framed for the current conspiratorial universe. So rather than 'don't trust the science,' it is much more 'don't trust the scientists.'"[19]

Even with an older generations' skepticism about climate change, young people across all political affiliations and levels of education are deeply worried about the rapidly escalating climate emergency. Catastrophic wildfires, floods, and hurricanes are hard to deny, and, for growing numbers of people, these horrific weather events make the climate crisis a personally experienced reality. This helps explain the extraordinary backlash by Republican-led state legislatures to push policies that outlaw teachers and students from discussing climate change across all levels of public education. For big fossil fuel corporations—including Koch Industries and the Texas fracking billionaires Farris and Dan Wilks—this backlash is great news, securing their future profits as they move full steam ahead opening gas and oil fields and ratcheting up their practices of extractive capitalism.

Rewriting Histories, Recolonizing Minds

Given efforts to silence information about environmental exploitation, it is not surprising that there are also significant efforts to silence or deny histories of human exploitation. Within the academy, this denialism of history often manifests in refusing to acknowledge what happened in the past or reinterpreting past events to favor a certain ideology or bias. The long-term goal of such denialism is to "recolonize" or reoccupy the thinking of a new generation of students and control what they know and how they can think. Silvia Federici, in her essay "The Recolonization of African Education," narrates how recolonizing occurred in African countries in the 1980s and 1990s under the structural adjustment loan programs imposed by the World Bank and the IMF, as discussed in chapter 4. This recolonization created conditions "whereby African academics cannot produce any intellectual work, much less be present in the world market of ideas, except at the service and under the control of the international agencies. Through targeted aid, these agencies determine what can be studied, written about, and voiced in the continent" (Federici 2000:19; see also Mamdani 2007; Ngũgĩ 1986).

In the United States, today's efforts to control historical narratives and what gets studied and discussed echo the intellectual recolonization strategies imposed by the global north on developing countries. These efforts became explicit over the journalist Nikole Hannah-Jones's revelations in her Pulitzer-winning report *The 1619 Project*, which first appeared in the *New York Times* in 2019. The report challenged the foundational myths of US society and argued that the country's history should start, not with the fight for American independence against the British in 1776, but with the landing in Jamestown of a Dutch ship carrying enslaved African peoples who were sold to the colonists in 1619 (Hannah-Jones 2021). Historians estimate that over centuries of transatlantic slave trade, approximately 12 million Africans were brought to the Americas, and more than 300,000 were sent to the 13 British colonies before 1776. The labor of slaves enabled the plantation economy to flourish in the South and made it possible for Northern manufacturers to establish the United States as a major industrial nation.

It is essential to acknowledge these previously silenced histories of colonialism, slavery, oppression, violence, and structural racism. They help us better understand the complexities of the past as well as to appreciate the enduring legacies of slavery that continue to shape racial discrimination and lack of opportunity for Black, Brown, and Indigenous peoples today. Yet despite the social benefits of learning from horrific histories and uncomfortable truths, *The 1619 Project* ignited a national crisis when it was first published. Many people considered it outrageous to suggest that racism played such a massive role in the building and shaping of the United States. This idea profoundly challenged their personal sense of identity based on a sanitized ideology of White Christian nationalism and manifest destiny. The wave of outraged indignation also underscored the deep racial exclusions and silences within society that continue to shape policies, laws, and access to health, education, housing, and employment.

In 2021, Hannah-Jones was offered a tenured professorship as the Knight Chair in Race and Investigative Journalism at the University of North Carolina (UNC). After Republican political interference, however, tenure was not forthcoming. Faculty and students loudly protested, condemning the politicization of higher education that undermined academic freedom and the right to pursue evidence-based knowledge and eventually forced the UNC Board of Trustees to offer tenure as per the original contract. Ultimately, Hannah-Jones declined the position, took up an endowed chair at Howard University, and founded the Center for Journalism and Democracy.

The racism of that episode erupted again when Dr. Kathleen McElroy was hired by Texas A&M University to lead its program in journalism in 2023. As a highly acclaimed Black scholar and journalist who had previously worked for the *New York Times*, her appointment was greeted with fanfare and celebration. External political forces interfered in the process, however, pressuring university leaders to revoke the terms of her contract and deny her tenure. The Rudder Association, an alumni group whose stated mission is to protect campus traditions and values, admitted to making complaints about

McElroy's work in promoting diversity within academia. Ultimately, McElroy rejected the revised contract and returned to her previous professorship. Under mounting public pressure, the university apologized, and a $1 million settlement was made to McElroy, who in a public statement said, "I hope the resolution of my matter will reinforce A&M's allegiance to excellence in higher education and its commitment to academic freedom and journalism."[20]

Together, the two incidents involving Hannah-Jones and McElroy expose the convergence of far-right goals to undermine evidence-based expertise through independent journalism, taint the credibility of Black scholars and particularly Black women, and reaffirm White nationalist values in higher education. Grotesquely, the racist attack against McElroy—even if it was publicly criticized—was authorized by a law signed by the Republican governor of Texas, Greg Abbott, which banned diversity, equity, and inclusion programming at the state's public universities.

Mobilizing Explicit Racism by the Far Right

Disturbingly, appealing to people's racist worldviews has proved to be a very effective political strategy for Trump and the wider MAGA Republican Party. Unlike previous presidents, Trump was explicit in his racial profiling and denigration of minorities and immigrants, knowing that this would please his core extremist supporters. As historian Ruth Ben-Ghiat writes in her book on authoritarian strongmen:

> Racism has long been an axis of Trump's national project and a space where the president's own long-held racist beliefs mingled with those of his heterodox group of backers. These include Confederate flag–waving Southerners who never accepted the end of segregation and GOP politicians who fear immigration

will cause "the browning of America." ... Muslims, Latinos, African Americans, and other people of color have been the target of the Trump administration's plan to remake American society in the image of White nationalism. (Ben-Ghiat 2020:85)

In the wake of the killing of numerous Black people by White police, including George Floyd in Minneapolis in 2020, and amid global political activism sparked by the reinvigorated Black Lives Matter movement, anti-Black racism was deliberately fostered by far-right politicians. These politicians took advantage of the wave of White rage and resentment against people of color that had been percolating since the Obama presidency and had been heightened by a report in 2018 predicting that Whites would be numerically a minority in the United States by 2045 (Anderson 2017).[21] This rage was further aggravated by *The 1619 Project* and renewed attempts on numerous college campuses to remove statues of Confederate soldiers and military figures that many students and faculty considered problematic for venerating a history of slavery and subjugation.

On the far right, taking down Confederate monuments is considered by many as the last straw in a long post–Civil War battle between Blacks and Whites. Those who defend the values of the "Old South" feel deeply threatened by the promotion of alternative histories and diverse worldviews that question their understanding of the present. As noted by historian Donald Yacovone, until the early 1960s most history textbooks in the United States presented slavery as a benevolent institution that benefited the enslaved Africans. These textbooks confirmed for White readers that they had done no harm in building a land of freedom and democracy at the expense of cruel exploitation and degradation of others over centuries. The textbooks "served as reservoirs of values, patriotism, and a national ethos ... creating a national identity that could serve as a road map to the future" (Yacovone 2022: xvii). Taking down Confederate monuments—for example, at the University of Mississippi in 2019—symbolically highlighted the ebbing away of that deeply cherished historical fantasy.

Targeting Critical Race Theory

With emotions running high, in September 2020, about three months after the murder of George Floyd, Christopher Rufo, a conservative political activist working for Governor Ron DeSantis of Florida, gave an interview on Fox News on the show *Tucker Carlson Tonight*.[22] There he declared that critical race theory was an "existential threat" to society and a dangerous ideology that had "infiltrated" the federal government. In an earlier tweet, he revealed his disinformation plan: "We have successfully frozen their brand—'critical race theory'—into the public conversation and are steadily driving up negative perceptions. We will eventually turn it toxic" (quoted in Taifha et al. 2023:10). In other words, Rufo deliberately weaponized CRT to mark colleges and universities as hotbeds of political activism and indoctrination that were teaching American history incorrectly.

Rufo's public attack mobilized a wide array of people to work as "foot soldiers" in the Republican cause—parents, school boards, college administrators, community members, philanthropists, and state decision-makers—to prevent any teaching about systemic racism in the classroom. This strategy was orchestrated by a very effective "national level political machine" led by conservative think tanks and institutes such as the Heritage Foundation, the American Enterprise Institute, and the Woodson Center (Brint 2023). The work of this behind-the-scenes far-right network was quickly reinforced by Trump's Executive Order 13950, issued later in

September 2020, which openly attacked CRT as a "divisive" and "destructive ideology," "grounded in misrepresentations of our country's history." According to the NAACP's Legal Defense Fund, which brought a lawsuit challenging the executive order, it had a "chilling effect on free speech and the dissemination of truthful information about systemic and structural inequalities, which undermines workplace equality for people of color, women, and LGBTQ individuals."[23]

Almost immediately, CRT became a dog whistle for the far right. In a remarkably coordinated attack, in 2021, more than 36 state legislatures introduced laws that restricted the teaching of race at all levels of public education, though most were aimed at grades K–12. These restrictions were used to police a wide range of books, curricula, and courses that took seriously the need to discuss and combat racism in contemporary society. In 2023, the Critical Race Studies Program at UCLA released a report, "Tracking the Attacking on Critical Race Theory," which noted that in every US state except Delaware, there are measures that outlaw CRT either as a matter of state policy or at local levels through school boards or regional school districts (Alexander et al. 2023). According to education scholars Francesca López and Chrstine Sleeter, CRT has become the new "villain" in the culture wars (López and Sleeter 2023; Goldberg 2023a; Khalid and Snyder 2023; for a comprehensive legislative account, see Kamola 2024).

So, even though Trump's executive order was revoked by the administration of President Joe Biden, Republicans have continued to use denunciation of CRT as code language to incite far-right legislation and political interference in classrooms. CRT was invoked, for example, by Governor DeSantis when he blocked Florida's new Advanced Placement course on African American studies in 2023. As noted by leading critical race scholar David Theo Goldberg, the attack on CRT has in practice silenced public discussion and teaching about racism and has emboldened racist rhetoric and attitudes (Goldberg 2023a).

Targeting LGBTQ+ Communities and Diversity in Higher Education

From the far right's perspective, the other "villains" are queer and transgender people and, by extension, anyone who defends their right to determine their own sexual orientation and gendered identity. Since 2020, a record number of bills have been passed that seek to limit LGBTQ+ rights and the opportunities and freedoms of queer and transgender people across the country. As of March 2024, the American Civil Liberties Union was tracking 484 anti-LGBTQ+ bills that were making their way through state legislatures and judicial review; even if not all the bills eventually become law, they still cause much injury to the people targeted.[24] The bills attack LGBTQ+ people in a wide variety of ways: making it harder for people to access health and mental care and even to be admitted to a hospital; preventing people from updating their gender on IDs, birth certificates, and passports; banning books that explore gender and LGBTQ+ issues; restricting access to bathrooms and public lockers; and preventing transgender youth from participating in school sports and feeling safe in classrooms. Cumulatively, the bills reflect a coordinated extremist attack on people who do not fit normative gender roles and are not legible—and so are deemed threatening—to a social system based on traditional patriarchal and gender-based values.

Building on the far right's success at mobilizing their core supporters around societal "villains" and chilling classroom discussion of issues of racism and sexuality, Republicans have also aggressively attacked diversity, equity, and inclusion

(DEI) programs in higher education. This attack didn't stem from any well-intentioned concerns about the efficacy of DEI programs to build inclusive academic communities.[25] Rather, the Republican attack has been driven by deeply embedded racism. In 2022, Governor DeSantis outlawed DEI programs in public higher education in Florida, and some other Republican-led state legislatures were quick to follow. Christopher Rufo went further in an article he published in the *New York Times* by calling for all states to outlaw DEI efforts in public education, claiming they are the antithesis of liberal education. Revealingly, Rufo argued that universities should not be used as a "vehicle for activism, liberation, and social change."[26]

But critics of Rufo have responded loudly, arguing that he is out of touch with the goals of higher education in the twenty-first century. According to Lynn Pasquerella, president of the American Association of Colleges and Presidents:

> Mr. Rufo's call for legislators to escalate the banning of diversity, equity and inclusion programs and curriculums constitutes an existential threat to the American tradition of liberal education. Essential to our nation's historic mission of educating for democracy, a liberal education for the 21st century requires active engagement with difference—in people, in the curriculum, and in the intellectual, social, cultural and geographical communities in which students connect.... He ignores data demonstrating that diversity on campuses is necessary for intellectual and social development and for preparing all students for work, citizenship and life in a multicultural, globally interdependent world.[27]

Another critic, recently graduated student Grady Martin, adds:

> A university's mission is to look forward by training people to create a better world. DEI does just that. Two months ago, I graduated from the University of Virginia. Over the past six

years, our student body has faced the violent Unite the Right Rally, the Covid pandemic, a series of hate crimes and a mass shooting. We would not have survived without leaning on, and learning from, our collective diversity in race, class, ideology, and background. I wouldn't have even attended UVA without expanded need-based financial aid programs—programs created by DEI advocates. Our diversity made us stronger, as students from all backgrounds are becoming the workers, thinkers and leaders of the future. I am proud that my university sees that as its mission.[28]

Together, the cumulative impact of far-right attacks on CRT discussion, LGBTQ+ communities, and DEI programs is to silence or distort past and present history, which includes colonialism, racism, patriarchy, discrimination, and persecution of marginalized populations. Arguably, removing DEI programming it is a form of pedagogical whitewashing or cleansing. Whatever name one wishes to use, these attacks are an explicit attempt to roll back critical thinking about the racial complexities of society, to rewrite history to suit a White nostalgic imaginary, and in effect to recolonize minds with sanitized narratives of plantation owners ultimately benefiting enslaved Africans.

The silencing of discussion around gender and the dismantling of DEI programs add further layers of legislative interference by making it more difficult for underrepresented students to enter colleges and universities in the first place. These moves by the far right are an effort to maintain a predominantly White learning environment in which the perspectives and worldviews of marginalized and immigrant communities—who will numerically be the majority in the United States by 2045—can be more easily sidelined. Karma Chávez, a member of the American Association of University Professors' executive committee at the University of Texas, argues that anti-DEI legislation discourages faculty from teaching about racial discrimination for fear of getting into trouble. She goes on, "Predominantly white departments are going to probably get whiter; male departments are probably going to be even more full of men."[29]

Undermining diversity on campus was a line of attack endorsed by the Supreme Court in *Students for Fair Admissions v. President and Fellows of Harvard College*. In this 2022 decision, a 6–3 conservative supermajority ruled against the use of race-conscious admissions and effectively dismantled affirmation action. As discussed in chapter 1, the federal decision is predicted to have far-reaching impacts by reducing the number of underrepresented students going to college and then going on to law, medical, business, and other professional and graduate programs. Tragically, this outcome is what is desired by the far right and its core White nationalist followers. They know that anti-racism starts with education. They know that Black, Brown, and Indigenous students from all sorts of cultural, social, and religious backgrounds are attending college and, in the words of former student Grady Martin, "becoming the workers, thinkers and leaders of the future." [30] This is exactly what the MAGA Republican movement is trying to stop. In a fiery dissenting opinion in *Students for Fair Admissions*, Justice Sonia Sotomayor wrote, "The Court subverts the constitutional guarantee of equal protection by further entrenching racial inequality in education, the very foundation of our democratic government and pluralistic society."[31]

Rewriting history to erase evidence of past injustices is not unique to the far right in the United States. Efforts to mislead generations of students and wider publics about violent colonial and national histories is occurring across Europe, as well as in India, Singapore, Turkey, Japan, China, and dozens of other places with antidemocratic regimes. One very disturbing example is the effort to deny the Holocaust and to claim that Hitler's racist extermination of millions of people never happened. This denial was legally denounced in a London courtroom in 2000 (Lipstadt 1994, 2016). Despite this internationally acclaimed legal victory for truth and evidence-backed historical accounts, the Holocaust denial movement has gained traction in the twenty-first century. It joins other attempts to erase from the record past injustices of violence, racism, slavery, and genocide. For instance, when the far-right Law and Justice Party came to power in Poland in 2015, it was determined to promote a positive and virtuous account of the country's past by removing records that, during World War II, some Poles had collaborated with the Nazis in the rounding up and extermination of Jews. In 2018, a law was introduced that threatened anyone pointing to the racist past in Polish history with a penalty of three years' imprisonment. In 2021, two historians were found guilty of writing a book about antisemitic atrocities by Poles, but fortunately their convictions were reversed by an appeals court. Historian Richard Evans notes, however, that "the struggle is far from over. . . . Populist politicians everywhere, from Victor Orbán in Hungary to Donald Trump in the United States, are trying to remold their nation's history into an uncritically patriotic narrative that involves massive denial of its negative aspects and brazen rejection of historical truth. This is a struggle that extends far beyond the borders of one country."[32]

Militarizing Campus Life

Since the mid 2010s, many colleges and university campuses have been roiled by a wide range of student protests and strikes. Student demands have included removing Confederate statues, defunding campus police, divesting university investments from fossil fuels, demanding better working conditions for adjunct teachers, and lowering tuition fees. Since 2020, some campuses have experienced student demonstrations against nonacademic speakers on campus, as well as protests against banning books and far-right legislation against CRT and DEI programs. Student protests erupted around the Israel–Hamas war in 2023–2024, pitting pro-Palestinian students against some Jewish student organizations and resulting in accusations of antisemitism that have chilled campus speech, particularly speech in support of Palestinian rights and a peaceful ceasefire. In response to the upswing in student activism, many universities, such as Johns Hopkins University, have established an armed private police department with the authority to make arrests and use force against student demonstrators—even though crime rates on most campuses have dropped in recent years (Anderson 2015).

This trend toward establishing private security forces on campuses, as well as arming existing campus police, is part of a larger national trend toward militarized policing of activists and political dissent. As politics scholar Paul Passavant reminds us, "Today we see, on the one hand, a growing militarization of protest policing and, on the other, the growing use of control technologies. . . . Neither the tendency toward a militarized response to protests nor the use of control technologies is compatible with the principles of constitutional democracy, which rejects interference with freedom of speech, political organization, and political participation" (Passavant 2021:242–243).

Unfortunately, the growing militarization with which public demonstrations are policed is not confined to the United States. With the global lean toward authoritarianism and growing political dissent among ordinary people resisting oppression, there has been a corresponding global rise in laws against protest. These antiprotest laws try to stop mass mobilizations of people demonstrating on the streets and have been passed in many countries, prohibiting political organizing and assembly on a wide number of issues including labor conditions, racial and gender discrimination, and the climate emergency. For instance, there has been a large uptick in criminalizing the acts of people who demonstrate outside oil company headquarters or near infrastructure such as gas pipelines and labeling environmental activists as "hooligans" and "eco-terrorists."

According to Civicus (a global civil society alliance that tracks restrictions on public protests), the use of excessive force and detention against people marching in the streets is escalating. Civicus found that in 2023, the right to peacefully protest, which is protected under international law, has been violated in more than 75 percent of countries where protests took place.[33] Many antidemocratic governments are using lawfare strategies that include the "overcriminalization" of targeted groups and activists. These strategies entail labeling public protests as "riots" and dissenters as "terrorists," who are heavily penalized and even criminalized for their behavior. Contributing to the rise of antiprotest laws was the COVID-19 pandemic, which enabled some governments to justify further crackdowns on political dissent in what scholars have called "governing through contagion" (Chua and Lee 2021). Disturbingly, the rise of antiprotest laws has escalated both in authoritarian regimes such as China and Russia and in more liberal democratic societies such as Britain, Australia, Germany, France, Italy, and the United States (Terwindt 2020: Weis 2022).

Militarizing Higher Education Since 9/11

Today's ramping up of armed police on US campuses is deeply entangled with the militarization of higher education in the wake of 9/11 and threats of global terrorism.[34] University security forces have become much more visible in terms of personnel numbers and military equipment. Many of the military-style uniforms and weapons are distributed through the federal 1033 Program, which transfers military surplus to law enforcement agencies, including university and college police units. Arguably, war equipment has no place on campuses supposedly devoted to research and learning. The most common items to show up in university police departments are semiautomatic rifles commonly known as M16s. Campus police often have a very menacing presence on campus, dressed in black riot gear, gloves, and metal helmets with visors, and carrying long M16 rifles along with a range of other firearms and batons swinging from their belts. This sense of menace is furthered by surveillance cameras and military-style equipment dotting campus grounds. There have been reports that military technology was used to monitor a graduate student strike on the University of California, Santa Cruz, campus in 2020, as well as evidence of university police using artificial intelligence technology and private security agencies to monitor students' social media communications.[35]

In the wake of George Floyd's murder in 2020, there was a wave of student activism in the United States and around the world demonstrating against police brutality and calling for the defunding of campus police. Studies have shown that campus police disproportionately scrutinize students of color and that they perpetuate racial profiling and discrimination against certain sectors of the campus community. In the context of the global Black Lives Matter movement, many students felt it was important to divest from police security and to think about the racist roots of campus policing as well as college connections to broader issues of mass incarceration and the prison-industrial complex (Watkins 2020; Chase and Suriel 2020; Cole 2021). Initially, many college leaders responded sympathetically to student demands. By 2023, however, most student concerns were ignored or overridden as college and university presidents increasingly turned to ramping up campus law enforcement. Not coincidentally, the panic about violence on campus has in part been manufactured by the very groups calling for armed campus police departments. In the United States, Britain, Australia, and other countries, far-right groups have invited extremist provocateurs and neofascist organizations to campus as a deliberate strategy to cause disruption and potential conflict.

One incident that helped create fear across an elite US campus was Yale University's message to its incoming first-year students in fall 2023. As new students arrived to start the academic year, a flyer was distributed to them as a "survival guide" by a union that represents Yale's campus police. The pamphlet described rising crime in the area and instructed students to remain on campus, avoid public transport, and stay off the streets after 8 p.m. These instructions were punctuated with a menacing image of the grim reaper. Mark Lawlor, a professor at another local university and a New Haven police commissioner, said the information about crime rates was inaccurate and that overall crime rates were lower than they had been two decades previously.[36]

Adding to the sense of imminent violence is the abundance of guns being carried by people—including students—walking around on many US college campuses. Republican-led state legislatures have introduced increasingly lax gun laws since the early 2000s, backed and encouraged by the powerful National Rifle Association. Utah started to allow concealed guns to be carried on college campuses in 2004 and became a model for many other states. Today, concealed guns are allowed on campuses in 34 states, with guns banned in only 16 states on the grounds that they would "have a chilling effect on freedom of thought and speech" (Lewis 2017).

Potential violence on campus cannot be easily dismissed, with mass shootings across the United States being a common event. Although only a small number of these shootings have occurred on college grounds, the threat of potential violence is enormously disconcerting for parents, students, faculty, staff, and administrators. Despite real safety concerns, however, armed campus police are highly problematic, precisely because they are largely unaccountable to anyone other than the college or university president. University police departments hold special jurisdictional authority, distinct from the accountability protocols of city and state law enforcement agencies. This means that campus police can treat students of color and LGBTQ+ students differently and get away with it. This was the case in the past at the University of Chicago, which was well-known for its campus police incessantly targeting Black students and extending anti-Black racism into the surrounding community (Cole 2021).

Today, with extremist Republican governors now feeling emboldened to fire college presidents and replace them with their own appointees, the ability to control a private armed campus police force is particularly disturbing. For instance, Richard Corcoran, former education secretary under Governor DeSantis, was appointed interim president of Florida's New College in early 2023. Corcoran was installed to implement DeSantis's agenda to dismantle the progressive curricula, appoint new faculty, and put into place a "classic" education that would be more appealing to White male students. This new interim president is also presumably within his authority to establish an armed campus police force that he alone controls and is responsible for. This was the case with Maurie

McInnis, former president of Stony Brook University (and new president of Yale starting in 2024), who established at Stony Brook a new security office with broad powers called the Division of Enterprise Risk Management. The office had jurisdiction over campus police and reported directly to McInnis. According to scholar of policing Robert Chase, "My concern is that this elevation of police to an executive-level authority in the university is one that's going to be adopted nationally."[37]

Concluding Comments

The heavy-handed enforcement of higher education through armed campus police should be understood against a bigger backdrop of policing political dissent more generally. As has been underscored throughout this book, what happens on college campuses often operates as a microcosm of the politics and material conditions that are going on within wider societies. The surveillance of student social media, activism, strikes, and public gatherings reflects what is happening to those living beyond the campus grounds who have also become subject to heightened militarized policing, digital surveillance, and antiprotest laws in recent years (Passavant 2021).

Intensified policing and crackdowns on political protests both on and off college campuses suggest that defending academic freedom and questioning the status quo will be very difficult in the years ahead. Within the US university setting, we are seeing deepening skepticism about science, the rewriting of histories of slavery and racism, and bans on discussion of so-called controversial subjects including gender, sexuality, and the climate crisis. Together, these strategies amount to aggressive policing—through legislation, surveillance technologies, and self-censorship—of people's ability to research, teach, and imagine alternative futures. Moreover, the US

Supreme Court has limited access to colleges for underrepresented students, ensuring that classrooms don't reflect the diversity of the general population. In the coming years, faculty will remain predominantly White and male, and the largely White student body they teach will go on to take up professions in law, health, finance, education, engineering, and so on, shaping policy and cultural values for decades to come. Opportunities to disrupt deeply embedded racist and sexist attitudes are declining, not rising, in higher education. This is a very gloomy scenario, and as I discuss in the next chapter, we need to radically revision public higher education to resist this antidemocratic full-scale assault.

Chapter Six

Fighting Back: Revisioning Higher Education

I teach at the University of California, a large 10-campus system of public higher education. In fall 2024, I taught a class on global environmental politics to 80 undergraduate students from across the campus. Some of the facts we covered were these:

- Climate scientists around the world agree that humans burning fossil fuels creates greenhouse gas emissions and they are causing unstoppable planetary warming.

- The year 2024 was the hottest globally on record, and 2025 is projected to be even hotter.

- Poorer and marginalized individuals and communities, often people of color, are disproportionately impacted by environmental degradation. This disproportionate impact is called environmental racism and is linked to intergenerational poverty as well as health disparities including reproductive problems around fertility and infant mortality.

- As the world leans toward antidemocracy and far-right leaders take control in many countries, there is a corresponding worldwide deregulation of environmental laws and policies.

- Under the Trump administration, 50 years of environmental regulations were dismantled. This enabled national parks to be opened for mining, corporations to ramp up greenhouse gas emissions, and protections for endangered animals to be removed.

- The Republican Party receives enormous campaign funding from energy corporations. In return, Trump gave these companies huge tax breaks and provided new mining leases and sale of lands for extracting gas and oil.

- Chevron, Shell, BP, and other Big Oil companies and groups such as the Koch family foundations give huge donations to universities. In return, they can influence what is researched and taught on a range of issues including the denial of planetary warming.

- Climate scientists can prove that if we don't stop burning fossil fuels, the planet will become uninhabitable for most of the world's population due to rising heat and lack of water by 2050.

- We can plan for a better future if we immediately stop burning fossil fuels and transition to renewable energy such as wind and solar.

On the last day of teaching the course, amid student applause, I hushed the lecture hall and told the students that if we were at a public university in Florida, Texas, Georgia, or North Carolina, I would not have been able to offer the class. The materials we had covered violated Republican legislation that prevented an instructor from talking about "controversial" subjects and policies, including slavery, sexuality, and climate warming. The students were shocked and outraged. Some gathered at the podium after class to continue the conversation. A number argued that it was my social responsibility to teach them facts about the environment that impacted their lives and those of their future children. I couldn't agree more.

Social Responsibility—a Special Duty in Higher Education

In the bitter culture wars impacting universities and colleges across the United States, there is much talk among the far right about professors having become "unpatriotic" and involved in the "indoctrination" of students. This rhetoric is strategically designed to raise a moral panic among the general population and drum up support for government oversight about what can be researched, taught, and discussed in classrooms. Silenced in this media frenzy is the idea that higher education is about communicating evidence-based knowledge—whether it is new knowledge or old knowledge newly revealed—as well as helping people think critically and ask questions about their place in the world and their relations to others. Even less discussed is that higher education is about scholars being socially responsible to students, present and future; that responsibility includes defending the sustainability of a flourishing planet in which all people thrive.

In chapter 1, I discussed how the Scholars at Risk organization states that one of the core values of higher education is social responsibility. SAR defines this as a duty "to seek and impart truth, according to ethical and professional standards, and to respond to contemporary problems and needs of all members of society" (SAR 2020). Given that we are living in extremely challenging times of massive economic inequality, rising political polarization, unending wars, mass migrations, looming ecological collapse, and the widespread use of disinformation by antidemocratic politicians and their allies, this duty is arguably more important than ever before.

In the past, Albert Einstein, after fleeing Nazi Germany in the early 1930s, talked about the special position of intellectuals, who have a social responsibility to the wider community that included fighting authoritarian interference in university life. In the 1960s, Noam Chomsky picked up this theme in the context of the Vietnam War and extreme student agitation over the CIA and the military draft that resulted in a heavy police presence on many university campuses. He, too, argued that scholars have a special responsibility to "seek the truth lying hidden behind the veil of distortion and misrepresentation, ideology and class interest." And Chomsky went on to say that intellectuals are in a position "to expose the lies of governments" (Chomsky 1967). As we saw in chapter 2, academic freedom grants scholars limited rights to speak the truth according to professional scholarly standards. Scholars are in a unique position, as knowledge experts, to pursue facts, ask probing questions, and challenge the status quo.

Today, scholars in the United States are confronted by the extremist MAGA movement within the Republican Party, which has endorsed plans to dismantle the constitutional checks and balances on a president's power and to usher in an antidemocratic government. Republican strategies align with the practices of other antidemocratic regimes around the world and new forms of societal fascism that are erupting across Europe, Africa, the Americas, the Middle East, and Asia. While these regimes may not fit traditional political categorizations of "authoritarianism" or "fascism," they share policies that seek to shut down representative forms of government, dismantle the basic principles of democracy that promote equality and social justice, and in the process privilege some people's lives over others.

As aggressive forms of racial, gender, religious, ethnic, and class discrimination creep into societies and across university communities, complacency or denial is no longer okay.

Universities are being attacked by a range of policing mechanisms that include external political pressure, legislative interference, replacement of trustees, defunding and disaccreditation, digital surveillance, disinformation campaigns, and overt and covert censorship and curriculum oversight, as well as a marked escalation in the presence of riot police on campus grounds. The stories told in chapter 3 of scholars and students being forced to flee their universities and homelands to escape harassment, persecution, and imprisonment should make everyone extremely fearful of what could happen in their own countries, including the United States. To remain silent is to be, in effect, complicit with far-right extremism.

We are at a pivotal and unprecedented moment, with a global rise in antidemocracy and a political landscape of disinformation disseminated through vast unregulated social media networks and amplified by AI algorithms. We are also confronted by a destabilized global political economy that has produced massive inequality and poverty and in the process robbed many millions of people of hope for a better future. Adding to the sense of despair are unfolding calamities of ecological collapse as we run for shelter from the burning sun or scramble to outpace rising oceans. Our current moment requires urgent action. As I argued at the start of this book, all scholars, from whatever discipline or training, can no longer hide behind their microscope, dataset, or archive; they must embrace their social responsibility to speak the truth about escalating crises if higher education and their future careers are to flourish.

Embracing social responsibility can require minimal effort. For instance, a 2023 report discussed in chapter 2, "Polarizing Times Demand Robust Academic Freedom," issued by the American Association of University Professors, argues that the "academic community's central mission of education, research, and service [is] to the broader society and to the public good." This statement emphasizes that universities and colleges are not simply producing knowledge as an objective or apolitical enterprise. Rather, as the AAUP report continues, while "college and university leaders have no obligation to speak out on the most controversial issues of the day," it is "their duty is to protect the academic freedom, free speech, and associational rights of faculty and students to speak on all topics of public or political interest without fear of intimidation, retaliation, or punishment."[1] In other words, university leaders do to have a responsibility to publicly speak out and protect scholars from external political pressure, censorship, and surveillance.

Similarly, not all scholars and teachers are obliged to start engaging with topics that may be deemed controversial. Every scholar doesn't have to change their syllabi or rush off to do a TED Talk or stream a podcast. On the contrary, scholars can continue their research and teaching without changing a thing, except to acknowledge the value of academic freedom, which up to this moment they have taken largely for granted. Ideally, this acknowledgment would mean accepting—or reclaiming—a more engaged role in shared university governance. Just as university leaders should, all scholars should be supporting those in their campus communities who conduct innovative research and teach evidence-based materials according to professional academic standards, however politically or emotionally unsettling it may be in practice. Defending the autonomy of the campus from external interference—and attempts to police and censor what gets studied and taught—is the most immediate and important responsibility anyone employed at a university should be engaged in.

Social Responsibility to Whom?

At this critical historical moment, scholars should also be asking themselves to whom they are socially responsible. This is a time to reflect on higher education and ask what we would like our colleges and universities to look like in the future. In defending the university from extremist political interference, it is important to articulate what scholars are fighting for. This is a complex and open question, to which there may be many answers. Two issues, however, should not be overlooked.

First, we must avoid nostalgia for a system of higher education that is embedded in long histories of colonialism, dispossession, elitism, sexism, racism, and exclusivity. Second, we must remember that university education historically excluded Black, Brown, Indigenous, and poorer students and scholars and that universities continue to serve a predominantly White and richer demographic. Sadly, in the United States today, the majority of university professors are still White men. And attending university for many young people, particularly those from economically or other disadvantaged groups, remains prohibitively expensive.

Given enduring legacies of racism, classism, and sexism in higher education, how should we revision the corporatized public university to be more accessible to middle- and working-class students and more receptive to intellectually diverse and culturally pluralist worldviews? How should we, as Marc Spooner and James McNinch urge us to do, "reclaim and reimagine the academy"? (Spooner and McNinch 2018:xxii). Below I list five ways to foster a more equitable and meaningful revisioning of higher education; I am sure others could contribute additional ideas. Each of these approaches will no doubt be deemed by far-right politicians in the United States and around the world as nonviable or unacceptable, which in my view speaks to their potential worth.

1. Responsibility and Freedom to Think Beyond the Euro-American Academy

In recent years, there has been an outpouring of scholarship about decolonizing the university and creating a more equitable learning community that represents a range of worldviews (Connell 2007; Mbembe 2016; Grosfoguel et al. 2016; Santos 2017; Bhambra et al. 2018; Rodríguez 2018; Schildermans 2021; Jansen 2019; Jansen and Walters 2022). This literature builds on postcolonial, decolonial, and feminist scholarship that for more than 40 years has called into question the violence of knowledge production and the repression of alternative voices within and beyond the Western academy (Spivak 1988; Shiva 1990).

Decolonialization can refer to various ideas and demands. For this reason, scholars calling for the decolonization of the university present different visions for a new kind of public higher education. Some focus on curricular reform, hiring practices, and campus outreach efforts to help build diverse and pluralist multiracial intellectual communities. Others question the very idea of the university itself, given its structural dependencies on settler colonial logic and racial capitalism that continue to marginalize certain members of society, particularly Indigenous scholars and students (Tuck 2018; Grande 2018:170; Cote-Meek and Moeke-Pickering 2020). Some remain pessimistic about ever overcoming the "institutional curriculum" (as opposed to the academic curriculum) that continues to shape what counts and is valued as legitimate knowledge in subtle and coercive ways (Lange 2019). This task is particularly difficult given institutional resistance to multilingual learning and the global lingua franca of the English language in education, technology, and social media across Africa and elsewhere (Parker 2019:259–260). Still others share a growing concern that "decolonization" has become a token buzzword among university administrators and managers, particularly in the United Kingdom. As Dalia Gebrial argues, we must not allow decolonization to "become the progressive face of a reactionary turn in the higher education sector" (Bhambra et al. 2020:514).

Despite anxieties about what it means to decolonize university spaces and break down barriers between those within and beyond the ivory tower, there is general agreement that any change "must make itself relevant and live to the current material struggles happening at universities across the world" (Bhambra et al. 2020:514). Doing so means acknowledging the dominance of the Euro-American academy in the global knowledge economy and recognizing valuable knowledge emanating from diverse non-Western epistemologies and worldviews (Collyer et al. 2019; Chatterjee and Maira 2014; Santos 2017). This change does not require erasing the Euro-American canon but rather promoting, in the words of political theorist Achille Mbembe, a "pluriversity":

> a process of knowledge production that is open to epistemic diversity. It is a process that does not necessarily abandon the notion of universal knowledge for humanity, but which embraces it via a *horizontal strategy of openness to dialogue among different epistemic traditions*. To decolonize the university is therefore to reform it with the aim of creating a less provincial and more open critical cosmopolitan pluriversalism—a task that involves the radical *re-founding* of our ways of thinking and a transcendence of our disciplinary divisions. (Mbembe 2015:14; author's italics)

In material terms, promoting pluriversalism means promoting accessibility to universities for underrepresented scholars and students and, once they are inside the academy, defending their scholarly contributions, which are often overlooked or deemed irrelevant (Popović 2022a). In other words, decolonizing the university includes building epistemologically diverse scholarly communities and curriculum and then connecting these dialogic and decentered ways of knowing to the lived conditions of the wider society, in turn promoting pathways for the next generations of students. Sociolegal Boaventura de Sousa Santos argues that this effort requires scholars involved in non-market-oriented knowledge to find or develop allies "outside the university walls" (Santos 2017:383). Otherwise, as has been the case with the corporatization of higher education over decades, "without external allies, non-market-oriented academics will easily be overpowered by market-oriented academics" (Santos 2017:383).

Along these lines, law scholar Folúkẹ́ Adébísí's book *Decolonisation and Legal Knowledge: Reflections on Power and Possibility* (2023) presents a remarkable discussion of the power structures embedded in scholarship and teaching of law that prioritize certain knowledge, and thus certain peoples, over others. Adébísí writes, "From the outset, it must be accepted that for the discipline to embrace decolonisation as praxis, academics must very deliberately acknowledge and oppose the problematic premises upon which the discipline has been advanced" (Adébísí's 2023:10). These premises operate to differentiate peoples and places, and law plays a central role in perpetuating historically oppressive logics of colonialism and racial capitalism. She goes on, "There is a difference, therefore, between 'decolonisation' (within and outside of academia) that merely *acknowledges* the colonial nature of the discipline and the decolonisation that seeks to *disrupt* and *dismantle* the colonial nature of the world" (Adébísí's 2023:11; author's italics; figure 15).

Figure 15. Removal of the statue of Cecil Rhodes from the campus of the University of Cape Town on April 9, 2015. Taking down the statue was part of the #FeesMustFall and #RhodesMustFall movements, motivated by earlier 1980s student movements in South Africa and calling for the decolonizing of knowledge in public education (see Willoughby-Herard 2025). The movement subsequently spread to campuses in the United Kingdom and United States, including Oxford and Harvard (Chigudu 2020). These student protests reflected a sense of alienation among Black and marginalized students and their efforts to challenge taken-for-granted modes of inquiry based in violent histories of racial capitalism, settler colonialism, and dispossession. Photo by Desmond Bowles. Licensed under the Attribution-NonCommercial-ShareAlike 2.0 International license. https://creativecommons.org/licenses/by/3.0/deed.en.

What Adébísí says about teaching in law schools applies more generally across the Euro-American academy. In other words, there is a need to disrupt and dismantle the hegemonic biases within research that prioritize Western knowledge as intrinsically superior. To echo bell hooks, we must be teaching to transgress the normative hierarchies that privilege Eurocentric knowledge and deny non-Westerners the ability to be knowledge-producing subjects (hooks 1994). We must overcome what Walter Mignolo calls "epistemic coloniality" and Geo Maher calls "colonial blindspots," in turn demanding "epistemic disobedience" and valuing and learning from "decolonial cunning" (Mignolo 2010; Maher 2022).

These contemporary scholars pick up earlier concerns expressed by Martin Luther King Jr. in 1967, a year before his assassination, when he called, in straightforward language that spoke to millions, for people to "develop a world perspective" and a "true revolution of values" (King 2010). King's leadership captured the turbulent years of the 1960s and student and faculty agitation concerning issues of racism, sexism, poverty and anti-environmentalism as well as the imperialist ambitions of the United States in overseas wars. As discussed in chapter 4, US student movements found allies in independence liberation movements across Africa, South Asia, and Central and South America, as well as antiwar movements and labor organizations across Europe and elsewhere, culminating in mass public demonstrations around the world in 1968.

It is important to remember, however, that the conservative backlash against student agitation was harsh and immediate in the 1970s and into the 1980s. The backlash forever changed public education in the United States and other global north countries by ushering in an era of university instrumentalization and the transformation of education into a commodity and students into consumers. Notably, this period also saw a transition away from faculty-led governance to governance by highly paid university administrators and managers. By making jobs for scholars increasingly precarious, these managers in practice controlled what was—and is—studied and taught. Concurrently, in the global south, newly independent university communities were brought to heel by the World Bank and International Monetary Fund through structural adjustment loans that expressly set out to dismantle public education and other much-needed social services, as explained in detail in chapter 4.

As we face decades-long institutional and economic challenges that are now escalating under a global wave of far-right regimes, it remains vital to critique the presumed superiority of the Westernized academy. We must "develop a world perspective" of inclusive collaboration, particularly given the challenges faced by the climate emergency and other pressing global issues that cannot be "fixed" by Western technology or assumed White intellectual brilliance. We can't bioengineer our way out of a warming planet, biodiversity extinction, massive migrations, and regional droughts. People in rich global north countries can, however, listen and learn from others who have had to live under colonial and neocolonial oppression for decades, if not centuries.

2. Responsibility and Freedom to Think with Inclusive Student Communities

Ngũgĩ wa Thiong'o, a renowned novelist, playwright and literary critic, takes the conversation about decolonizing the university in a different direction. Instead of examining what it may mean for the Western academy to look beyond its intellectual borders, he explores this notion in the context of African universities. As a political prisoner in postindependence Kenya, Ngũgĩ turned away from his training at an English university to embrace his native language, Gikuyu, and completed a novel written on toilet paper while incarcerated by the authoritarian regime. In his groundbreaking book *Decolonising the Mind: The Politics of Language in African Literature*, he wrote about decolonizing as a process of struggle over what should be taught and how it should be done. He argued that colonialism imposed its control through "military conquest and subsequent political dictatorship," but he went on to say that "the most important area of domination was the mental universe of the colonized, the control, through culture, of how people perceived themselves and their relationship to the world. Economic and political control can never be complete or effective without mental control" (Ngũgĩ 1986:16).

To counter political oppression, Ngũgĩ argued that African children need to break free from the Eurocentric learning that was imposed under colonialism and study and learn in their own native language, whatever that may be. Doing so would entail reorienting the academy with Africa—not Europe—at the center. According to Ngũgĩ, this reorientation does not require rejecting Western learning but rather mapping new "directions and perspectives" within the African university. This reorientation is "liberating," enabling Africans "to see ourselves clearly in relationship to ourselves and other selves in the universe." In language that elegantly sums up his vision for public education in schools and universities, Ngũgĩ calls this decentering a "quest for relevance" (Ngũgĩ 1986:87).

Back in the United States, efforts to recenter curriculum to include the histories, cultures, and worldviews of marginalized and non-Western peoples are precisely what the far right objects to. Under Florida's Republican governor, DeSantis, legislation now allows the prosecution of anyone teaching about slavery and its enduring legacies of racial oppression. Even the 2024 Republican presidential candidate Nikki Haley, when asked about the cause of the Civil War, failed to mention slavery, despite clear evidence that Confederate leaders left the Union because President Lincoln assumed the "equality of the races."[2] This denial is shocking but not surprising. Rewriting histories of violence and stoking national myths of racial (White) supremacy are both tactics in a playbook shared among many antidemocratic leaders across the Americas, Europe, Africa, and Asia, as explored in chapter 5.

3. Responsibility and Freedom to Think Across National Borders

Notably, Ngũgĩ' developed his thinking further in his book *Globalectics: Theory and the Politics of Knowing*. Here he argues for the study of world literatures and the transcending of "national and linguistic prisons" (Ngũgĩ' 2014:61). This transcendence requires expanding the center of knowing to include a postcolonial synthesis of "African, Caribbean, African-American literature and kindred literatures of Asia and Latin America" to create "a new order of knowing" (Ngũgĩ 2014:43).

Ngũgĩ' would probably agree with Evyn Lê Espiritu Gandhi's argument, in her 2022 book *Archipelago of Resettlement: Vietnamese Refugee Settlers and Decolonization Across Guam and Israel-Palestine*, that the goal of decoloniality is to be able to think beyond national borders, "not to collapse difference, but to recognize and communicate across it," to "render legible emergent solidarities between seemingly incommensurable subject positions" (Gandhi 2022:158; see also Tamale 2022:44). This argument acknowledges that knowledge production is both a global and a local phenomenon. It is in effect borderless, drawing from numerous worldviews and positionalities in which there is no hierarchy of knowing determined by Western criteria or the nation in which scholarship is produced. In the writings of Gandhi, and in fact in all scholarship calling for the decolonization of the university, the freedom to think across national borders is a central element. This freedom is based in a duty, not to any one country or nationalist identity, but to a collective humanity, echoing the African ethic of *ubuntu* (Waghid 2023; Waghid et al. 2023) and the sentiment of "commoning," as discussed by Silvia Federici (Federici 2019). Moreover, it speaks to the material realities of diverse demographics in most countries, due to the many millions of people around the world who have migrated, and the intercultural dynamics in any one society that profoundly disrupt an essentialized and homogeneous nationalism.

Such societal realities are not well received by the far right, however—in the United States or elsewhere. For instance, it is predicted that immigrants and racially marginalized peoples will numerically be the majority population in the United States by 2045. This prediction has caused an outpouring of anxiety among many who think that White civilization is being replaced by Black and Brown peoples. Racism toward others shows up in widespread support for the "Great Replacement" conspiracy theory pushed by radical conservative Renaud Camus and widespread conspiracy groups such as QAnon. And racism energizes ugly discourse and attitudes against immigrants, as calls for stronger border controls and anti-immigration policy have become popular rallying cries on the part of Republicans and all far-right political leaders, particularly those in Europe.

4. Responsibility and Freedom to Think with Nonhuman Worlds

Growing numbers of scholars, especially those associated with environmental research, argue that academic freedom means being responsible not just to humans but to nonhuman entities as well. In other words, decolonizing the university requires fostering new modes of knowledge production among a diverse range of people that includes non-Western understandings of human and nonhuman relations of interconnectedness, codependence, and reciprocity.

For those holding this view, decolonizing the university requires disrupting the dominance of Enlightenment thinking, which posits humans as distinct from and superior to the natural world, with the right to possess, control, and exploit it

(Plumwood 1993:42). This human–nature binary historically justified colonialism and extractive capitalism, including exploitation of both human and natural resources. In the pursuit of profit, some people (deemed nonhuman) could be exploited, enslaved, bred, and exterminated, and natural landscapes and animal species could be mined, deforested, polluted, hunted, and driven to extinction.

Again, Achille Mbembe offers a perceptive commentary, arguing that the human–nature binary is deeply embedded in Western thinking. Moreover, it has enabled knowledge to be understood as objective and decontextualized from its surroundings and then to be carried around the world as if it had universal application. Mbembe writes that "the problem—because there is a problem indeed—with this tradition is that it has become hegemonic. This hegemonic notion of knowledge production has generated discursive scientific practices and has set up interpretative frames that make it difficult to think outside of those frames. But this is not all. This hegemonic tradition also actively represses anything that actually is articulated, thought and envisioned from outside of these frames" (Mbembe 2016:30–31).

Today, the human–nature binary continues to be dominant in the Euro-American academy and frames ways of thinking about people's place in the world. The natural world continues to be seen by many—especially those living in the global north—as a resource to be owned and plundered for profit. This way of knowing denies the relationality all human beings share with the natural world in which they live and on which they ultimately depend—a relationship Donna Haraway calls *natureculture* (Haraway 2008, 2016; Merrick 2017). As Ailton Krenak, a Brazilian writer, journalist, public intellectual, and Indigenous activist poetically argues, we need to "reforest our imagination," reconnecting alliances between people living in concrete sterile cities with the living "wild" entities of the natural world (Krenak 2024:43). Reminding us of this relationality, Jack Forbes, a leading Indigenous scholar and founder of one of the first Native American studies programs, at UC Davis, writes:

> I can lose my hands, and still live. I can lose my legs and still live. I can lose my eyes and still live. I can lose my hair, eyebrows, nose, arms, and many other things and still live. But if I lose the air I die. If I lose the sun I die. If I lose the earth I die. If I lose the water I die. If I lose the plants and animals I die. All of these things are more a part of me, more essential to my every breath, than is my so-called body. What is my real body? (Forbes 2001)

Thinking about everyone's relations with the nonhuman world is vital if we are going to seriously address the climate emergency on a global scale. Focusing on the relationality between peoples, animals, birds, and places brings into question the centuries-old logic of extractive capitalism that prioritizes profits over people. Challenging the status quo is precisely why this kind of relational thinking between humans and nonhumans is being forcefully, sometimes violently, attacked by the far right in concert with major corporate sectors such as Big Oil, technology, defense, and finance. As the planet continues to heat and burn, policing university research and curriculum that challenges this dominant extractive logic has become essential for corporations, lobbyists, and conservative think tanks and philanthropic foundations, as discussed in chapter 5. Research and teaching about the realities of the climate emergency—including discussions of the negative impacts of free-market economics—have become an intensified battlefront in the war over higher education.

5. Responsibility and Freedom to Think About Collective Futures

In the context of the climate crisis and looming ecological collapse, dismantling the human–nature binary is a matter of survival for the human species (Kolbert 2014; Darian-Smith 2022, 2023b, 2023c). In the coming years, we will all be faced with mass movements of people fleeing environmental degradation and related economic and political conflict. Already hundreds of thousands of environmental refugees are on the move—despite not yet being recognized as refugees in international law. And within countries such as the United States, we are seeing a new phenomenon in the wave of internally displaced environmental refugees, with escalating catastrophic weather events forcing people from their homes and communities.

The global climate emergency needs colleges and universities to play a central role in thinking through solutions for our collective futures. The development of solutions requires thinking critically about our capitalist system, which "is the mortal enemy of global aspirations for a sustainable economy that satisfies needs rather than stock portfolios."[3] Thinking through solutions also requires rethinking relations within and beyond national borders to focus on humanity's interconnections and reciprocity with one another and the natural world. Finally, the development of solutions entails adopting a longer time horizon, beyond annual gross domestic product reports and election cycles. Only by extending our thinking to long-term potentials and solutions can we imagine a better future for younger generations and their future children.

The reality, however, is that far-right politicians and their corporate allies do not want the university to be reclaimed and reimagined for more just collective futures. Students demanding divestment from fossil fuel companies, scholars protesting funding for research that serves corporate interests, and student-led demonstrations against escalating racial and ethnic violence at home and wars overseas are all evidence of a rising mood of campus resistance. Mounting protests within campus communities, including demands for campus unionization, seek to *disrupt*—to borrow Folúkẹ́ Adébísí's terminology. These protests evoke earlier efforts in the 1960s to forge a more inclusive and diverse higher education sector. And as with the conservative backlash against higher education in the 1970s, today's agitation on campuses has helped galvanize Republicans to take repressive political action. This time, however, the backlash has taken on an unprecedented scale and is being prosecuted with a new ferocity, as the far right aggressively weaponizes the university, steps up police presence on campuses, bans books, promotes self-censorship, chills conversation, and limits what can be studied, taught, and imagined in college classrooms, as discussed in chapter 5.

Concluding Comments

By way of conclusion, let's return to a question raised earlier in this chapter: To whom should scholars be socially responsible? Are scholars responsible to students, colleagues, adjunct lecturers, and the staff they work with? Beyond the campus, what about the local communities that surround the university? What about the wider society, including people who can't afford or don't intend to go to college? What about being responsible for homelands—the places where people are born and the villages to which they belong? What about the international community and displaced peoples caught in borderlands between unending regional conflicts and wars? What about the polar bears, rainforests, and honeybees we live together with on our fragile planet? What about everyone's kids and the coming generations who will fill our collective futures?

The answer is that scholars are responsible for all these things, whether or not they recognize their unique duty. As demonstrated by the extraordinary bravery of many thousands of scholars forced to flee persecution by authoritarian leaders around the world, this responsibility is the cost of occupying the privileged positions of "scholar" and "educator," especially those who are tenured professors and work at an elite university. This responsibility is based on integrity, professionalism, and truth-searching. It amounts to the deceptively simple task of defending the right of all scholars and students to pursue evidence-based knowledge and to "speak on all topics of public or political interest without fear of intimidation, retaliation, or punishment" (AAUP 2023).

Given widespread disinformation and declining public trust in science and expertise, coupled with the hostile far-right assault on higher education, revisioning new strategies for the university in the twenty-first century is essential. My modest solution is to reframe universities as institutions committed to social responsibility and, by extension, to social justice. My reasons for this reframing have been explored throughout the book. In sum, whether speech is "academic" and protected under the principle of academic freedom depends on whether the speech passes professionally determined scholarly standards. This can be difficult to explain and, in practice, to sort out from an individual's constitutional right to free speech. If, however, we revision the university as an institution of collective social responsibility, then the need for academic freedom becomes easier for students and the wider society to grasp. Legibility to broader audiences is vital for informing people why they should care about public education more generally. Specifically, it makes it easier to link the value of education to flourishing and equitable societies that promote the basic principles of democracy such as the right to vote, health care, clean water, affordable housing, and job opportunities, as well as a more radical imagining of democracy that transcends national borders and promotes the idea of an interdependent global humanity. As the sociologist Raewyn Connell argues, a powerful first step is to "recognize the modern university as a shared social resource, a collective asset" (Connell 2019:188–189).

To this end, all scholars, no matter what they study or teach, should be able to explain to themselves why their work is important. On that basis, scholars should also be able to explain to others why their work is important and an asset to society, even if they disagree on how their work matters or to whom they are responsible. This ability to explain their work's importance at least starts a conversation that links the value of higher education to communities both inside and outside the academy. Currently, under the antidemocratic assault on higher education, scholars and students are fearful of speaking out. Many self-censor rather than be called before a university administrator or subjected to online harassment, trolling, and doxing. Many, especially adjunct and contract-based teachers, fear they might lose their jobs. In this increasingly oppressive environment, we must create pathways for people to speak without fear about their work and its significance for building more just collective futures. We must not give up on public education's "quest for relevance."

Acknowledgments

The most important people to acknowledge and thank are the many thousands of scholars, students, staff, and administrators who have been targeted by extremist governments and forced to compromise their research and teaching. Still others have been prosecuted, jailed, exiled, and even killed. To these courageous people I give my most heartfelt thanks. I also give huge thanks to the organizations and groups that are committed to helping scholars in need and to hosting and welcoming those forced to flee and live in new academic communities.

I especially want to acknowledge Jane O. Newman, a colleague at my university, for her work over many years in helping scholars at risk to be received within the University of California system. Jane has been a shining light and an inspiration to me and numerous others. Thanks also to the wonderful participants in the First Conference on Academic Freedom in the Americas, sponsored by the Coalition for Academic Freedom in the Americas and held in Monterrey, Mexico, in November 2022. This was an illuminating event, where I met new and inspiring colleagues including (in alphabetical order) Catalina Arango Patiño, Viviana Fernandez, Salvador Herencia-Carrasco, Rafael Ibarra, Jessie Levine, Robert Quinn, and Clare Robinson, among others.

Special thanks to my editor, Greg Britton, for his enthusiasm for this book project when I first pitched it to him and for his constant support throughout the production process, as well as the very helpful comments from anonymous reviewers. Specific people who gave me feedback on the manuscript are (again in alphabetical order) Jeffrey Bachman, Matt Canfield, Jon Goldberg-Hiller, Isaac Kamola, Anne McCall, Ellen Schrecker, and Jeffrey Snyder. I thank them all for their generous and insightful input.

People who have inspired and helped shape my thinking over many years also dwell in the pages of this book—love and deep appreciation go to Peter Fitzpatrick, Wes Pue, Donna Merwick, Greg Dening, Jane Collier, George Collier, Sally Falk Moore, and Sally Merry. Thanks also to the amazing scholars, students, and staff in the Department of Global and International Studies at UC Irvine, who keep me on my toes intellectually by challenging my preconceived ideas, which I greatly appreciate.

Finally, I thank my wonderfully loving, supportive and engaging partner, Philip McCarty; our crazy twins, Ellie and Sam; my amazing twin sister, Corinna; and our much-loved and much-missed parents, Pammie and Ian, who always encouraged us to think of education as a cherished privilege.

Appendix

PEN America: Principles on Campus Free Speech

PEN America's Principles on Campus Free Speech were originally developed as part of our landmark 2016 report, *And Campus for All*. We add to these principles here to reflect changing dynamics and new challenges on US campuses.*

OVERVIEW

- While free speech is alive and well on campus, it is not free from threats, and must be vigilantly guarded if its continued strength is to be assured.

- Current campus controversies merit attention and there have been a significant number of troubling instances of speech curtailed amid what seems to be an increasingly tense campus environment. But these controversies in many cases represent campus communities sorting out differences in values, however heatedly. They represent an area of serious concern but not a wholesale "crisis" for free speech on campus.

- At times, protests and forms of expression are treated as if they are incursions on free speech when in fact they are manifestations of free speech.

---

* This statement of principles was reproduced with the permission of PEN America.

- Many of today's campus controversies that implicate free speech and the First Amendment are fueled by legitimate concerns about racism, discrimination, inclusion, and inequality. The failure at times to recognize these factors may impair efforts to defuse conflict and safeguard free speech.

- Free expression should be recognized as a principle that will overwhelmingly serve not to exclude or marginalize minority voices, but rather to amplify them. Free speech protections have been essential to the movements to counter racism, redress inequalities and advance social justices.

- By acknowledging and addressing legitimate concerns regarding racism and bigotry in the context of free speech debates, universities can help ensure that the defense of freedom of expression is not misconstrued as a cause that is at odds with movements for social justice.

THE CAMPUS CLIMATE

- Administrators must look hard at how physical barriers, historical traditions, inequalities, prejudices, and power dynamics can weigh against openness, and take concrete steps to alleviate those burdens.

- Campus discourse should be predicated on the presumption of respect for differences, including differences of view that cause disagreement.

- Respect entails an obligation to listen to understand what words may cause offense to others and why, and to conscientiously consider avoiding such words when no offense is intended.

- The duty of care involved in understanding different perspectives and learning to anticipate where offense might be caused is heightened for administrators and faculty when they are carrying out institutional duties.

- Violence, threats, and harassment are never appropriate. However, vociferous, adamant, and even contentious argument and protest have their place.

- College should be acknowledged as a time for students to engage with new ideas and participate in robust debates, which can involve testing boundaries and experimenting with forms of speech and activism. As such, consequences for errors of judgment should be commensurate, and geared toward the possibility of learning and future improvement.

- An environment where too many offenses are considered impermissible or even punishable becomes sterile, constraining, and inimical to creativity.

- So-called "free speech zones," wherein schools limit activities such as pamphleteering or spontaneous demonstrations to contained areas on campus, may violate the First Amendment and contravene principles of free speech.

- Schools should refrain from establishing policies or imposing facially neutral rules that either intend or have the effect of discriminating against speakers based upon the content of their speech.

- Administrators should ensure equitable space and opportunities for diverse political perspectives and thought.

HATEFUL SPEECH

- Hateful speech that is intended to menace, intimidate or discriminate against an individual based upon a personal characteristic or membership in a group can impair equal access to the full benefits of a college education and the ability of all students to participate in campus discourse.

- In an environment of rising incidences of hateful speech and hate crimes nationally, the potency of individual instances of hateful speech on campus can be heightened, increasing the psychological harm that such speech can cause and underscoring the importance of effective institutional responses.

- That some individuals may experience offense or insult or negative feelings such as anger, resentment, frustration, or discouragement in response to others' speech is not sufficient grounds to limit that speech, because by its nature speech frequently does give rise to such feelings.

- Conflating the expression of controversial or even offensive viewpoints with hateful speech can result in the suppression of open discourse and trigger a backlash from groups whose expression is deterred or punished despite not being intentionally hateful.

- Administrators have an imperative to be responsive to threats, hateful intimidation, and students' encounters with overt racism and other forms of discrimination. This responsiveness is imperative to nurturing an environment where all feel empowered to participate in the free exchange of ideas and opinions.

- Effective responses to hateful speech include counter-messaging, condemnations, direct support to targeted individuals and groups, dialogue, and education. In the case of hate crimes, harassment and any other conduct that violates the law, aggressive disciplinary response is warranted.

CAMPUS SPEAKERS

- Campuses, both public and private, should keep their platforms accessible to a wide variety of academic and popular opinions, while fostering a culture where speech and reasoned debate are seen as the best tools for confronting mistaken, wrongheaded or hateful ideas.

- A decentralized approach to campus speakers, where student groups, academic departments, classroom teachers and others are free to invite whom they wish to campus without having to receive prior administrative approval can help foster exposure to the widest breadth of ideas, although student groups will usually benefit from consultation with a faculty adviser.

- When an invited speaker is likely to be controversial, those issuing the invitation should consider whether outreach to other stakeholders, facilitating counter-speech or other measures are appropriate to ensure that the speech is aired without negative repercussions.

- Once a body has decided to extend an invitation to a campus speaker, the decision by administrators' to override that choice and rescind the invitation should be made only in the rarest of circumstances.

- Except in the most extreme cases, concerns over threats of violence or the potential outbreak of violence should not be grounds for withdrawing an invitation or canceling a controversial speech or event.

- That a campus event may meet with protests should not be considered a reason to suspend it.

- Wherever possible, campuses should not allow security costs to be grounds for withdrawing a speaking invitation, recognizing that such costs are unavoidably linked to the anticipated reaction to the content of speech and are thus viewpoint specific.

- If security costs for campus events are born by inviting organizations or speakers themselves, they must be apportioned based on content and viewpoint neutral policies.

- When a speaking invitation sparks protests, those who object and wish to protest should have an opportunity to make themselves heard.

- Protesters should not be permitted to shut down, shout down or obstruct speech, preventing others from hearing the speaker.

- Some speakers invited to campus fall into the category of professional provocateurs, whose primary aim is to shock, offend, and build their own notoriety when they are silenced or censored. While there is no obligation to invite such speakers, when invitations are made through proper, authorized campus channels such speakers should be permitted to speak.

- When a university provides a platform to a figure who contradicts its values, leaders should strenuously and unequivocally affirm their values, explaining their position in considerable detail, while still permitting the speaker to speak.

CALLS TO PUNISH SPEECH

- Institutions should be careful to avoid any form of discipline or punishment solely for legally protected speech.

- While demands for punishment themselves constitute protected speech, calls to punish speakers for their speech have a chilling effect and are usually inimical to an open environment for ideas.

- As forums and guardians of open debate, campuses must resist pressure from external actors and campus constituencies to curtail and punish speech. Campus leaders should engage legitimate complaints through dialogue, counter-speech and support while defending the rights of speakers to voice their opinions without fear of official reprimand or discipline.

- Administrators and campus leaders must be consistent in coming to prompt, full-throated defense of a faculty member's right to exercise academic freedom without fear of dismissal, retaliation, or loss of position even when the speech in question is controversial.

- When campus constituents are targeted by doxxing, online harassment or other unofficial reprisals for speech, they should enjoy the support of campus administrators in safeguarding themselves from such reprisals, including through the pursuit of disciplinary action against those responsible.

- Universities should not shy away from commenting on or denouncing the content of a faculty member's speech when it contravenes a university's stated values. It does not constitute retaliation or chilling for a university president or leader merely to criticize, without seeking punishment, the content of a faculty member's speech in such cases. Such counter-speech can be an effective reassurance to various university constituencies when hateful speech arises from faculty. Doing so, however, should never preclude the campus from doing everything in its power to shield faculty from threats to their safety or position as a result of such speech.

FACULTY SPEECH AND EXPRESSION

- With the rise of social media and new methods of recording and distributing information, faculty members should not expect privacy when it comes to their public online speech and expression and should recognize that anything they say may be construed to reflect upon their ability to carry out their institutional responsibilities.

- When considering a response to faculty speech, universities should take into account whether a faculty member had a reasonable expectation of privacy in expressing his or her views.

- Academic freedom is a core tenet of the academy and faculty should be encouraged to push the bounds of knowledge without fear of retaliation for exploring ideas that might offend.

- Extramural speech by faculty members is considered protected by most definitions of academic freedom.

Administrators should resist pressures to engage in disciplinary actions in response to such speech except in instances where the content of the speech calls into question whether a faculty member can adequately execute their duties.

- Where faculty members serve in an institutional capacity that may be negatively affected by the content of speech that raises questions about their ability to fulfill duties fairly and with equal respect for all students, universities should strive to ensure that any reallocation of duties is not punitive do not spill over to impair the faculty member's academic career.

MICROAGGRESSIONS AND THE LANGUAGE OF HARM

- The increasing diversity of college populations requires a wider conscientiousness of how words are understood by different groups of listeners.

- The task of fostering a more inclusive environment—and calling out language that undercuts it—cannot be left only, or even primarily, to students who are members of marginalized groups.

- University administrators should encourage all students to be sensitive to the ways that their words can unintentionally hurt others and should show sensitivity in their own communications.

- The onus to consider the impact of words, images and messages on diverse groups of students is heightened for administrators and faculty in that their professional duties encompass the creation and maintenance of an open and equal learning environment.

- University policies regulating everyday speech or attempting to define insults for the entire community are intrusive and risk prohibiting or even simply disfavoring permissible speech.

TRIGGER WARNINGS

- If professors wish to offer students a preview of troubling content to come in a syllabus, the university should not prevent them from doing so.

- Universities cannot and should not position themselves institutionally to ensure that every possibly upsetting encounter with course material is averted.

- Universities should therefore leave the question of trigger warnings or any other sort of alerts about course material up to individual faculty members.

SAFE SPACES

- It is the obligation of the university to foster an environment in which violent, harassing, and reckless conduct does not occur and respect is encouraged.

- It is neither possible nor desirable for the campus to offer protection from all ideas and speech that may cause a measure of damage.

- Campuses should acknowledge and respond to the impact of hateful speech and hate crimes in terms of creating an environment of safety and belonging on campus, taking affirmative steps to make sure that affected students are supported and that the campus culture fosters mutual respect for individual differences.

- It is reasonable to designate some spaces "safe" for particular groups on a campus but these must always be entered into voluntarily by those wishing to associate with the group. It is unreasonable to impose such constraints on public or communal areas of a campus as a way to exclude certain words or ideas.

- Campuses should enable and even support the creation and protection of spaces established by students—such as clubs, organizations, or even small gathering areas based on common themes and lifestyles.

- The campus as a whole and segments thereof that are intended for all—such as dorms, residential colleges, classrooms, and cafeterias—must be kept physically safe but intellectually and ideologically open.

SPEECH AND SEXUAL HARASSMENT

- There is no contradiction between advocating for more stringent measures to address sexual harassment and assault on campus and insisting on measures to protect free speech and academic freedom.

- Universities should reiterate the centrality of academic freedom when they address issues of harassment.

EDUCATION AND DIALOGUE

- There is both a need and an opportunity for expanded education and mobilization on issues of free speech on campus.

- All groups supportive of free speech should redouble their efforts to ensure that campus free speech is a cause that engages students from across the political spectrum.

- Institutions and funders with an interest in supporting free speech should invest in the next generation by underwriting grants for work to build awareness and appreciation for free speech on campus.

- Whether it is on racial, gender, ethnic or ideological grounds, those who may feel marginalized in campus discourse should be supported by the universities in finding avenues for full participation in campus life.

- Campuses should take full advantage of the diversity of their student bodies to ensure opportunities for dialogue are maintained for students who have different views from one another. Principles of free speech should be adhered to as central to such endeavors.

CAMPUS SPEECH LEGISLATION

- State and federal bodies invested in defending speech on campus should take care to avoid overreach, especially in the form of guiding campuses' responses to various free speech incidents. This includes ensuring campuses are free to affirm and articulate the values of open discourse, academic freedom, diversity and inclusion, and other principles integral to the institutional role of the university in society.

- Legislation seeking to address free speech on campus should avoid the use of overbroad and vague definitions that have the potential curtail free speech or otherwise render legitimate topics of academic deliberation effectively off-limits.

- Legislation should not dictate disciplinary requirements or penalties, and should leave decisions about discipline to the discretion of school administrators who have a full understanding of the context in which events have occurred.

- Legislation should preserve the ability of public colleges to prevent discrimination based on race, ethnicity, religion, or other protected class by publicly funded student organizations.
- Legislative efforts to address campus free speech should include or be accompanied by the appropriation of funds for orientation and ongoing education on the importance of free expression.

Notes

Introduction

1. Alberto Toscano, "The Rise of the Far Right Is a Global Phenomenon," *In These Times*, November 21, 2023, https://inthesetimes.com/article/global-far-right-meloni-milei-putin-bannon-orban.

2. American Association of University Professors, "1940 Statement of Principles on Academic Freedom and Tenure," 1940, https://www.aaup.org/report/1940-statement-principles-academic-freedom-and-tenure.

3. Michael Sainato "'Many of Us Are Struggling': Why US Universities Are Facing a Wave of Strikes," *The Guardian*, April 21, 2023, https://www.theguardian.com/us-news/2023/apr/21/us-universities-wave-strikes.

4. Talloires Network; see https://talloiresnetwork.tufts.edu/who-we-are/.

5. The Talloires Network echoes earlier efforts that emerged in the post–World War II period. For instance, a UNESCO conference was convened in 1950 in Nice, France, and the International Association of Universities (IAU) was founded with a global mandate "to provide a centre of cooperation at the international level among the universities and similar institutions of higher education of all countries." The IAU Constitution, signed on December 9, 1950, stated that every university must enable knowledge to be pursued openly, must tolerate divergent opinions and resist state interference, and must promote the "principles of freedom and justice, of human dignity and solidarity, and to develop mutually material and moral aid on an international level" (Land et al. 2021:1). In other words, universities were understood to have a global role in supporting one another across national borders in defense of scholars' academic freedom to promote democracy, justice, and freedom for all.

6. Inter-American Commission on Human Rights, Special Rapporteur for Freedom of Expression, and Special Rapporteur for Economic, Social, Cultural and Environmental Rights, *Inter-American Principles on Academic Freedom and University Autonomy*, 2021, https://www.oas.org/en/iachr/reports/questionnaires/2021_principiosinteramericanos_libertadacademica_autonomiauniversitaria_eng.pdf.

7. Kalven Committee, *Report on the University's Role in Political and Social Action*, University of Chicago Office of the Provost, November 1967, https://provost.uchicago.edu/reports/report-universitys-role-political-and-social-action.

8. Fears are increasing that college enrollments will drop dramatically in the coming years, however, particularly among small private colleges and those serving lower-income student populations. These fears stem in part from a stable labor market, which makes it possible for young people to find a job after leaving high school. These fears are also in part due to rising tuition costs, which promise to make a college degree even less affordable in the United States in the foreseeable future and which disproportionately impact lower-income and minority students (see Grawe 2018, 2022).

9. Eric Kelderman, "What the Public Really Thinks About Higher Education," *Chronicle of Higher Education*, September 5, 2023, https://www.chronicle.com/article/what-the-public-really-thinks-about-higher-education?sra=true&cid=gen_sign_in.

10. For instance, Silicon Valley computer technology developed geographically where it did in large part because of its proximity to students graduating from the University of California, Berkeley and Stanford University, which are both nearby.

11. Nao Matsukata, "Letter to the Editor," *New York Times*, December 6, 2023, https://www.nytimes.com/2023/12/06/opinion/humanities-college.html.

Chapter 1. Intersecting Global Trends

1. Quoted in "On Loving Trump: A CounterPunch Dialogue on the Grand Flirtation with Fascism," *CounterPunch*, November 9, 2023, https://www.counterpunch.org/2023/11/09/on-loving-trump-a-counterpunch-dialogue-on-the-grand-flirtation-with-fascism/.

2. Vijay Prashad, "The Dangerously Appealing Style of the Far Right: The Forty-Eighth Newsletter (2023)," *TriContinental*, November 30, 2023, https://thetricontinental.org/newsletterissue/argentina-elections-and-the-rise-of-the-far-right/.

3. In Operation Condor, the US government worked with Latin American oligarchies to suppress the political left through murder, imprisonment, torture, and regime change. Numerous coups were carried out in the Dominican Republic (1965), Chile (1973), Uruguay (1973), Argentina (1976), and El Salvador (1980). The puppet military governments that were put in place supported a Western neoliberal agenda that proved highly profitable to US-led multinational corporations.

4. Still, many countries continue to be involved in violence and coercion, and military coups have not gone away. Africa alone experienced seven coups since August 2020.

5. The concept of "lawfare" evolved in the wake of 9/11; it involves the use of legal systems and lawsuits to attack enemies of the state in defense of national security interests. For instance, the United States made an international law claim about weapons of mass destruction to justify its invasion of Iraq and Afghanistan. Since the early 2010s, there has been much debate about how to define "lawfare," as its usage has moved beyond the international security context. I use the term throughout the book in reference to the Republican Party's open support of a "war" on public education. In my usage, "lawfare" refers to the abuse and exploitation of law by the far right to bolster Republican power as well as to attack those they consider domestic enemies, such as scholars, teachers, and students.

6. Joe Biden, "Remarks by President Biden Honoring the Legacy of Senator John McCain and the Work We Must Do Together to Strengthen Our Democracy," White House, November 10, 2023, https://www.whitehouse.gov/briefing-room/speeches-remarks/2023/09/28/remarks-by-president-biden-honoring-the-legacy-of-senator-john-mccain-and-the-work-we-must-do-together-to-strengthen-our-democracy/.

7. Sam Levine, "Trump Suggests He Would Use FBI to Go After Political Rivals If Elected in 2024," *The Guardian*, November 10, 2023, https://www.theguardian.com/us-news/2023/nov/10/trump-fbi-rivals-2024-election.

8. Tom Nichols, "Trump Plots Against His Enemies," *The Atlantic*, November 6, 2023, https://www.theatlantic.com/newsletters/archive/2023/11/trump-plot-military-election/675922/.

9. Baher Kamal, "Extremist Ideology Spreading like an Oil Spill in Europe," *Global Issues*, June 22, 2023, https://www.globalissues.org/news/2023/06/22/34082.

10. Anne Mailliet, Raphael Kominis, Willy Mahler, and Nick Spicer, "Germany: 'Citizens of the Reich' Refuse to Recognise Post-war Federal State," *Focus*, France 24, January 17, 2023, https://www.france24.com/en/tv-shows/focus/20230117-germany-citizens-of-the-reich-refuse-to-recognise-post-war-federal-state.

11. For instance, Arthur Levine and Scott Pelt, who have studied higher education for decades, argue in their book that the forces driving a "great upheaval" in US higher education are "changing demographics, the rise of the knowledge economy, and the advance of digital technology and globalization" (Levine and Pelt 2021:x). Oddly, however, there is no mention of the far-right attack on universities. Similarly, Wanda Teays and Alison Renteln, in their edited volume on higher education, examine a range of challenges, such as privacy, accountability, shared governance, and adjunct professors, but fail to mention the Republican attack and how this is upturning the higher education sector (Teays and Renteln 2022).

12. Quoted in Anna Betts and Nichole Manna, "Grief and Anger Continue to Reverberate from Jacksonville Shootings," *New York Times*, August 28, 2023, https://www.nytimes.com/2023/08/28/us/jacksonville-shooting-florida-hbcu.html.

13. Steven Lee Myers and Sheera Frenkel, "G.O.P. Targets Researchers Who Study Disinformation Ahead of 2024 Election," *New York Times*, June 19, 2023, https://www.nytimes.com/2023/06/19/technology/gop-disinformation-researchers-2024-election.html.

14. The Supreme Court ruled against the affirmative action policies of Harvard University and the University of North Carolina, with the court majority stating that these reflected "elite" interests and expertise rather than attempts over decades to dismantle systemic racism in higher education.

15. Ai Weiwei, "How Censorship Works," *New York Times*, May 17, 2017, https://www.nytimes.com/2017/05/06/opinion/sunday/ai-weiwei-how-censorship-works.html.

16. Anna Fazackerley, "Climate Crisis Deniers Target Scientists for Vicious Abuse on Musk's Twitter," *The Guardian*, May 14, 2023, https://www.theguardian.com/environment/2023/may/14/climate-crisis-deniers-target-scientists-abuse-musk-twitter.

17. Quoted in Vimal Patel, "At UChicago, a Debate over Free Speech and Cyberbullying," *New York Times*, July 3, 2023, https://www.nytimes.com/2023/07/03/us/university-of-chicago-whiteness-free-speech.html.

18. Quoted in Megan Zahneis and Beckie Supiano, "Fear and Confusion in the Classroom," *Chronicle of Higher Education*, June 9, 2023, https://www.chronicle.com/article/fear-and-confusion-in-the-classroom?sra=true&cid=gen_sign_in.

19. See Faculty First Responders, "What We Do," accessed August 28, 2024, https://facultyfirstresponders.com/whatwedo/.

20. Quoted in Patrica Cohen, "Why It Seems Everything We Knew About the Global Economy Is No Longer True," *New York Times*, June 18, 2023, https://www.nytimes.com/2023/06/18/business/economy/global-economy-us-china.html.

21. Martin-Brehm Christensen, Christian Hallum, Alex Maitland, Quentin Parrinello, and Chiara Putaturo, *Survival of the Richest: How We Must Tax the Super-Rich Now to Fight Inequality*, Oxfam International, January 2023, https://oxfamilibrary.openrepository.com/bitstream/handle/10546/621477/bp-survival-of-the-richest-160123-en.pdf.

22. Quoted in Michael Roberts, "Davos and the Melting World Economy," *Climate&Capitalism*, January 20, 2024, https://climateandcapitalism.com/2024/01/20/davos-and-the-melting-world-economy/.

23. Scholars at Risk, "'There Were No Fatalities . . . [but] If This Happens Again, I Am Not So Sure': Discussing the Forcible Violation of the Universi-

dad Nacional de San Marcos, Lima, Peru, with Salvador Herencia-Carrasco," *Free to Think*, podcast, episode 29, February 7, 2023, https://www.scholarsatrisk.org/resources/podcast/.

24. American Library Association, *The State of America's Libraries 2024*, accessed August 28, 2024, https://www.ala.org/news/state-americas-libraries-report-2024.

25. Quoted in Chris Walker, "Report: Attempts to Ban Books in 2023 Are Outpacing Previous Year by 20 Percent," *Truthout*, September 21, 2023, https://truthout.org/articles/report-attempts-to-ban-books-in-2023-are-outpacing-previous-year-by-20-percent/.

26. Michelle Goldberg, "At a College Targeted by DeSantis, Gender Studies Is Out, Jocks Are In," *New York Times*, August 14, 2023, https://www.nytimes.com/2023/08/14/opinion/columnists/gender-studies-ron-desantis-florida.html.

27. Quoted in Kenny Stancil, " 'Race to the Bottom': GOP Has Introduced 84 Educational Gag Orders So Far in 2023," *Common Dreams*, February 16, 2023, https://www.commondreams.org/news/gop-educational-gag-orders-2023.

28. Irene Mulvey, "Florida's Stop WOKE Act Must Be Rejected by the Court," AAUP, October 13, 2022, https://www.aaup.org/news/floridas-stop-woke-act-must-be-rejected-court#.ZCB_GnbMLEY.

29. David Robinson, "Executive Director's Corner / Fear and Loathing in Florida," CAUT, March 2023, https://www.caut.ca/bulletin/2023/03/executive-directors-corner-fear-and-loathing-florida.

Chapter 2. The Politics of Knowledge Production

1. Lyss Welding, "College Enrollment Statistics in the US," *Best Colleges*, February 7, 2024. https://www.bestcolleges.com/research/college-enrollment-statistics/.

2. American Association of University Professors, "Polarizing Times Demand Robust Academic Freedom," *AAUP Updates*, November 15, 2023, https://www.aaup.org/news/polarizing-times-demand-robust-academic-freedom.

3. Quoted in Nathan M. Greenfield, "Where Universities Face Emerging Threats and Crises," *University World News*, September 15, 2023, https://www.universityworldnews.com/post.php.

4. Quoted in Karin Fischer, "The Power and Vulnerability of Colleges Amid Rising Authoritarianism," *Chronicle of Higher Education*, February 8, 2023, https://www.chronicle.com/newsletter/latitudes/2023-02-08.

5. Gigi Lee and Siyan Cheung, "Hong Kong University Fires Tiananmen Historian After Visa Denial," *Radio Free Asia*, October 30, 2023, https://www.rfa.org/english/news/china/hongkong-professor-fired-10302023172045.html.

6. This hearing resulted in the quick resignation of Penn's president and, a few weeks later, the resignation of Harvard's president. The hearing should be understood as part of a wider well-organized attack on higher education, led to a large degree by far-right activist Christopher Rufo, who worked for years on the weaponization of critical race theory to force curriculum reform and the whitewashing of Black histories of slavery and exploitation in Florida, Texas, and other Republican-led states.

7. For instance, groups such as the Patriot Front and the Proud Boys, who have been backed by Trump and other political figures on the far right, have all embraced racism, sexism, ignorance, cruelty, and in some cases violence. It would be extremely hard, if not impossible, to change their attitudes and their entitled White belief that they should control how society functions and how its members—particularly women, people of color, and those identifying as part of the LGBTQ+ and trans communities—should behave and think.

8. The Manhattan Project was the code name for a research and intelligence enterprise that developed the first nuclear weapons in World War II, led by the United States and backed by Canada and Britain. The project was located at the Los Alamos National Laboratory, New Mexico, built on lands formerly presided over by the San Ildefenso Pueblo and staffed by scientists from the University of California, Berkeley (Platt 2023:30, 64–70). The project developed a range of nuclear weaponry and resulted in the atomic bombing of Hiroshima and Nagasaki in 1945, instantly killing tens of thousands of people, mostly civilians, and a further 226,000 people in the first four months after the bombs were dropped on Japan.

9. While living in Princeton, Einstein became openly agitated about racial oppression in the United States and was a public supporter of Paul Robeson, an African American whose illustrious career as a legal scholar, footballer, and musician was brought to a halt when he was blacklisted as a traitor and "subversive" (Sayen 1985; Jerome 2004).

10. Quoted in Hank Reichman, "Einstein on Academic Freedom and Political Inquisitions," *Academe Blog*, June 11, 2017, https://academeblog.org/2017/06/11/einstein-on-academic-freedom-and-political-inquisitions/.

11. For many less-famous scholars fleeing Nazi Germany, it was not easy to find academic jobs in the United States. Some universities and colleges had policies that allowed them to hire only one Jewish scholar, and the obstacles to employment were great. Writes the historian Laurel Leff, "To be hired by an American university, a refugee scholar had to be world-class and well connected, not too old and not too young, not too right and not too left, and, most important, not too Jewish" (see Leff 2019).

12. Richard Amesbury and Catherine O'Donnell, "Dear Administrators: Enough with the Free Speech Rhetoric!," *Chronicle of Higher Education*,

November 16, 2023, https://www.chronicle.com/article/dear-administrators-enough-with-the-free-speech-rhetoric?.

13. See Stacy Hawkins "Sometimes Diversity Trumps Academic Freedom," *Chronicle of Higher Education*, February 28, 2023, https://www.chronicle.com/article/sometimes-diversity-trumps-academic-freedom.

14. Arjun Guneratne, "Letter to the Editor: How 'Care' Compromises a Macalester Education," *Mac Weekly*, February 16, 2023, https://themacweekly.com/81858/opinion/how-care-compromises-a-macalester-education/.

15. Amna Khalid and Jeffrey Snyder, "The Point of Education Is Not to Reduce Harm," *Chronicle of Higher Education*, February 23, 2023, https://www.chronicle.com/article/the-point-of-education-is-not-to-reduce-harm.

16. David Lat, "Yale Law Is No Longer #1—for Free-Speech Debacles," *Original Jurisdiction*. March 11, 2023, https://davidlat.substack.com/p/yale-law-is-no-longer-1for-free-speech.

17. David Lat, "7 Updates On Judge Kyle Duncan and Stanford Law," *Original Jurisdiction*, March 14, 2023, https://davidlat.substack.com/p/7-updates-on-judge-kyle-duncan-and-stanford-law.

18. Rabia Ali, "'Scholasticide': How Israel Is Systematically Destroying Palestinian Education in Gaza," *Anadoluu Agency*, February 14, 2024, https://www.aa.com.tr/en/education/-scholasticide-how-israel-is-systematically-destroying-palestinian-education-in-gaza/3135127.

Chapter 3. Classrooms as Global Battlegrounds

1. Arundhati Roy, "Approaching Gridlock: Arundhati Roy on Free Speech and Failing Democracy," *Literary Hub*, March 24, 2023, https://lithub.com/approaching-gridlock-arundhati-roy-on-free-speech-and-failing-democracy/.

2. Aurélia Dondo, Ross Holder, Nduko o'Matigere, Alicia Quiñones, and Mina Thabet, *War, Censorship and Persecution: PEN International Case List 2023/2024*, PEN International, accessed August 29, 2024, https://www.pen-international.org/research/war-censorship-persecution-case-list-2023.

3. By the mid-twentieth century, after two devasting world wars, defending academic freedom from possible future attacks by oppressive governmental interference took on great urgency. Strategies were designed that linked academic freedom to the idea of global democracy to sustain scholarly independence despite the persecution of scholars in any one country. In the wake of World War II, academic freedom was granted recognition and protection in international law (United Nations Universal Declaration of Human Rights [1948, Articles 19 and 26] and International Covenant on Economic, Social, and Cultural Rights [1966, Articles 13 and 15]).

4. For a more critical assessment of these organizations, see Adebayo 2022.

5. For instance, CAFA loudly condemned Bill 32, which was passed in June 2022 by the far-right government of Quebec. While the bill ostensibly protects academic freedom, it allows a politically appointed outsider—the minister for higher education—to manage all internal affairs and totally undermines the autonomy of universities.

6. U.S. Mission to International Organizations in Geneva, "Joint Statement on Behalf of a Group of 70 Countries on Academic Freedom," 52nd Session of the Human Rights Council, March 29, 2023, https://geneva.usmission.gov/2023/03/29/joint-statement-academic-freedom-hrc52/.

7. Scholars at Risk Network, "UN Human Rights Council: 72 Countries Urge Greater Cooperation to Protect Academic Freedom," March 29, 2023, https://www.scholarsatrisk.org/2023/03/un-human-rights-council-72-countries-urge-greater-cooperation-to-protect-academic-freedom/.

8. Readers who would like to listen to voices instead of reading text can follow the links to the podcasts from this page: Scholars at Risk Network, *Free to Think*, podcast, https://www.scholarsatrisk.org/resources/podcast/.

9. Scholars at Risk Network, "2022 Annual Report," accessed August 29, 2024, https://www.scholarsatrisk.org/annual-report-2022/.

10. Scholars at Risk Network, "2022 Annual Report."

11. Rosa Schwartzburg, "These Hungarian Students Are Fighting for Their Country's Democracy," *The Nation*, January 16, 2019, https://www.thenation.com/article/archive/these-hungarian-students-are-fighting-for-their-countrys-democracy/.

12. Scholars at Risk Network, "'Weaponization' of Higher Education," *Free to Think*, podcast, episode 16, December 2021.

13. Scholars at Risk Network, "A Virtual Target Painted on My Back . . . ," *Free to Think*, podcast, episode 22, April 2022.

14. According to Vatansever, at the time of writing her book, 542 peace academics had been indicted, and another 64 had been sentenced to imprisonment ranging from 9 to 30 months (Vatansever 2020:1).

15. Quoted in Joseph Contreras, "'I'm Not Wanted': Florida Universities Hit by Brain Drain as Academics Flee," *The Guardian*, July 30, 2023, https://www.theguardian.com/us-news/2023/jul/30/florida-universities-colleges-faculty-leaving-desantis.

16. Quoted in Jocelyn Gecker, "A College in Upheaval: War on 'Woke' Sparks Fear in Florida," AP Press, March 29, 2023, https://apnews.com/article/ron-desantis-new-college-florida-woke-15d61ab52724dc447ba6d03238f7719e.

17. Personal conversation with Liz Leininger, November 3, 2023. Drexel University.

18. Quoted in Popescu and Seymour-Jones 2007:199–205.

19. Melissa Faye Green, "'They Can't Kill Us All': These Scholars Lost Their Countries and Found Each Other," *Mother Jones*, November 23, 2022, https://www.motherjones.com/politics/2022/11/they-cant-kill-us-all-these-scholars-lost-their-countries-and-found-each-other/.

Chapter 4. Higher Education and Democratic Dreams

1. Against these efforts toward democratization, the growth of higher education is deeply entangled with settler colonialism, land grabs, and dispossession of Indigenous peoples. It should not be forgotten that land-grant universities were founded on racism and inequality, and enduring legacies of these histories continue to impact campuses to this day (Mettler 2014).

2. On the East Coast, public lands were no longer available, so colleges were awarded cash from sales of lands in the West in what were called certificates of scrip. In thinking through colonial extractivism and its impacts on Indigenous peoples, colleges in Western states should acknowledge that they benefited from the land they now stand on, while colleges in Eastern states should acknowledge that they financially benefited from the dispossession of lands hundreds of miles away.

3. The Carlisle Indian School became a template for the Indigenous residential school system that was established across the United States and in other British settler-colonial states such as Canada, Australia, and New Zealand. In the United States, the logic behind forcibly removing Indigenous children from their families continues up to the present day, legally justified under the Indian Child Welfare Act (1978). For decades, this legislation has enabled the removal of Indian children from their parents to be placed in non-Indian families or institutional facilities where they have often been abused and exploited. The act was shamefully upheld by the far-right super majority Supreme Court in *Haaland v Brackeen* in 2023 (Blackhawk 2023).

4. Note that a few years later in 1954, when Bundy was dean of Harvard's Faculty of Arts and Sciences, he succumbed to the pressures of McCarthyism and didn't reappoint Professor Sigmund Diamond, who had refused to give names to the Federal Bureau of Investigation (Schrecker 1980:313).

5. As Frantz Fanon argued in *The Wretched of the Earth* (1961), efforts to decolonize the university, or more accurately to "Africanize" the university after independence, were not always able to throw off colonial legacies that continued to be imposed through coopted African elites.

6. At a well-documented conference in 1957, academic leaders and administrators spelled out the need for academic freedom. The concept was further expanded upon in Academic Freedom Committees of the University

of Cape Town and the University of the Witwatersrand, *The Open Universities in South Africa and Academic Freedom 1957–1974* (Cape Town: Juta, 1974).

7. In the United States, racial segregation under Jim Crow was formally made illegal with the passing of the Civil Rights Act of 1964 (expanded in 1968) and the Voting Rights Act of 1965. It was many years, however, before desegregation was underway, and often it was not achieved in practice. The legacies of slavery and racial discrimination have continued to the current moment through institutional inequities and social biases, with today's MAGA movement in the Republican party explicitly and proudly embracing anti-Black racism.

8. "List of 15 Demands, Part 1," San Francisco State College Strike Collection, accessed August 29, 2024, https://diva.sfsu.edu/collections/strike/bundles/187915.

9. Historian Angela Woollacott argues that these demonstrations were very important for opening up local debate in Australia about discriminatory gerrymandering and ushering in more democratic electoral reform (Woollacott 2021).

10. As early as 1961, Dwight Eisenhower, in the final days of his presidency, warned the public in a farewell speech on television of the "rise of the military-industrial complex"; he also warned that "free" universities had become dominated by "the power of money" and government contracts. Apparently, "Eisenhower had originally named this mortal threat to American democracy as the 'miliary-industrial-academic-complex' though he deleted that phrase from the final draft of his speech" (Zwerling 2011:3–4).

11. Ellen Schrecker, "The 50-Year War on Higher Education," *Chronicle of Higher Education*, October 13, 2022, https://www.chronicle.com/article/the-50-year-war-on-higher-education.

12. Racial tension in the United States was displayed on the international stage when, in October 1968, two US Black athletes raised their fists in a "Black Power" salute at the Mexico City Olympic medal ceremony. Tommie Smith (gold medalist) and John Carlos (bronze medalist) were joined by Australian Peter Norman (silver medalist) in wearing a badge promoting human rights. All three athletes received harsh criticism from their respective conservative governments.

13. This suggests that in addition to the common critiques of neoliberalism that focus on privatization, deregulation, financialization, individualism, and the dominance of free-market logic, it is important to recognize a deeply rooted ideology within capitalism that rejects liberal democratic principles of inclusiveness and equality and at its core is bound up with racial hierarchy and patriarchy (see Duggan 2003; Giroux 2004; Ayers and Saad-Filho 2015; Shaxson 2019).

14. Schrecker, "50-Year War on Higher Education."

15. David D. Kirkpatrick, "The 2004 Campaign: The Conservatives; Club of the Most Powerful Gathers in Strictest Privacy," *New York Times*, August 28, 2004, https://www.nytimes.com/2004/08/28/us/2004-campaign-conservatives-club-most-powerful-gathers-strictest-privacy.html.

16. Quoted in James Rushing Daniel, "The-Ever-More-Corporate University," *Chronicle of Higher Education*, November 6, 2023, https://www.chronicle.com/article/the-ever-more-corporate-university.

17. Rewarding certain kinds of "performance," such as publication in highly ranked journals, also devalues teaching, mentoring, and professionalization, which are harder to quantify numerically even though they are vital elements in training graduate students and fulfilling the mission of higher education.

18. As universities hustle to raise their rankings, assessment criteria have come under heated debate. There is clear consensus that ranking organizations use a variety of methodologies that may favor certain factors and distort overall outcomes. This problem is exacerbated when it comes to ranking universities around the world, an effort that assumes that all higher education systems are somehow commensurable and equivalent. Sally Merry pointedly notes that forms of global measurement created in the global north "generally reinforce the power differentials between rich and poor countries" and that the global rankings of universities must be considered in this light (commentary by Merry in Shore and Wright 2015:436–437).

19. For instance, some universities and colleges in Florida, Texas, Virginia, and other Republican-led states now require additional materials for tenure or have imposed post-tenure reviews without faculty consultation.

20. Schrecker, "50-Year War on Higher Education."

Chapter 5. Weaponizing Universities in the Twenty-First Century

1. Paul Krugman, "Climate Is Now a Culture War Issue," *New York Times*, August 7, 2023, https://www.nytimes.com/2023/08/07/opinion/climate-is-now-a-culture-war-issue.html.

2. Suzanne Goldenberg. "Exxon Knew of Climate Change in 1981, Email Says—but It Funded Deniers for 27 More Years," *The Guardian*, July 8, 2015, https://www.theguardian.com/environment/2015/jul/08/exxon-climate-change-1981-climate-denier-funding.

3. John Vidal, "Climate Sceptic Willie Soon Received $1M from Oil Companies, Papers Show," *The Guardian*, June 28, 2011, https://www.theguardian.com/environment/2011/jun/28/climate-change-sceptic-willie-soon.

4. George Monbiot, "The Hard Right and Climate Catastrophe Are Intimately Linked. This Is How," *The Guardian*, June 15, 2023, https://www

.theguardian.com/commentisfree/2023/jun/15/hard-right-climate-catastrophe-extreme-weather-refugees.

5. Austin Sarat and Dennis Aftergut, "Is America on the Brink of Tyranny? Trump's Plan if Elected in 2024 Should Frighten Us All," *USA Today*, July 20, 2023, https://www.usatoday.com/story/opinion/2023/07/20/trump-campaign-presidential-power-grab-2024-election/70430661007/.

6. "Project 2025 Presidential Transition Project," accessed August 29, 2024, https://www.project2025.org/.

7. Lisa Friedman, "A Republican 2024 Climate Strategy: More Drilling, Less Clean Energy," *New York Times*, August 4, 2023, https://www.nytimes.com/2023/08/04/climate/republicans-climate-project2025.html.

8. EarthDay.org, "Our History," accessed August 29, 2024, https://www.earthday.org/history/.

9. United States Environmental Protection Agency, "National Environmental Education Act," accessed August 31, 2024, https://www.epa.gov/education/national-environmental-education-act.

10. Quoted in Matt Shipman, "Climate Impacts Are Increasing; Textbooks Aren't Keeping Pace," press release, NC State University, December 21, 2022, https://news.ncsu.edu/2022/12/climate-change-and-textbooks/.

11. Stephanie M. Lee, "Big Oil Helped Shape Stanford's Latest Climate-Research Focus," *Chronicle of Higher Education*, May 4, 2023, https://www.chronicle.com/article/big-oil-helped-shape-stanfords-latest-climate-research-focus.

12. Institute for Humane Studies, "Promoting Intellectual Discovery and Human Flourishing," accessed August 31, 2024, https://www.theihs.org/about-ihs/.

13. In the context of deepening financial insecurity and declining student enrollments at many universities and colleges, donor-controlled academic programs are increasingly common in the United States and to a lesser degree in Britain, Canada, and Australia (Wilson and Kamola 2021).

14. At the time the new center was being set up, faculty and students voiced concerns about Koch funding and potential political interference. A letter from Pitt faculty and students to the administration stated that "on corporate academic lobbying, the University appears to be completely asleep at the wheel. While philanthropic donations from questionable donors has historically been a norm, the use of that financial power to influence ideology at universities is a recent phenomenon." The letter went on, "Academic freedom and academic integrity can and must work together. But allowing corporate influence to stomp over our contract vetting process under the guise of protecting individual career ambitions protects neither." Quoted in Susan Jones, "Koch Foundation Gift Sparks Heated Faculty Assembly

Meeting," *University Times* (University of Pittsburgh), December 5, 2019, https://www.utimes.pitt.edu/news/koch-foundation-gift.

15. Peter Stone, "US 'University' Spreads Climate Lies and Receives Millions from Rightwing Donors," *The Guardian*, September 6, 2023, https://www.theguardian.com/us-news/2023/sep/06/prageru-climate-change-denier-republican-donors.

16. The evidence is now clear that fossil fuel funding of university centers produces scholarship that favors natural gas over renewable energy, while academic centers that do not receive such funding are less favorable toward natural gas and promote wind and solar energy production (Almond et al. 2022).

17. For a full list of more than 140 US universities that have divested from fossil fuels, see Evan Castillo, "These Colleges Have Divested from Fossil Fuels," *Best Colleges*, September 19, 2023, https://www.bestcolleges.com/news/list-of-colleges-divested-from-fossil-fuels/. In the United Kingdom, 100 universities have also divested in a surge of student activism in support of the environment. Kevri, "100 UK Universities Divest from Fossil Fuels," December 6, 2022, https://insight.kevri.co/100-uk-universities-fossil-free/.

18. Fossil Free Research website, accessed August 31, 2024, https://www.fossilfreeresearch.org/.

19. Quoted in Kristoffer Tigue, "Experts Warn of 'Denialism Comeback' Ahead of November's Global Climate Talks," *Inside Climate News*, September 8, 2023, https://insideclimatenews.org/news/08092023/experts-warn-of-denialism-comeback-ahead-of-cop28-global-climate-talks/.

20. Stephanie Saul, "Texas A&M Agrees to $1 Million Settlement with Journalism Professor," *New York Times*, August 8, 2023, https://www.nytimes.com/2023/08/03/us/texas-am-mcelroy-settlement.html.

21. William H. Frey, "The US Will Become 'Minority White' in 2045, Census Projects," Brookings, March 14, 2018, https://www.brookings.edu/articles/the-us-will-become-minority-white-in-2045-census-projects/.

22. Heritage Foundation, "Critical Race Theory Has Infiltrated the Federal Government: Christopher Rufo on Fox News," video, September 2, 2020, https://www.youtube.com/watch?v=rBXRdWflV7M.

23. Legal Defense Fund, "LDF Files Amended Complaint in Lawsuit Challenging Trump Administration Executive Order; American Association for Access, Equity and Diversity Joins as Plaintiff," January 12, 2021, https://www.naacpldf.org/press-release/ldf-files-amended-complaint-in-lawsuit-challenging-trump-administration-executive-order-american-association-for-access-equity-and-diversity-joins-as-plaintiff/.

24. American Civil Liberties Union, "Mapping Attacks on LGBTQ Rights in U.S. State Legislatures in 2024," accessed August 31, 2024, https://www.aclu.org/legislative-attacks-on-lgbtq-rights?impact=school.

25. As some progressive scholars have argued, DEI programs that are based on identity politics and a student's perceived "harm" can at times work against the principle of academic freedom. Amna Khalid and Jeffrey Aaron Snyderm, "Yes, DEI Can Erode Academic Freedom. Let's Not Pretend Otherwise," *Chronicle of Higher Education*, February 6, 2023, https://www.chronicle.com/article/yes-dei-can-erode-academic-freedom-lets-not-pretend-otherwise?sra=true&cid=gen_sign_in.

26. Christopher F. Rufo, "D.E.I. Programs Are Getting in the Way of Liberal Education," *New York Times*, July 27, 2023, https://www.nytimes.com/2023/07/27/opinion/christopher-rufo-diversity-desantis-florida-university.html.

27. Lynn Pasquerella, "University D.E.I. Programs: Do They Help or Harm Education?," *New York Times*, August 19, 2023, https://www.nytimes.com/2023/08/19/opinion/letters/diversity-equity-inclusion-college.html.

28. Grady Martin, "University D.E.I. Programs: Do They Help or Harm Education?," *New York Times*, August 19, 2023, https://www.nytimes.com/2023/08/19/opinion/letters/diversity-equity-inclusion-college.html.

29. Quoted in Maggie Hicks, "Texas Officials Scramble, Advocates Fret, Weeks Before DEI Funding Expires," *Chronicle of Higher Education*, July 20, 2023, https://www.chronicle.com/article/texas-officials-scramble-advocates-fret-weeks-before-dei-funding-expires.

30. Martin, "University D.E.I. Programs."

31. Quoted in Olivia B. Waxman, "Read Justice Sotomayor and Jackson's Dissents in the Affirmative Action Case," *New York Times*, June 29, 2023, https://time.com/6291230/affirmative-action-dissent-jackson-sotomayor/.

32. Richard J. Evans, "The Holocaust in Poland and the Erasures of the Past," *New York Times*, October 12, 2023, https://www.nytimes.com/2023/07/12/books/review/jews-in-the-garden-judy-rakowsky.html.

33. Civicus, "In Numbers," *Monitor: Tracking Civic Space*, accessed August 31, 2024, https://monitor.civicus.org/globalfindings_2023/innumbers/.

34. Apart from the greater police presence on campus, many scholars and researchers have also been funded through federal defense programs for work that involves security strategies, surveillance technology, drones, robotics, and chemical and biological munitions that help support and expand the United States' enormous military-industrial complex. What the militarization of research agendas signals is a much greater tolerance among faculty and students for a culture of violence and warfare, along with a receptivity to propaganda about potential enemies (see Giroux 2008; Saltman and Gabbard 2011).

35. Lauren Kaori Gurley, "California Police Used Military Surveillance Tech at Grad Student Strike." *Vice*, May 15, 2020. https://www.vice.com/en/article/california-police-used-military-surveillance-tech-at-grad-student-strike/.

36. Amelia Nierenberg, "Yale Students Got a Terrifying Message. From the Campus Police," *New York Times*, August 25, 2023, https://www.nytimes.com/2023/08/25/nyregion/yale-police-fliers.html.

37. Stephanie Saul, "Yale's New President Pushed Policing as Leader of Stony Brook," *New York Times*, July 5, 2024, https://www.nytimes.com/2024/07/02/us/politics/yale-maurie-mcinnis-police-protest-stony-brook.html.

Chapter 6. Fighting Back

1. American Association of University Professors, "Polarizing Times Demand Robust Academic Freedom," *AAUP Updates*, November 15, 2023, https://www.aaup.org/news/polarizing-times-demand-robust-academic-freedom.

2. Steven Inskeep, "What Nikki Haley Didn't Say," *New York Times*, December 23, 2023, https://www.nytimes.com/2023/12/29/opinion/nikki-haley-civil-war.html.

3. Mark Bray, "How Capitalism Stokes the Far Right and Climate Catastrophe," *Truthout*, October 30, 2018, https://truthout.org/articles/how-capitalism-stokes-the-far-right-and-climate-catastrophe/.

References

Abel, Richard L. 2024. *How Autocrats Attack Expertise: Resistance to Trump and Trumpism*. New York: Routledge.

Aby, Stephen A. 2009. "Discretion over Valor: The AAUP during the McCarthy Years." *American Educational History Journal* 36 (1–2): 121–132.

Adams, David Wallace. 2020. *Education for Extinction: American Indians and the Boarding School Experience, 1875–1928*, 2nd ed. Kansas: University Press of Kansas.

Adebayo, Kudus Oluwatoyin. 2022. "The State of Academic (Un)Freedom and Scholar Rescue Programs: A Contemporary and Critical Overview." *Third World Quarterly* 43 (8): 1817–1836.

Adébísí, Folúké. 2023. *Decolonisation and Legal Knowledge: Reflections on Power and Possibility*. Bristol, UK: Bristol University Press.

Alatas, Syed Hussein. 2000. "Intellectual Imperialism: Definition, Traits, Problems." *Southeast Asian Journal of Social Science* 28 (1): 23–45.

Al-Bulushi, Yousuf. 2023. "Dar es Salaam on the Frontline: Red and Black Internationalisms." *Third World Thematics: A TWQ Journal* 8 (1–3): 21–37.

Alexander, Michelle. 2012. *The New Jim Crow: Mass Incarceration in the Age of Colorblindness*. New York: The New Press.

Alexander, Neville. 1992. "Address Given at the National Consultation on Education for Affirmation, 27 August 1986." In *Education and the Struggle for National Liberation in South Africa*, 25–48. Trenton, NJ: Africa World Press.

Alexander, Taifha, LaToya Baldwin Clark, Kyle Reinhard, and Noah Zatz. 2023. *CRT Forward: Tracking the Attack on Critical Race Theory*. CRT Forward's Tracking Project, an initiative of the Critical Race Studies Program, University of California, Los Angeles. https://crtforward.law.ucla.edu/wp-content/uploads/2023/04/UCLA-Law_CRT-Report_Final.pdf.

Allen, Danielle. 2016. "What Is Education For?" Forum. *Boston Review*, April 26. https://www.bostonreview.net/forum/danielle-allen-what-is-education-for/.

Allott, Nicholas, Chris Knight, and Neil Smith (eds.). 2019. *The Responsibility of Intellectuals: Reflections by Noam Chomsky and Others after 50 years*. London: UCL Press.

Almond, Douglas, Xinming Du, and Anna Papp. 2022. "Favourability towards Natural Gas Relates to Funding Source of University Energy Centres." *Nature Climate Change* 12 (12): 1–7.

Altbach, Philip G. and Geraldo Blanco. 2024. "Editorial: Authoritarian Threats to Higher Education Require a Response." *International Higher Education*, no. 117 (Winter): 3.

Altbach, Philip G., Liz Reisberg, and Laura E. Rumbley. 2019. *Trends in Global Higher Education: Tracking a Revolution*. Rotterdam: Sense Publishers and UNESCO Publishing.

Altschuler, Glenn, and Stuart Blumin. 2009. *The GI Bill: The New Deal for Veterans* (Pivotal Moments in American History). Oxford: Oxford University Press.

American Association of University Professors. 1915. "General Report of the Committee on Academic Freedom and Tenure." *Bulletin of the AAUP* 1 (1): 15–43.

Anderson, Carol. 2017. "The Policies of White Resentment." *New York Times*, August 5.

Anderson, Melinda D. 2015. "The Rise of Law Enforcement on College Campus." *Atlantic*, September 28. https://www.theatlantic.com/education/archive/2015/09/college-campus-policing/407659/.

Apple, Michael W. (ed.). 2010. *Global Crises, Social Justice, and Education*. New York: Routledge.

Applebaum, Anne. 2020. *Twilight of Democracy: The Seductive Lure of Authoritarianism*. New York: Doubleday.

Axyonova, Vera, Florian Kohstall, and Carola Richter (eds.). 2022. *Academics in Exile: Networks, Knowledge Exchange, and New Forms of Internationalization*. Bielefeld, Germany: transcript Verlag.

Ayers, Alison J., and Alfredo Saad-Filho. 2015. "Democracy against Neoliberalism: Paradoxes, Limitations, Transcendence." *Critical Sociology* 41 (4–5): 597–618.

Baker, John. 2014. "Academic Freedom as a Constraint on Freedom of Religion." In *Academic Freedom in Conflict: The Struggle over Free Speech Rights in the University*, edited by James L. Turk, 127–144. Toronto: James Lorimer & Co.

Barbour, John D. 2007. "Edward Said and the Space of Exile." *Literature and Theology* 21 (3): 293–301.

Barrow, Clyde W. 1990. *Universities and the Capitalist State: Corporate Liberalism and the Reconstruction of American Higher Education, 1894–1928*. Madison: University of Wisconsin Press.

Beetham, David. 2015. "Authoritarianism and Democracy: Beyond Regime Types." *Comparative Democratization* 13 (2): 2, 12–13.

Bello, Walden. 2019. *Counterrevolution: The Global Rise of the Far Right*. Halifax, Nova Scotia, Canada: Fernwood Publishing.

Ben-Ghiat, Ruth. 2020. *Strongmen: Mussolini to the Present*. New York: W.W. Norton & Company.

Ben-Porath, Sigal R. 2023. *Cancel Wars: How Universities Can Foster Free Speech, Promote Inclusive, and Renew Democracy*. Chicago: University of Chicago Press.

Berberoglu, Berch (ed.). 2020. *The Global Rise of Authoritarianism in the 21st Century: Crisis of Neoliberal Globalization and the Nationalist Response*. New York: Routledge.

Berrett, Dan. 2015. "The Day the Purpose of College Changed." *Chronicle of Higher Education*, January 26.

Bérubé, Michael, and Jennifer Ruth. 2022. *It's Not Free Speech: Race, Democracy, and the Future of Academic Freedom*. Baltimore: Johns Hopkins University Press.

Bhambra, Gurminder K., Dalia Gebrial, and Kerem Nişancioğlu (eds.). 2018. *Decolonising the University*. London: Pluto Press.

Bhambra, Gurminder K., Kerem Nişancioğlu, and Dalia Gebrial. 2020. "Decolonising the University in 2020." *Identities: Global Studies in Culture and Power* 27 (4): 509–516.

Binder, Amy J., and Jeffrey L. Kidder. 2022. *The Channels of Student Activism: How the Left and Right Are Winning (and Losing) in Campus Politics Today*. Chicago: University of Chicago Press.

Black, Derek W. 2016. *Ending Zero Tolerance: The Crisis of Absolute School Discipline*. New York: New York University Press.

Blackhawk, Maggie. 2023. "The Constitution of American Colonialism." *Harvard Law Review* 137 (1): 2–152.

Blight, David W., with Yale and Slavery Research Project. 2024. *Yale and Slavery*. New Haven, CT: Yale University Press.

Borstelmann, Thomas. 2012. *The 1970s: A New Global History from Civil Rights to Economic Inequality*. Princeton, NJ: Princeton University Press.

Bosio, Emiliano, and Gustavo Gregorutti (eds.). 2023. *The Emergence of the Ethically-Engaged University*. New York: Palgrave Macmillan.

Brandenburg, Uwe, Hans de Wit, Elspeth Jones, and Betty Leask. 2019. "Internationalisation in Higher Education for Society." *University World News*, April 20. https://www.universityworldnews.com/post.php?story=20190414195843914.

Brint, Steven. 2023. "The Political Machine Behind the War on Academic Freedom: How Conservative Activists Use State Legislatures to Control What Colleges Can Teach." *Chronicle of Higher Education*, August 28.

Brown, Wendy. 2019. *In the Ruins of Neoliberalism: The Rise of Antidemocratic Politics in the West*. New York: Columbia University Press.

Brunner, Claudia. 2021. "Conceptualizing epistemic violence: an interdisciplinary assemblage for IR." *International Politics Reviews* 9: 193–212.

Buckley, William F. 1951. *God and Man at Yale: The Superstitions of Academic Freedom*. Chicago: Regnery.

Bullard, Robert D. 2000. *Dumping in Dixie: Race, Class, and Environmental Quality*, 3rd ed. New York: Routledge.

Bunch, Bill. 2022. *After the Ivory Tower Falls: How College Broke the American Dream and Blew Up Our Politics—and How to Fix It*. New York: William Morrow.

Bundy, McGeorge. 1951. "The Attack on Yale." *Atlantic*. https://www.theatlantic.com/magazine/archive/1951/11/the-attack-on-yale/306724/.

Burden-Stelly, Charisse. 2023. *Black Scare / Red Scare: Theorizing Capitalist Racism in the United States*. Chicago: University of Chicago Press.

Burlyuk, Olga, and Ladan Rahbari. 2023. *Migrant Academics' Narratives of Precarity and Resilience in Europe*. Cambridge: Open Book Publishers.

Butler, Judith. 2004. *Precarious Life: The Powers of Mourning and Violence*. London: Verso.

Butler, Judith. 2017. "Academic Freedom and the Critical Task of the University." *Globalizations* 14 (6): 857–861.

Cantwell, Brendan, and Ilkka Kauppinen (eds.). 2014. *Academic Capitalism in the Age of Globalization*. Baltimore: Johns Hopkins University Press.

Carvalho, Edward J. 2010. "Preserving the Democratic Experiment: Moral Courage and the Role of Intellectual Activism; Interview with Cornel West." In *Academic Freedom in the Post-9/11 Era*, edited by Edward J. Carvalho and David B. Downing, 267–283. New York: Palgrave Macmillan.

Carvalho, Edward J., and David B. Downing (eds.). 2010. *Academic Freedom in the Post-9/11 Era*. New York: Palgrave Macmillan.

Chappell, Bill. 2022. "Penn State Cancels Proud Boys Founder's Speech, Citing the Threat of Violence." NPR, October 25. https://www.npr.org/2022/10/25/1131300978/penn-state-cancels-proud-boys-speech-protests.

Chase, Robert, and Yalile Suriel. 2020. "Black Lives Matter on Campus—Universities Must Rethink Reliance on Campus Policing and Prison Labor." *Black Perspectives*, June 15. https://www.aaihs.org/black-lives-matter-on-campus-universities-must-rethink-reliance-on-campus-policing-and-prison-labor/.

Chatterjee, Piya, and Maira, Sunaina (eds.). 2014. *The Imperial University: Academic Repression and Scholarly Dissent*. Minneapolis: University of Minnesota Press.

Chemerinsky, Erwin, and Howard Gillman. 2018. *Free Speech on Campus*. New Haven, CT: Yale University Press.

Cherniavsky, Eva. 2021. "Against the Common Sense: Academic Freedom as a Collective Right." *Journal of Academic Freedom* 12.

Chigudu, Simukai. 2020. "Rhodes Must Fall in Oxford: A Critical Testimony." *Critical African Studies* 12 (3): 302–312.

Chomsky, Noam. 1967. "The Responsibility of Intellectuals." *New York Review of Books*, February 23, 1967. https://chomsky.info/19670223/.

Chomsky, Noam. 1999. *Profit over People: Neoliberalism and Global Order*. New York: Seven Stories Press.

Chomsky, Noam, Ira Katznelson, R. C. Lewontin, et al. 1997. *The Cold War and the University: Toward an Intellectual History of the Postwar Years*. New York: New Press.

Choudry, Aziz, and Salim Vally (eds.). 2020. *The University and Social Justice: Struggles Across the Globe*. London: Pluto Press.

Chua, Lynette J., and Jack Jin Gary Lee. 2021. "Governing Through Contagion." In *Covid-19 in Asia: Law and Policy Contexts*, edited by Victor V. Ramraj, 115–132. New York: Oxford University Press.

Churchill, Ward. 2004. *Kill the Indian, Save the Man: The Genocidal Impact of American Indian Residential Schools*. San Franscico: City Lights.

Cohen, Robert. 2009. *Freedom's Orator: Mario Savio and the Radical Legacy of the 1960s*. Oxford: Oxford University Press.

Cohen, Stan. 1972. *Folk Devils and Moral Panics: The Creation of Mods and Rockers*. London: MacGibbon and Kee.

Cole, Eddie. 2021. "The Racist Roots of Campus Policing." *Washington Post*, June 2.

Collyer, Fran, Raewyn Connell, João Maia, and Robert Morrell. 2019. *Knowledge and Global Power: Making New Sciences in the South*. Clayton, Victoria, Australia: Monash University.

Connell, Raewyn. 2007. *Southern Theory: The Global Dynamics of Knowledge in Social Science*. Sydney: Allen and Unwin.

Connell, Raewyn. 2019. *The Good University: What Universities Actually Do and Why It's Time for Radical Change*. London: Zed Books.

Corbett, Anne, and Claire Gordon. 2018. "Academic Freedom in Europe: The Central European University Affair and the Wider Lessons." *History of Education Quarterly* 58 (3): 467–474.

Corrales, Javier. 2015. "The Authoritarian Resurgence: Autocratic Legalism in Venezuela." *Journal of Democracy* 26 (2): 37–51.

Cote-Meek, Shiela, and Taima Moeke-Pickering. 2020. *Decolonizing and Indigenizing Education in Canada*. Toronto: Canadian Scholars' Press.

Crook, Paul. 2002. "American Eugenics and the Nazis: Recent Historiography." *European Legacy* 7 (3): 363–381.

Daniels, Ronald J. 2021. *What Universities Owe Democracy*. Baltimore: Johns Hopkins University Press.

Darian-Smith, Eve. 2012. "Re-reading W.E.B. Du Bois: The Global Dimensions of the US Civil Rights Struggle." *Journal of Global History* 7 (3): 485–505.

Darian-Smith, Eve. 2021. "Dying for the Economy: Disposable People and Economies of Death in the Global North." *State Crime Journal* 10 (1): 61–79.

Darian-Smith, Eve. 2022. *Global Burning: Rising Antidemocracy and the Climate Crisis*. Redwood City, CA: Stanford University Press.

Darian-Smith, Eve. 2023a. "United States Academic Freedom in Regional and Global Contexts." *Revista Internacional de Derecho y Ciencias Sociales / International Journal of Law and Social Sciences*, no. 33: 129–148.

Darian-Smith, Eve. 2023b. "Entangled Futures: Big Oil, Political Will, and the Global Environmental Movement." *Perspectives on Global Development and Technology* 21 (3): 403–425.

Darian-Smith, Eve. 2023c. "Deadly Global Alliance: Antidemocracy and Anti-environmentalism." *Third World Quarterly* 44 (2): 284–299.

Darian-Smith, Eve. 2024. "Knowledge Production at a Crossroads: Rising Antidemocracy and Diminishing Academic Freedom." *Studies in Higher Education*, 1–15. https://doi.org/10.1080/03075079.2024.2347562.

Darian-Smith, Eve, and Philip C. McCarty. 2017. *The Global Turn: Theories, Research Designs, and Methods for Global Studies*. Berkeley: University of California Press.

De Groot, Gerard J. 1996. "Ronald Reagan and Student Unrest in California, 1966–1970." *Pacific Historical Review* 65 (1): 107–129.

de Wit, Hans, and Elspeth Jones. 2022. "A New View of Internationalization: From a Western, Competitive Paradigm to a Global Cooperative Strategy." *Journal of Higher Education Policy and Leadership Studies* 3 (1): 142–152.

Doğan, Sevgi, and Ervjola Selenica. 2022. "Authoritarianism and Academic Freedom In Neoliberal Turkey." *Globalisation, Societies and Education* 20 (2): 163–177.

Douglass, John Aubrey (ed.). 2021. *Neo-nationalism and Universities: Populists, Autocrats, and the Future of Higher Education*. Baltimore: Johns Hopkins University Press.

Duggan, Lisa. 2003. *The Twilight of Equality? Neoliberalism, Cultural Politics, and the Attack on Democracy*. Boston: Beacon Press.

Dunlap, Jr., Charles J. 2001. "Law and Military Interventions: Preserving Humanitarian Values in 21st Conflicts." Presented at Humanitarian Challenges in Military Interventions Conference (November 29). https://scholarship.law.duke.edu/faculty_scholarship/3500/.

Dunlap, Riley E., and Peter J. Jacques. 2013. "Climate Change Denial Books and Conservative Think Tanks: Exploring the Connection," *American Behavioral Scientist* 57 (6): 699–731.

Eaton, Charlie. 2022. *Bankers in the Ivory Tower: The Troubling Rise of Financiers in U.S. Higher Education.* Chicago: University of Chicago Press.

Ehsanipour, Asal. 2020. "Ethnic Studies: Born in the Bay Area from History's Biggest Student Strike." KQED. https://www.kqed.org/news/11830384/how-the-longest-student-strike-in-u-s-history-created-ethnic-studies, accessed August 29, 2024. Erakat, Noura. 2020. *Justice for Some: Law and the Question of Palestine.* Stanford, CA: Stanford University Press.

Federici, Silvia. 2000. "The Recolonization of African Education." In *A Thousand Flowers: Social Struggles Against Structural Adjustment in African Universities,* edited by Silvia Federici, George Caffentzis, and Ouseina Alidon, 19–23. Trenton, NJ: Africa World Press.

Federici, Silvia. 2019. *Re-enchanting the World: Feminism and the Politics of the Commons.* Oakland, CA: PM Press.

Federici, Silvia, George Caffentzis, and Ouseina Alidon (eds.). 2000. *A Thousand Flowers: Social Struggles Against Structural Adjustment In African Universities.* Trenton, NJ: Africa World Press.

Feldblum, Sammy. 2023. "How Stanford Helped Capitalism Take Over the World." *Chronicle of Higher Education,* July 20.

Ferguson, Roderick. 2017. *We Demand: The University and Student Protests.* Oakland: University of California Press.

Ferrall, Victor E. 2011. *Liberal Arts at the Brink.* Cambridge, MA: Harvard University Press.

Findlay, Len. 2014. "Institutional Autonomy and Academic Freedom in the Managed University." In *Academic Freedom in Conflict: The Struggle over Free Speech Rights in the University,* edited by James L. Turk, 49–61. Toronto: James Lorimer & Co.

Finkin, Matthew W., and Robert C. Post. 2009. *For the Common Good: Principles of American Academic Freedom.* New Haven, CT: Yale University Press.

Fish, Stanley. 2014. *Versions of Academic Freedom: From Professionalism to Revolution.* Chicago: University of Chicago Press.

Fisher, Max. 2023. *The Chaos Machine: The Inside Story of How Social Media Rewired Our Minds and Our World.* New York: Back Bay Books.

Fitzpatrick, Kathleen. 2021. *Generous Thinking: A Radical Approach to Saving The University.* Baltimore: Johns Hopkins University.

Fleming, Peter. 2021. *Dark Academia: How Universities Die.* London: Pluto Press.

Forbes, Jack D. 2001. "Indigenous Americans: Spirituality and Ecos." *Dedalus* 130 (4): 283–300.

Foucault, Michel. 1979. *Discipline and Punish: The Birth of the Prison.* New York: Vintage.

Freedom House. 2021. *Nations in Transit: The Antidemocratic Turn.* https://freedomhouse.org/report/nations-transit/2021/antidemocratic-turn.

Freese, Barbara. 2020. *Industrial-Strength Denial: Eight Stories of Corporations Defending the Indefensible, from the Slave Trade to Climate Change*. Oakland: University of California Press.

Gabbert, Mark A. 2014. "The Right to Think Otherwise." In *Academic Freedom in Conflict: The Struggle over Free Speech Rights in the University*, edited by James L. Turk, 89–109. Toronto: James Lorimer & Co.

Gambetti, Zeynep. 2022. "The Struggle for Academic Freedom in an Age of Post-truth." *South Atlantic Quarterly* 121 (1): 178–187.

Gamper-Rabindran, Shanti. 2022. *America's Energy Gamble: People, Economy and Planet*. Cambridge: Cambridge University Press.

Gandhi, Evyn Lê Espiritu. 2022. *Archipelago of Resettlement: Vietnamese Refugee Settlers and Decolonization Across Guam and Israel-Palestine*. Oakland: University of California Press.

Ghosh, Amitav. 2017. *The Great Derangement: Climate Change and the Unthinkable*. Chicago: Chicago University Press.

Giroux, Henry A. 2004. *The Terror of Neoliberalism: Authoritarianism and the Eclipse of Democracy*. Boulder, CO: Paradigm Publishers.

Giroux, Henry A. 2008. "The Militarization of US Higher Education After 9/11." *Theory, Culture & Society* 25 (5): 56–82.

Giroux, Henry A. 2014. *Neoliberalism's War on Higher Education*. Chicago: Haymarket Books.

Giroux, Henry A. 2016. "Neoliberal Savagery and the Assault on Higher Education as a Democratic Public Sphere." *Café Dissensus*, September 15. https://cafedissensus.com/2016/09/15/neoliberal-savagery-and-the-assault-on-higher-education-as-a-democratic-public-sphere/.

Giroux, Henry A. 2018. *The Public in Peril: Trump and the Menace of American Authoritarianism*. New York: Routledge.

Giroux, Henry A. 2021. *Race, Politics, and Pandemic Pedagogy: Education in a Time of Crisis*. London: Bloomsbury.

Giroux, Henry A., and Emiliano Bosio. 2021. "Critical Pedagogy and Global Citizenship Education." In *Conversations on Global Citizenship Education: Perspectives on Research, Teaching, and Learning in Higher Education*, edited by Emiliano Bosio, 3–12. New York: Routledge.

Glasius, Marlies. 2018. "What Authoritarianism Is . . . and Is Not: A Practice Perspective." *International Affairs* 94 (3): 515–533.

Godrej, Farah. 2014. "Neoliberalism, Militarization, and the Price of Dissent: Policing Protest at the University of California." In *The Imperial University: Academic Repression and Scholarly Dissent*, edited by Piya Chatterjee and Sunaina Maira, 125–143. Minneapolis: University of Minnesota Press.

Goldberg, David Theo. 2023a. *The War on Critical Race Theory*. New York: Polity Press.

Goldberg, Michelle. 2023b. "DeSantis's 'Apocalyptic' Attack on Higher Education." *New York Times*, February 23.
Goldrick-Rab, Sarah. 2017. *Paying the Price: College Costs, Financial Aid, and the Betrayal of the American Dream*. Chicago: University of Chicago Press.
Gomez Gamboa, David, and Ricardo Villalobos Fontalvo. 2023. "Academic Freedom: A View from the Inter-American System of Human Rights." *Netherlands Quarterly of Human Rights* 41 (2).
González, Roberto J. 2014. "Militarizing Education: The Intelligence Community's Spy Camps." In *The Imperial University: Academic Repression and Scholarly Dissent*, edited by Piya Chatterjee and Sunaina Maira, 79–98. Minneapolis: University of Minnesota Press.
Gordon, Daniel. 2023. *What Is Academic Freedom? A Century of Debate, 1915–Present*. New York: Routledge.
Grande, Sally. 2018. "Refusing the University." In *Dissident Knowledge in Higher Education*, edited by Marc Spooner and James McNinch. Regina, 168–192. Saskatchewan, Canada: University of Regina Press.
Grawe, Nathan D. 2018. *Demographics and the Demand for Higher Education*. Baltimore: Johns Hopkins University Press.
Grawe, Nathan D. 2022. *The Agile College: How Institutions Successfully Navigate Demographic Changes*. Baltimore: Johns Hopkins University Press.
Grosfoguel, Ramón. 2013. "The Structure of Knowledge in Westernized Universities: Epistemic Racism/Sexism and the Four Genocides/ Epistemicides of the Long 16th Century." *Human Architecture: Journal of the Sociology of Self-Knowledge* 11 (1): article 8.
Grosfoguel, Ramón, Roberto Hernández, and Ernesto Rosen Valásquez (eds.). 2016. *Decolonizing the Westernized University*. London: Lexington Books.
Gross, Neil, and Solon Simmons. 2006. "American's Views on Political Bias in the Academy and Academic Freedom," Working Paper, American Association of University Professors, May 22.
Gueorguiev, Dimitar D. (ed.). 2023. *New Threats to Academic Freedom in Asia*. New York: Columbia University Press.
Halffman, Willem, and Hans Radder. 2015. "The Academic Manifesto: From an Occupied to a Public University." *Minerva* 53 (2): 165–187.
Hall, Budd L. 2018. "Beyond Epistemicide: Knowledge Democracy and Higher Education." In *Dissident Knowledge in Higher Education*, edited by Marc Spooner and James McNinch, 84–101. Regina, Saskatchewan, Canada: University of Regina Press.
Hall, Budd, and Rajesh Tandon (eds.). 2021. *Socially Responsible Higher Education: International Perspectives on Knowledge Democracy*. Boston: Brill.

Hall, Stuart, Chas Critcher, Tony Jefferson, John Clarke, and Brian Roberts. 1978. *Policing the Crisis: Mugging, the State, and Law and Order*. London: Macmillan.

Hannah-Jones, Nikole. 2021. *The 1619 Project: A New Origin Story*. New York: One World.

Haraway, Donna J. 2008. *When Species Meet*. Minneapolis: University of Minnesota Press.

Haraway, Donna J. 2016. *Staying with the Trouble: Making Kin in the Chthulucene*. Durham, NC: Duke University Press.

Harris, Adam. 2023. "The Decision That Upends the Equal-Protection Clause." *Atlantic*. June 29. https://www.theatlantic.com/ideas/archive/2023/06/scotus-affirmative-action-ruling-implications/674567/.

Harris, Malcolm. 2023. *Palo Alto: A History of California, Capitalism, and the World*. New York: Little, Brown and Company.

Haynes, Dina Francesca. 2019. "Subordinating Women and Demonizing Immigrants on the Altar of Regressive Politics." *Human Rights Quarterly* 41: 777–822.

Herbold, Hilary. 1994–1995. "Never a Level Playing Field: Blacks and the GI Bill." *Journal of Blacks in Higher Education*, no. 6 (Winter): 104–108.

Hickel, Jason. 2018. *The Divide: Global Inequality from Conquest to Free Markets*. New York: W.W. Norton & Company.

Hoffman, Andrew. 2015. *How Culture Shapes the Climate Change Debate*. Stanford, CA: Stanford University Press.

Hoggan, James, with Richard Littlemore. 2009. *Climate Cover-Up: The Crusade to Deny Global Warming*. Vancouver: Greystone Books.

hooks, bell. 1994. *Teaching to Transgress: Education as the Practice of Freedom*. New York: Routledge.

Hutcheson, Philo, Marybeth Gasman, and Kijua Sanders-McMurtry. 2011. "Race and Equality in the Academy: Rethinking Higher Education Actors and the Struggle for Equality in the Post-World War II Period." *Journal of Higher Education* 82 (2): 121–153.

Huzzard, Tony, Mats Benner, and Dan Kärreman (eds.). 2017. *The Corporatization of the Business School: Minerva Meets the Market*. New York: Routledge.

Ivancheva, Mariya, Kathleen Lynch, and Kathryn Keating. 2019. "Precarity, Gender and Care in the Neoliberal Academy." *Gender Work & Organization* 26: 448–462.

Jansen, Jonathan D. (ed.). 2019. *Decolonisation in Universities: The Politics of Knowledge*. Johannesburg: Wits University Press.

Jansen, Jonathan D., and Cyrill A. Walters. 2022. *The Decolonization of Knowledge: Radical Ideas and the Shaping of Institutions in South Africa and Beyond*. Cambridge: Cambridge University Press.

Jerome, Fred. 2004. "Einstein, Race, and the Myth of the Cultural Icon." *History of Science Society* 95: 627–639.

Jerome, Fred, and Rodger Taylor. 2005. *Einstein on Race and Racism*. Newark, NJ: Rutgers University Press.

Johnson, Jake. 2022. "Chilling": GOP Has Introduced 136 "Educational Gag Order" Bills in 37 States Just This Year." *Salon*, August 17. https://www.salon.com/2022/08/17/chilling-has-introduced-136-educational-gag-order-bills-in-37-states-just-this-year_partner/.

Kaczmarska, Katarzyna, and Yeşim Yaprak Yıldız. 2022. "Introduction to the Special Issue on Academic Freedom and Internationalization." *International Journal of Human Rights* 26 (10): 1691–1697, https://www.doi.org/10.1080/13642987.2022.2152573.

Kamola, Isaac A. 2019a. "The LONG '68: African Anticolonialism and the Emergence of a World University System." *Cultural Politics* 15 (3): 303–314.

Kamola, Isaac A. 2019b. *Making the World Global: US Universities and the Production of the Global Imaginary*. Durham, NC: Duke University Press.

Kamola, Isaac A. 2024. "Manufacturing Backlash: Right-Wing Think Tanks and Legislative Attacks on Higher Education, 2021–2023." White Paper, American Association of University Professors, May 2024. https://www.aaup.org/article/manufacturing-backlash.

Kaufam-Osborn, Timothy V. 2023. *The Autocratic Academy: Reenvisioning Rule Within America's Universities*. Durham, NC: Duke University Press.

Kaye, David. 2020. *United Nations Report of the Special Rapporteur on the Promotion and Protection of the Right to Freedom of Opinion and Expression*. https://digitallibrary.un.org/record/3833657?ln=en.

Keim, Wiebke, Ercüment Çelik, and Veronika Wöhrer (eds.). 2014. *Global Knowledge Production in the Social Sciences: Made in Circulation*. New York: Routledge.

Kendi, Ibram X. 2012. *The Black Campus Movement: Black Students and the Racial Reconstitution of Higher Education, 1965–1972*. New York: Palgrave Macmillan.

Kezar, Adrianna, Tom DePaola, and Daniel T. Scott. 2019. *The Gig Academy: Mapping Labor in the Neoliberal University*. Baltimore: Johns Hopkins University Press.

Khalid, Amna, and Jeffrey Aaron Snyder. 2023. "The War Against 'Woke Indoctrination': How Anti-Critical Race Theory Bills Threaten Academic Freedom in the United States." *Revista Internacional de Derecho y Ciencias Sociales*, no. 33: 149–163.

Kimball, Bruce A., and Sarah M. Iler. 2023. *Wealth, Cost, and Price in American Higher Education*. Baltimore: Johns Hopkins University Press.

Kimber, Megan, and Lisa C. Ehrich. 2015. "Are Australia's Universities in Deficit? A Tale of Generic Managers, Audit Culture, and Casualization." *Journal of Higher Education Policy and Management* 37 (1): 83–97.

King, Martin Luther, Jr. (1967) 2010. *Where Do We Go From Here? Chaos or Community*, illustrated ed. Boston: Beacon Press.

Kittrie, Orde. 2016. *Lawfare: Law as a Weapon of War*. New York: Oxford University Press.

Kiwan, Dina. 2023. *Academic Freedom and the Transnational Production of Knowledge*. Cambridge: Cambridge University Press.

Knijnik, Jorge. 2021. "To Freire or Not to Freire: Educational Freedom and the Populist Right-Wing 'Escola sem Partido' Movement in Brazil." *British Educational Research Journal* 47 (2): 355–371.

Kolbert, Elizabeth. 2014. *The Sixth Extinction: An Unnatural History*. New York: Henry Holt and Company.

Kornbluh, Peter. 2003. *The Pinochet File: A Declassified Dossier on Atrocity and Accountability*. New York: New Press.

Kraus, Neil. 2023. *The Fantasy Economy: Neoliberalism, Inequality, and the Education Reform Movement*. Philadelphia: Temple University Press.

Krenak, Ailton. 2024. *Ancestral Future*. Cambridge: Polity Press.

Land, Hilligje van't, Andreas Corcoran, and Diana-Camelia Iancu. 2021. "Introduction." *In The Promise of Higher Education: Essays in Honour of 70 Years of IAU*, edited by Hilligje van't Land, Andreas Corcoran, and Diana-Camelia Iancu, 1–7. Cham, Switzerland: Springer.

Lange, Lis. 2019. "The Institutional Curriculum, Pedagogy and the Decolonisation of the South African University." In *Decolonisation in Universities: The Politics of Knowledge*, edited by Jonathan D. Jansen, 79–99. Johannesburg: Wits University Press.

Latour, Bruno. 2017. *Down to Earth: Politics in the New Climatic Regime*. New York: Polity Press.

Lee, Robert, and Tristan Ahtone. 2020. "Land-Grab Universities." *High Country News*, March 30. https://www.hcn.org/issues/52-4/indigenous-affairs-education-land-grab-universities/.

Leff, Laurel. 2019. *Well Worth Saving: American Universities' Life-and-Death Decisions on Refugees from Nazi Europe*. New Haven, CT: Yale University Press.

Levine, Arthur, and Scott J. Van Pelt. 2021. *The Great Upheaval: Higher Education's Past, Present, and Future*. Baltimore: Johns Hopkins University Press.

Levitsky, Steven, and Daniel Ziblatt. 2018. *How Democracies Die*. New York: Crown.

Levitsky, Steven, and Daniel Ziblatt. 2023. *Tyranny of the Minority: Why American Democracy Reached the Breaking Point*. New York: Crown.

Lewis, Philip. 2024. *The Public Humanities Turn: The University as an Instrument of Cultural Transformation.* Baltimore: Johns Hopkins University.

Lewis, Shaundra K. 2017. "Crossfire on Compulsory Campus Carry Laws: When the First and Second Amendments Collide." *Iowa Law Review* 102 (5): 2109–2144.

Lipstadt, Deborah E. 1994. *Denying the Holocaust: The Growing Assault on Truth and Memory.* New York: Plume.

Lipstadt, Deborah E. 2016. *Denial: Holocaust History on Trial.* New York: Ecco.

López, Francesca, and Christine E. Sleeter. 2023. *Critical Race Theory and Its Critics: Implications for Research and Teaching.* New York: Teachers College Press.

Lopez, Patricia. J., and Gillespie, Kathryn. A. (eds.). 2015. *Economies of Death: Economic Logics of Killable Life and Grievable Death.* Routledge Frontiers of Political Economy. London: Routledge.

Lorinc, John. 2023. "Academic Freedom Amidst Global Instability." *CAUT*, January 2023. https://www.caut.ca/bulletin/2023/01/academic-freedom-amidst-global-instability.

Maassen, Peter, Dennis Martinsen, Mari Elken, Jens Jungblut, and Elisabeth Lackner. 2023. *State of Play of Academic Freedom in the EU Member States.* Brussels, Belgium: European Parliamentary Research Service. https://www.europarl.europa.eu/RegData/etudes/STUD/2023/740231/EPRS_STU2023740231_EN.pdf.

MacLean, Nancy. 2018. *Democracy in Chains: The Radical Right's Stealth Plan for America.* New York: Penguin Books.

Madely, Benjamin. 2017. *An American Genocide: The United States and the California Indian Catastrophe, 1846–1873.* New Haven, CT: Yale University Press.

Maher, Geo. 2022. *Anticolonial Eruptions: Racial Hubris and the Cunning of Resistance.* Oakland: University of California Press.

Mamdani, Mahmood. 2007. *Scholars in the Marketplace: The Dilemmas of Neo-liberal Reform at Makerere University, 1989–2005.* Dakar, Senegal: Council for the Development of Social Science Research in Africa.

Mamdani, Mahmood, and Mamadou Diouf (eds.). 1995. *Academic Freedom in Africa.* Dakar, Senegal: Conseil pour le Développement de LA.

Marcinkowski, Thomas J. 1991. "The New National Environmental Education Act: A Renewal of Commitment." *Journal of Environmental Education* 22 (2): 7–10.

Mayer, Jane. 2017. *Dark Money: The Hidden History of the Billionaires Behind the Rise of the Radical Right.* New York: Anchor Books.

Mbembe, Achille. 2015. *Decolonization and the Question of the Archive*. New York: Africa is a Country, p. 14. https://worldpece.org/content/mbembe-achille-2015-%E2%80%9Cdecolonizing-knowledge-and-question-archive%E2%80%9D-africa-country.

Mbembe, Achille. 2016. "Decolonizing the University: New Directions." *Arts & Humanities in Higher Education* 15 (1): 29–45.

Mbembe, Achille. 2019. *Necropolitics*. Durham, NC: Duke University Press.

McCarthy, Samantha, and Isaac Kamola. 2022. "Sensationalized Surveillance: Campus Reform and the Targeted Harassment of Faculty." *New Political Science* 44 (2): 227–247.

McGoey, Linsay. 2016. *No Such Thing as a Free Gift: The Gates Foundation and the Price of Philanthropy*. London: Verso.

McSherry, J. Patrice. 2005. *Predatory States: Operation Condor and Covert War in Latin America*. New York: Rowman & Littlefield.

Merrick, Helen. 2017. "Naturecultures and Feminist Materialism." In *Routledge Handbook of Gender and Environment*, edited by Sherilyn MacGregor, 101–14. New York: Routledge.

Mettler, Suzanne. 2014. *Degrees of Inequality: How the Politics of Higher Education Sabotaged the American Dream*. New York: Basic Books.

Michel, Gregg L. 2024. *Spying on Students: The FBI, Red Squads, and Student Activists in the 1960s South*. Baton Rouge, LA: Louisiana State University Press.

Mignolo, Walter D. 2010. "Epistemic Disobedience, Independent Thought and Decolonial Freedom." *Theory, Culture & Society* 26 (7–8): 159–181.

Mignolo, Walter D. 2023. "The Explosion of Globalism and the Advent of the Third Nomos of the Earth." In *Globalization: Past, Present, Future.* edited by Manfred B. Steger, Roland Benedikter, Harald Pechlaner, and Ingrid Kofler, 193–206. Berkeley: University of California Press. Miller-Idriss, Cynthia. 2019. *The Extreme Gone Mainstream: Commercialization and Far Right Youth Culture in Germany*. Princeton, NJ: Princeton University Press.

Milosz, Czeslaw. (1953) 1990. *The Captive Mind*, international ed. London: Vintage.

Minton, Stephen. 2019. *Residential Schools and Indigenous Peoples: From Genocide via Education to the Possibilities for Processes of Truth, Restitution, Reconciliation, and Reclamation*. New York: Routledge.

Mirowski, Philip, and Dieter Plehwe. 2009. *The Road from Mount Pèlerin: The Making of the Neoliberal Thought Collective*. Cambridge, MA: Harvard University Press.

Moore, MariJo (ed.). 2003. *Genocide of the Mind: New Native American Writing*. New York: Nation Books.

Morrish, Liz. 2017. "Why the Audit Culture Made Me Quit." *Times Higher Education*, March 2. https://www.timeshighereducation.com/features/why-audit-culture-made-me-quit.

Naím, Moisés. 2022. *The Revenge of Power: How Autocrats Are Reinventing Politics for the 21st Century*. New York: St. Martin's Press.

Nash, Margaret A. 2019. "Entangled Pasts: Land-Grant Colleges and American Indian Dispossession." *History of Education Quarterly* 59 (4): 437–467.

Neem, Johann N. 2019. *What's The Point of College? Seeking Purpose in an Age of Reform*. Baltimore: Johns Hopkins University Press.

Neiman, Susan. 2019. *Learning from the Germans: Race and the Memory of Evil*. New York: Farrar, Straus and Giroux.

Nelson, Anne. 2019. *Shadow Network: Media, Money, and the Secret Hub of the Radical Right*. London: Bloomsbury.

Newfield, Christopher. 2008. *Unmaking the Public University: The Forty-Year Assault on the Middle Class*. Cambridge, MA: Harvard University Press.

Newfield, Christopher. 2021. "California Dreaming: Clark Kerr and the University of California." In *Utopian Universities: A Global History of the New Campuses of the 1960s*, edited by Jill Pellew and Miles Taylor, 251–267. London: Bloomsbury.

Newman, Jane O. 2020. "Scholar Rescue: The Past of the Future." In *Refugee Routes*, edited by Vanessa Agnew, Kader Konuk, and Jane O. Newman, 285–297. Bielefeld, Germany: transcript Verlag.

Ngũgĩ wa Thiong'o. 1986. *Decolonising the Mind: The Politics of Language in African Literature*. Portsmouth, NH: Heinemann Educational.

Ngũgĩ wa Thiong'o. 2014. *Globalectics: Theory and the Politics of Knowing*. New York: Columbia University Press.

Nocella, Anthony, Steven Best, and Peter McLaren. 2010. *Academic Repression: Reflections from the Academic-Industrial Complex*. Chico, CA: AK Press.

Nocella, Anthony J., and David Gabbard. 2013. *Policing the Campus: Academic Expression, Surveillance, and the Occupy Movement*. New York: Peter Lang Publishing.

Nussbaum, Martha C. 2016. *Not for Profit: Why Democracy Needs the Humanities*, updated ed. Princeton, NJ: Princeton University Press.

Nyberg, Daniel. 2021. "Corporations, Politics, and Democracy: Corporate Political Activities as Political Corruption." *Organization Theory* 2 (1): 1–24.

O'Keefe, Theresa, and Aline Courtois. 2019. "'Not One of the Family': Gender and Precarious Work in the Neoliberal University." *Gender, Work & Organization* 26 (4): 463–479.

Okihiro, Gary Y. 2016. *Third World Studies: Theorizing Liberation*. Durham, NC: Duke University Press.

Oreskes, Naomi, and Erick M. Conway. 2010. *Merchants of Doubt: How a Handful of Scientists Obscured the Truth on Issues from Tobacco Smoke to Global Warming.* London: Bloomsbury.

Oreskes, Naomi, and Erick M. Conway. 2023. *The Big Myth: How American Business Taught Us to Loathe Government and Love the Free Market.* London: Bloomsbury.

Özdemir, Seçkin Sertdemir, Nil Mutluer, and Esra Özyürek. 2019. "Exile and Plurality in Neoliberal Times: Turkey's Academics for Peace." *Public Culture* 31 (2): 235–259.

Özkirimli, Umut. 2017. "How to Liquidate a People? Academic Freedom in Turkey and Beyond." *Globalizations* 14 (6): 851–856.

paperson, la. 2017. *A Third University is Possible.* Minneapolis: University of Minnesota Press.

Parker, Grant. 2019. "Afterword: Decolonising Minds via Curricula?" In *Decolonisation in Universities: The Politics of Knowledge,* edited by Jonathan D. Jansen, 255–264. Johannesburg: Wits University Press.

Passavant, Paul. 2021. *Policing Protest: The Post-Democratic State and the Figure of Black Insurrection.* Durham, NC: Duke University Press.

Peck, Jamie. 2010. *Constructions of Neoliberal Reason.* Oxford: Oxford University Press.

Pellew, Jill and Miles Taylor (eds.). 2021. *Utopian Universities: A Global History of the New Campuses of the 1960s.* London: Bloomsbury.

Platt, Tony. 2023. *The Scandal of Cal: Land Grabs, White Supremacy, and Miseducation at Berkeley.* Berkeley, CA: Heyday.

Plumwood, Val. 1993. *Feminism and the Mastery of Nature.* New York: Routledge.

Popescu, Lucy, and Carole Seymour-Jones (eds.). 2007. *Writers Under Siege: Voices of Freedom from Around the World; A PEN Anthology.* New York: New York University Press.

Popović, Milica. 2022a. "Academic Freedom and Epistemic Injustice." *Alternator* April 21. https://doi.org/10.3986/alternator.2022.16.

Popović, Milica. 2022b. "The Legitimate Demand for Justice Within Our Universities." *University World News,* October 1. https://www.universityworldnews.com/post.php?story=20220929113013991.

Popović, Milica, Liviu Matei, and Daniele Joly. 2022. *Changing Understandings of Academic Freedom in the World in a Time of Pandemic.* OSUN Global Observatory on Academic Freedom, Central European University.

Post, Robert C. 2016. "Free Speech and Academic Freedom." Lecture delivered at Columbia Law School, March 7. https://www.law.columbia.edu/news/archive/free-speech-and-academic-freedom.

Powell, Lewis F., Jr. 1971. "'The Memo': Powell Memorandum; Attack on American Free Enterprise System." Lewis F. Powell Jr. Papers. https://scholarlycommons.law.wlu.edu/powellmemo/1/.

Prashad, Vijay. 2009. "Oppressive Pedagogy: Some Reflections on Campus Democracy." In *Dangerous Professors: Academic Freedom and the National Security Campus*, edited by Malini Johar Schueller and Ashley Dawson, 175–186. Ann Arbor: University of Michigan Press.

Price, Richard H. 2004. *Threatening Anthropology: McCarthyism and the FBI's Surveillance of Activist Anthropologists*. Durham, NC: Duke University Press.

Price, Richard H. 2011. "Uninvited Guests: A Short History of the CIA on Campus." In *The CIA on Campus: Essays on Academic Freedom and the National Security State*, edited by Philip Zwerling, 33–60. London: McFarland & Company.

Priest, Goerge L. 2020. *The Rise of Law and Economics: An Intellectual History*. New York: Routledge.

Quinn, Robert. 2021. "Academic Self-Censorship Is a 'Brain Drag' on Arab Universities and Societies." Al-Fanar Media.

Rabban, David M. 2014. "Professors Beware: The Evolving Threat of 'Institutional' Academic Freedom." In *Academic Freedom in Conflict: The Struggle over Free Speech Rights in the University*, edited by James L. Turk, 23–48. Toronto: James Lorimer & Co.

Rachman, Gideon. 2022. *The Age of the Strongman: How the Cult of the Leader Threatens Democracy Around the World*. New York: Other Press.

Rajah, Jothie. 2012. *Authoritarian Rule of Law: Legislation, Discourse and Legitimacy in Singapore*. Cambridge: Cambridge University Press.

Readings, Bill. 1996. *The University in Ruins*. Cambridge, MA: Harvard University Press.

Reeves, Michelle. 2010. "'Obey the Rules or Get Out': Ronald Reagan's 1966 Gubernatorial Campaign and the 'Trouble in Berkeley.'" *Southern California Quarterly* 92 (3): 275–305.

Reichman, Henry. 2021. *Understanding Academic Freedom*. Baltimore: Johns Hopkins University Press.

Repucci, Sarah. 2020. *Freedom in the World 2020: A Leaderless Struggle for Democracy*. Freedom House. https://freedomhouse.org/report/freedom-world/2020/leaderless-struggle-democracy.

Reyes, Victoria. 2022. *Academic Outsider: Stories of Exclusion and Hope*. Stanford, CA: Stanford University Press.

Robinson, William I. 2016. "Global Capitalism and the Restructuring of Education: The Transnational Capitalist Class' Quest to Suppress Critical Thinking." *Social Justice* 43 (3): 1–24.

Robinson, William I. 2020. *The Global Police State*. London: Pluto Press.

Robinson, William I. 2023. "The Violent Crackup of the Post-WWII International Order." *Journal of World-Systems Research* 29 (1): 227–232.

Rodríguez, Clelia. O. 2018. *Decolonizing Academia: Poverty, Oppression and Pain*. Halifax, Nova Scotia, Canada: Fernwood Publishing.

Roth, Michael S. 2015. *Beyond the University: Why Liberal Education Matters*. New Haven, CT: Yale University Press.

Said, Edward. 1996. "Identity, Authority, and Freedom: The Potentate and the Traveler." In *The Future of Academic Freedom*, edited by Louis Menand, 214–228. Chicago: University of Chicago Press.

Said, Edward. 2000. *Reflections on Exile and Other Essays*. Cambridge, MA: Harvard University Press.

Saloojee, Anver. 2014. "Balancing Academic Freedom and Freedom from Discrimination in Contested Spaces." In *Academic Freedom in Conflict: The Struggle over Free Speech Rights in the University*, edited by James L. Turk, 205–217. Toronto: James Lorimer & Co.

Salper, Roberta. 2011. "San Diego State 1970: The Initial Year of the Nation's First Women's Studies Program." *Feminist Histories and Institutional Practices* 37 (3): 656–682.

Saltman, Kenneth J. and David A. Gabbard (eds.). 2011. *Education as Enforcement: The Militarization and Corporatization of Schools*, 2nd ed. New York: Routledge.

Samuels, Sarah. 2019. " 'An Outstanding and Unusual Contribution': The Emergency Committee in Aid of Displaced Foreign Scholars." *Penn History Review* 24 (2): 71–99.

Santos, Boaventura de Sousa. 2001. "Nuestra America: Reinventing a Subaltern Paradigm of Recognition and Redistribution." *Theory Culture Society* 18 (2–3): 185–217.

Santos, Boaventura de Sousa. 2014. *Epistemologies of the South: Justice Against Epistemicide*. New York: Routledge.

Santos, Boaventura de Sousa. 2017. *Decolonising the University: The Challenge of Deep Cognitive Justice*. Newcastle upon Tyne, UK: Cambridge Scholars Publishing.

Santos, Boaventura de Sousa. 2023. *Law and the Epistemologies of the South*. Cambridge: Cambridge University Press.

Sayen, Jamie. 1985. *Einstein in America: The Scientist's Conscience in the Age of Hitler and Hiroshima*. New York: Crown Publishers.

Scheppele, Kim L. 2018. "Autocratic Legalism." *University of Chicago Law Review* 85 (2): 545–583.

Schildermans, Hans. 2021. *Experiments in Decolonizing the University: Towards an Ecology of Study*. London: Bloomsbury.

Scholars at Risk. 2020. *Promoting Higher Education Values: A Guide for Discussion.* Accessed August 29, 2024. https://www.scholarsatrisk.org/wp-content/uploads/2020/05/SAR_PHV_DiscussionGuide_v20_ONLINE.pdf.

Scholars at Risk. 2022. *Free to Think 2022* (summary). November 2022.

Schrecker, Ellen. 1980. "Academic Freedom and the Cold War." *Antioch Review* 38 (3): 313–327.

Schrecker, Ellen. 1986. *No Ivory Tower: McCarthyism and the Universities.* Oxford: Oxford University Press.

Schrecker, Ellen. 2010. *The Lost Soul of Higher Education: Corporatization, the Assault on Academic Freedom, and the End of the American University.* New York: New Press.

Schrecker, Ellen. 2021. *The Lost Promise: American Universities in the 1960s.* Chicago: University of Chicago Press.

Schrum, Ethan. 2019. *The Instrumental University: Education in the Service of the National Agenda After World War II.* Ithaca, NY: Cornell University Press.

Schueller, Malini Johar, and Ashley Dawson (eds.). 2009. *Dangerous Professors: Academic Freedom and the National Security Campus.* Ann Arbor: University of Michigan Press.

Scott, Joan Wallach. 1996. "Academic Freedom as an Ethical Practice." In *The Future of Academic Freedom*, edited by Louis Menand, 163–180. Chicago: University of Chicago Press.

Scott, Joan Wallach. 2019. *Knowledge, Power, and Academic Freedom.* New York: Columbia University Press.

Shahjahan, Riyad A., and Adrianna J. Kezar. 2013. "Beyond the 'National Container': Addressing Methodological Nationalism in Higher Education Research." *Educational Researcher* 42 (1): 20–29. https://doi.org/10.3102/0013189X12463050.

Shahjahan, Riyad A., and Adam Grimm. 2023. "Bringing the 'Nation-State' into Being: Affect, Methodological Nationalism and Globalization of Higher Education." *Globalisation, Societies and Education* 21 (2): 293–305.

Shaxson, Nicholas. 2019. *The Finance Curse: How Global Finance Is Making Us All Poorer.* New York: Grove Atlantic.

Shefner, Jon, Harry F. Dahms, Robert Emmet Jones, and Asafa Jalata (eds.). 2014. *Social Justice and the University: Globalization, Human Rights and the Future of Democracy.* New York: Palgrave Macmillan.

Shelton, Jon. 2023. *The Education Myth: How Human Capital Trumped Social Democracy.* Ithaca, NY: Cornell University Press.

Shepherd, Lauren Lassabe. 2023. *Resistance from the Right: Conservatives and the Campus Wars in Modern America.* Chapel Hill: University of North Carolina Press.

Shiva, Vandana. 1990. "Reductionist Science as Epistemological Violence." In *Science, Hegemony and Violence: A Requiem for Modernity*, edited by A. Nandy, 232–256. Oxford: Oxford University Press.

Shore, Cris. 2008. "Audit Culture and Illiberal Governance: Universities and the Politics of Accountability." *Anthropological Theory* 8 (3): 278–298.

Shore, Cris, and Susan Wright. 2015. "Audit Culture Revisited: Rankings, Ratings, and the Reassembling of Society." *Current Anthropology* 56 (3): 421–444.

Shore, Cris, and Susan Wright. 2024. *Audit Culture: How Indicators and Rankings are Reshaping the World*. London: Pluto Press.

Sitze, Adam. 2017. "Academic Unfreedom, Unacademic Freedom: Part One of Two." *Massachusetts Review* 58 (4): 589–607.

Slaughter, Sheila. 2019. "Challenges to Academic Freedom: Academic Capitalism and Neonationalism." In *The Three Cs of Higher Education: Competition, Collaborations and Complementarity*, edited by Rosalind M.O. Pritchard, Mark O'Hara, Clare Milsom, James Williams and Liviu Matei, 27–50. Budapest and New York City: Central European University Press.

Slaughter, Shiela, and Gary Rhoades. 2004. *Academic Capitalism and the New Economy: Markets, State, and Higher Education*. Baltimore: Johns Hopkins University Press.

Slaughter, Shiela, and Larry L. Leslie. 1997. *Academic Capitalism: Politics, Policies, and the Entrepreneurial University*. Baltimore: Johns Hopkins University Press.

Slobodian, Quinn. 2018. *Globalists: The End of Empire and the Birth of Neoliberalism*. Cambridge, MA: Harvard University Press.

Snyder, Jeffrey Aaron. 2022. "What Are the Limits of Academic Freedom? A Maddening New Book Fumbles an Important Debate." *Chronicle of Higher Education*, May 5.

Snyder, Jeffrey Aaron. 2023. "Is Academic Freedom a Human Right?" *Chronicle of Higher Education*, January 11. https://www.chronicle.com/article/is-academic-freedom-a-human-right.

Spannagel, Jankia. 2024. "The Constitutional Codification of Academic Freedom over Time and Space." *Global Constitutionalism*, 1–27. https://doi.org/10.1017/S2045381724000108.

Spivak, G. C. 1988. "Can the Subaltern Speak?" In *Marxism and the Interpretation of Culture*, edited by N. Carry and L. Grossberg, 271–313. Urbana-Champaign: University of Illinois Press.

Spooner, Marc. 2023. "Backsliding Toward Illiberal Democracy and Authoritarianism: Qualitative Inquiry, Academic Freedom, and Technologies of Governance." In *The Sage Handbook of Qualitative Research*, 6th ed., edited by Norman K. Denzin, Yvonna S. Lincoln, Michael D. Giardina and Gaile S. Canella, 567–593. Thousand Oaks, CA: Sage Publications.

Spooner, Marc, and James McNinch. 2018. "Introduction." In *Dissident Knowledge in Higher Education*, edited by Marc Spooner and James McNinch, xxiii–xxxii. Regina, Saskatchewan, Canada: University of Regina Press.

Spring, Joel. 2018. *The American School: From the Puritans to the Trump Era*, 10th ed. New York: Routledge.

Stein, Sharon. 2022. *Unsettling the University: Confronting the Colonial Foundations of US Higher Education*. Baltimore: Johns Hopkins University Press.

Steiner, H. Arthur. 1936. "The Fascist Conception of Law." *Columbia Law Review* 36 (8): 1267–1283.

Stoesz, David. 1992. "The Fall of the Industrial City: The Reagan Legacy for Urban Policy." *Journal of Sociology & Social Welfare* 19 (1): 149–167.

Sunstein, Cass R. (ed.). 2018. *Can It Happen Here? Authoritarianism in America*. New York: Dey St.

Tamale, Sylvia. 2022. *Decolonization and Afro-Feminism*. Quebec: Daraja Press.

Teays, Wanda, and Alison Dundes Renteln (eds.). 2022. *The Ethical University: Transforming Higher Education*. Lanham, MD: Rowman & Littlefield.

Terwindt, Carolijn. 2020. *When Protest Becomes Crime: Politics and Law in Liberal Democracies*. London: Pluto Press.

Thornton, Patricia M. 2023. "Afterword: Canary in the Coal Mine." In *New Threats to Academic Freedom in Asia*, edited by Dimitar D. Gueorguiev. New York: Columbia University Press.

Tobias, Sarah, and Arlene Stein (eds.). 2022. *The Perils of Populism*. Newark, NJ: Rutgers University Press.

Tourish, Dennis, Russell Craig, and Joel Amernic. 2017. "A Mania for Assessment: How an Audit Culture Undermines the Purpose of Universities." In *The Corporatization of the Business School: Minerva Meets the Market*, edited by Tony Huzzard, Mats Benner, and Dan Kärreman, 34–55. New York: Routledge.

Tuck, Eve. 2018. "Biting the University That Feeds Us." In *Dissident Knowledge in Higher Education*, edited by Marc Spooner and James McNinch, 149–167. Regina, Saskatchewan, Canada: University of Regina Press.

Turk, James L. (ed.). 2014. *Academic Freedom in Conflict: The Struggle over Free Speech Rights in the University*. Toronto: James Lorimer & Co.

Turner, James Morton, and Andrew C. Isenberg. 2018. *The Republican Reversal: Conservatives and the Environment from Nixon to Trump*. Cambridge, MA: Harvard University Press.

United Nations. 2023. *A New Agenda for Peace*. Policy Brief 9. https://www.un.org/sites/un2.un.org/files/our-common-agenda-policy-brief-new-agenda-for-peace-en.pdf.

Vatansever, Asli. 2018. "Academic Nomads: The Changing Conception of Academic Work Under Precarious Conditions." *Cambio* 8 (15): 153–165.

Vatansever, Asli. 2020. *At the Margins of Academia: Exile, Precariousness, and Subjectivity.* Boston: Brill.

V-Dem. 2022a. *Democracy Report 2022.* Executive Summary, p. 6. h https://v-dem.net/documents/19/dr_2022_ipyOpLP.pdf.

V-Dem. 2022b. *Academic Freedom Index: Update 2022.* Friedrich-Alexander Universität, Institute of Political Science. https://www.pol.phil.fau.eu/files/2022/03/afi-update-2022.pdf?emci=686bb990-519e-ec11-a22a-281878b85110&emdi=96c5ee28-429f-ec11-a22a-281878b85110&ceid=1647205.

Waghid, Yusef. 2023. "Cultivating an Ubuntu University of Ethical Engagement in Africa." In *The Emergence of the Ethically-Engaged University*, edited by Emiliano Bosio and Gustavo Gregorutti, 105–135. New York: Palgrave Macmillan.

Waghid, Yusef, Judith Terblanche, Lester Brian Shawa, Joseph Pardon Hungwe, Faiq Waghid, and Zayd Waghid (eds.). 2023. *Towards an Ubuntu University: African Higher Education Reimagined.* New York: Palgrave-MacMillan.

Watkins, Grace. 2020. "'Cops Are Cops': American Campus Police and the Global Carceral Apparatus." *Comparative American Studies: An International Journal* 17 (3–4): 242–256.

Weis, Valerie Vegh (ed.). 2022. *Criminalization of Activism: Historical, Present and Future Perspectives.* New York: Routledge.

West, Cornel. 2005. *Democracy Matters: Winning the Fight Against Imperialism.* New York: Penguin.

Whittington, Keith E. 2018. *Speak Freely: Why Universities Must Defend Free Speech.* Princeton, NJ: Princeton University Press.

Whittington, Keith E. 2024. *You Can't Teach That!: The Battle over University Classrooms.* New York: Polity Press.

Wilder, Craig Steven. 2014. *Ebony and Ivy: Race, Slavery, and the Troubled History of America's Universities.* London: Bloomsbury.

Williamson-Lott, Joy Ann. 2018. *Jim Crow Campus: Higher Education and the Struggle for a New Southern Social Order.* New York: Teachers College Press.

Williamson-Lott, Joy Ann. 2024. "The AAUP and the Black Freedom Struggle, 1955–1965." Spring 2024: Race and the AAUP. *Academe*. https://www.aaup.org/article/aaup-and-black-freedom-struggle.

Willoughby-Herard, Tiffany. 2025. *"I Meant for you to be free": Pedagogies for Young South Africans, the Post-1994 Generation.* Oxford: Oxford University Press.

Wilsdon, James, Liz Allen, Eleonora Belfiore, et al. 2015. *The Metric Tide: Report of the Independent Review of the Role of Metrics in Research Assessment and Management*. Technical report. https://www.doi.org/10.13140/RG.2.1.4929.1363.

Wilson, Ralph, and Isaac Kamola. 2021. *Free Speech and Koch Money: Manufacturing a Campus Culture War*. London: Pluto Press.

Wolff, Michael. 2010. *The Man Who Owns the News: Inside the Secret World of Rupert Murdoch*. New York: Broadway Books.

Woollacott, Angela. 2021. "1968 and the Fight for Democracy in Australia: Don Dunstan, Student Activism, and the End of the South Australian 'Playmander.'" *Australian Journal of Politics and History* 67 (2): 246–259.

Worth, Katie. 2021. *Miseducation: How Climate Change Is Taught in America*. New York: Columbia Global Reports.

Yacovone, Donald. 2022. *Teaching White Supremacy: America's Democratic Ordeal and the Forging of Our National Identity*. New York: Pantheon.

Zahneis, Megan, and Audrey Williams June. 2023. "In These Red States, Professors Are Eying the Exits." *Chronicle of Higher Education*, September 7.

Zakaria, Fareed. 2016. *In Defense of a Liberal Education*. New York: W.W. Norton & Company.

Zanin, Cristiano, Valeska Martins, and Rafael Valim. 2022. *Lawfare: Waging War Through Law*. New York: Routledge.

Zwerling, Philip (ed.). 2011. *The CIA on Campus: Essays on Academic Freedom and the National Security State*. London: McFarland & Company.

Index

Page numbers in italics refer to figures and tables.

Abbott, Greg, 200
abortion, 150, 158
academic freedom: acknowledging value of, 221; collective, 71–72, 91–92; epistemic justice and, 94–96, 175; free speech vs., 83–89; history and definitions of, 5–8; human rights and, 68–71; meaning and definitions of, 71–74, 79, 89, 103; social justice and, 89–94; as social responsibility, 12–18. *See also* PEN America Principles on Campus Free Speech
academic freedom, attacks on: global pattern of, 3–4; repressive strategies, 34–44; structural drivers of, 50–55. *See also* authoritarianism; lawfare strategies; persecution of scholars; violence; *specific places*
activism. *See* protests and activism
Adébísí, Folúkẹ́, 225–26, 235
adjunct labor, 174–76
admissions, race-conscious, 42–43, 207
affirmative action, 258n14
Afghanistan, 106–7, 178
African Americans: censorship of Black female scholars, 199–200; GI Bill unfilled for, 138; Jim Crow and Black Freedom struggle, 143, 264n7; King assassination, 149; slavery, censorship of, 198–99, 229. *See also* NAACP; racism
Age of the Strongman, The (Rachman), 27
AI (artificial intelligence), 48, 211, 220
Ai Weiwei, 48
Alexander, Neville, 144–45
Allende, Salvador, 161
American Association of University Professors (AAUP): on academic freedom, 6–7, 71–72; on donor interference, 194; "Polarizing Times Demand Robust Academic Freedom," 63, 220–21
America's Censored Classrooms (PEN America), 57–58
Amesbury, Richard, 84
antidemocracy: academic freedom and response to, 91–92; historical fascist regimes and, 74; *Inter-American Principles* and, 102–4; knowledge production and, 64–68; rising, 25–34; US embrace of, xvi, 10–11. *See also* authoritarianism; censorship; lawfare strategies; neoliberalism and free-market ideology
anti-politics orthodoxy, 18, 19–20
Apple, Michael, 51
Arab Spring, 178
audit culture, 170–74
austerity policies, 114, 162
Australia, 127, 129–31, 148, 185, 212

authoritarianism: academic freedom, assault on, 64–67; capitalism and, 180; Einstein on, 79; fascism and, 26; free-market, 31; global lean toward, xx, 22, 27, 33, 82, 100, 124; illiberal democracy and, 40; insecurity and, 50; oil industry and, 186–87; PEN on, 99; resistance against, 103–4, 128; states supporting one another in, 132; strategies of, 30; strongman leaders, 27–28, 200–201; US and, 19, 31, 186–87; weaponization of higher education and, 54–55, 113. *See also* antidemocracy; censorship; fascism; persecution of scholars; policing; surveillance

Baldwin, James, 9
Beauvoir, Simone de, 149
Becker, Jonathan, 64–65
Bello, Walden, 26
Ben-Ghiat, Ruth, 30, 31, 200–201
Berrett, Dan, 152
Biden, Joe, 31, 203
Biden v. Nebraska, 43
Big Oil, 184–87, 190–96, *191*
Biko, Steve, 14
Black Lives Matter movement, 13, 179, 201, 211
Boğaziçi University, 82
Bolsonaro, Jair, xiv, 28, 33, 38, 114–15, 132
book bans and burnings, xiv, 55–59, 75, 75, *163*
Bosio, Emiliano, 16
Brazil: Freire and, 13–14, 55; Nobrega/ Medeiros interview, 113–18; right-wing demonstrators, 33, *34. See also* Bolsonaro, Jair
Brown, Wendy, 2, 160
Brown v. Board of Education, 157
Brunner, Claudia, 96
Buchanan, James M., 159
Bucher, Gabriela, 52
Buckley, William, 140–41
Bundy, McGeorge, 141, 263n4
Burden-Stelly, Charisse, 77

Bush, George W., 127–28, 181, 189
Butler, Judith, 7

Caldwell-Stone, Deborah, 56
California Technical University (Caltech), 159
Camus, Renaud, 231
Canada, 59, 182, 260n8, 262n5
capitalism: anti-capitalism movements, 77, 141; antidemocracy and, 47, 180; authoritarianism and, 180; extractive, 51–52, 177, 182–83, 197, 232–33; Giroux on hyper-capitalism, 36; market logics and reshaping higher education, 164–67; neoliberalism and, 264n13; Powell memo, 160; racial, 223, 225; sustainable economy vs., 234; transnational capitalist class, 52–54. *See also* neoliberalism and free-market ideology
Carlisle Indian Industrial School, 139, 263n3
Carlos, John, 264n12
Carson, Rachel, 151
Carvalho, Edward, 164–65
censorship: of Black female scholars, 199–200; book bans and burnings, xiv, 55–59, 75, 75, *163*; in Brazil, 113–15; of controversial subjects, 183, 217; of curriculum, 57–59; gag order measures, 57–58, 183; history denialism, 197–200, 207–8, 229; self-censorship, 47–48, 122
Center for Governance and Markets (Pitt), 194
Center for International Studies, MIT, 165
Central European University, 54, 66, 108–13
Central Intelligence Agency (CIA), 148–49
Chase, Robert, 214
Chatterjee, Piya, 10
Chávez, Karma, 206–7
Cherniavsky, Eva, 71–72, 89
Chile, 161–62
China, 67–68, *68*, 207
Chomsky, Noam, 81, 219

Citizens of the Reich movement, 33
Civil Rights Act (1964), 143, 264n7
civil rights movement, 143, 147–48, 149, 156
Clemson University, 193–94
climate denialism: environmental education, donor interference, and, 190–95; history of, 183–86; PragerU edutainment and, 195; pre-Reagan environmental legislation and, 187–89; resistance, fossil fuel divestment, and skepticism, 195–97
climate refugees, 234
climate science facts, 216
Coalition for Academic Freedom in the Americas (CAFA), 55, 96, 104, 262n5
Cohen, Robert, 143
Cold War, 141, 148–49, 162
collective futures, 234–35
colonialism and imperialism: anticolonialist activism, 143–47, 164, 263n5; epistemicide, 96; Freire on, xiv; global north, colonial logics within, 14, 73; human–nature binary and, 232; neocolonial exploitation, 161–62, 179; neoliberalism and, 161–63; settler colonialism, 29, 44, 138–39, 263n3; universities as political and, 61–62. *See also* decolonization
Columbia University, 149
commoning, 82–83, 97, 230
Confederate monuments, 201
Connell, Raewyn, 62, 90, 237
conspiracy theories, xvii, 24, 33, 120, 186, 196, 231
Corcoran, Richard, 213
corporatism, 167–70. *See also* oil industry
Corvinus University of Economics, 109–10
Council for National Policy (CNP), 166
COVID-19 pandemic, 182, 210
critical race theory (CRT), 202–4
critical thinking: collaborative, 65; disavowal of, 64, 70; efforts to control, 9, 44, 46, 172, 206; exiles and, 123; humanities education and, 23; self-censorship and, 47

culture wars, 181–82, 218
curricula: controlled by US states, 55–59, 58; as "government speech," 57, 59; neoliberalism and, 161
cyberbullying of teachers, 48–49
Czechoslovakia, 147–48

Daniels, Ronald, 60
Dartmouth College, 196
deadly global alliance, 186
Decolonising the Mind (Ngũgĩ), 228–29
decolonization: beyond the Euro-American academy, 223–28; human–nonhuman relations and, 231–33; with inclusive student communities, 228–29; knowledge production as global and local, 230–31
defense interests, 76, 158–59, 260n8
defunding, 157, 167, 176
democracy: capitalism and, 47; commoning and, 82; concept called into question, 19; conservative takeover of higher education and, 166–67; *Democracy Report* (V-Dem), 26; dissent and, 66–68; illiberal, 40, 123–24; importance of higher education to, 60, 237; Ivory Coast and, 128; MAGA Movement and, 31; neoliberalism as opposition to, 160; public spheres and, 36. *See also* antidemocracy
Democracy Report (V-Dem), 26
DeSantis, Ron, 41, 55–57, 125–26, 203, 205, 229
Diamond, Sigmund, 263n4
digital surveillance, 48–49
disinformation: on campus violence, 212–13; challenging, 122; on climate change, 184–95; concept of democracy and, 19; free speech and, 85; history denialism and rewriting, 197–200, 207–8, 229; media literacy and, 24; moral panics and, 181; political landscape of, 220; science denialism, 182–83, 184. *See also* climate denialism

diversity, equity, and inclusion (DEI) programs, 200, 204–7, 268n25
donor interference, 190–95, *191*
Douglass, John, 50–51
Downing, David, 164–65
Du Bois, W. E. B., 77
Duncan, Kyle, 87–88

Earth Day, 188
Eaton, Charlie, 165, 168
economic ideology. *See* neoliberalism and free-market ideology
edutainment, 195
Einstein, Albert, 71, 74–80, *78*, 218–19
Eisenhower, Dwight, 264n10
enrollment trends, 256n8
environmental activism, 151
environmental education, 187–95
Eötvös Lorand University (ELTE), 109–10
epistemicide, 96
epistemic justice, 94–96, 175
equity, private, 168–69
Erdoğan, Recep, 29–30, 82
Ethiopia, 107–8
Evans, Richard, 208
exile, 122–27. *See also* persecution of scholars
ExxonMobile, 184

facts, weaponization of, 64
Faculty First Responders, 50
Faison, A. Zachary, Jr., 41
Falk, Richard, 27–28
Fanon, Frantz, 263n5
fascism: Citizens of the Reich movement (Germany), 33; lawfare and, 28; past vs. current, 80–81; societal, 26, 81, 105; Trump and, 31–32
Federal Bureau of Investigation (FBI), 142–43
Federici, Silvia, 82–83, 97, 197–98, 230
feminist movement, 149–50, 157–58
First Amendment, 83, 84–85, 242, 243
Fish, Stanley, 19–20
Fleming, Peter, 171

Florida: critical race theory and, 202; curricula control and book banning, 55–59; internal exile and brain drain, 125–26; militarization, 213; "Stop Woke Act" and "Don't Say Gay Act," 57–59; violence in, 41
Florida State University, 193–94
Floyd, George, 201, 202, 211
Forbes, Jack, 233
Fossil Free Research Coalition, 196
fossil fuels industry, 184–87, 190–96, *191*
Foucault, Michel, 47
France, 148
free-market authoritarianism, 31
free-market ideology. *See* neoliberalism and free-market ideology
Free Speech Movement, 142–43
free speech principles. *See* PEN America Principles on Campus Free Speech
free speech vs. academic freedom, 83–89
Free to Think 2023 report (SAR), 39
Freire, Paulo, xiv, 13–14, 55
Friedan, Betty, 149
Friedman, Milton, 35, 159, 162

gag order measures, 57–58, 183. *See also* censorship
Galschiot, Jens, 67–68, *68*
Gambetti, Zeynep, 82
Gandhi, Evyn Lê Espiritu, 230
Gebrial, Dalia, 224
gender studies, 57
George Mason University, 35, 161, *191*, 193
George Washington University, 196
Germany: Citizens of the Reich, 33; Nazi regime, 71, 74–76, 80, 100, 208
Geyer, Michel, 30
GI Bill (1944), 18, 137–38
Gill, Indermit, 52
Giroux, Henry, 17, 36, 70
Global Climate Coalition, 184
Globalectics (Ngũgĩ), 230
globalization, concept of, 165. *See also* neoliberalism and free-market ideology

Global Observatory on Academic Freedom (GOAF), 93, 95
God and Man at Yale (Buckley), 141
Godrej, Farah, 168
Goldberg, David Theo, 203–4
Goldberg, Michelle, 57
Greene, Melissa Fay, 131–33
Gregorutti, Gustavo, 16
Guneratne, Arjun, 86–87
gun laws, 212–13

Haley, Nikki, 229
Hall, Stuart, 56
Hannah-Jones, Nikole, 198–99
Hansen, James, 184
Haraway, Donna, 232
Harvard Business School, 165
Harvard University, 69, 159, 191, 195–96, 260n6
Harvey, Colin, 118–22
hateful speech, 244–45
Hawkins, Ed, 48
Hawkins, Stacy, 85–86
Hayek, Friedrich, 35, 159
He, Rowena, 68
Herbold, Hilary, 138
Herencia-Carrasco, Salvador, 55
Heritage Foundation, 35, 84, 187
higher education. *See specific topics, such as* persecution of scholars
Historically Black Colleges and Universities (HBCUs), 41, 77–78, 78, 102
history denialism and rewriting, 197–200, 207–8, 229
history of public higher education: audit culture, 170–74; conservative backlash, 151–55; corporatism, 167–70; defense and economic interests, 158–64; end of utopian universities, 155–56; labor force, precarious and adjunct, 174–76; market logics and neoliberal educational agenda, 164–67; minority students, blocking of, 156–58; overview, 135–37; post-WWII utopian universities, 137–42; student activism, 142–51

Hitler, Adolf, 71, 74–76, 100, 208
Holocaust denial movement, 208
Hong Kong, 67–68, *68*
hooks, bell, 91, 150, 226
House Committee on Education and Workforce hearing (2023), 69
Howard University, 199
human–nature binary, 231–34
human rights, 68–71
Humboldt, Wilhelm von, 6
Humboldt University of Berlin, 72, 74
Hungary, 54, 66, 108–13. *See also* Orbán, Viktor

identity, weaponization of, 98
immigration centers and camps, 127–31
Imperial College London, 196
India, 98, 100–101, 207. *See also* Modi, Narendra
Indian Child Welfare Act (1978), 263n3
Indigenous peoples, 116, 138–39, 232–33, 263n3
inequality: in global political economy, 52–53, 220; income inequality, 174–76, 179; land-grant universities and, 263n1. *See also* neoliberalism and free-market ideology
Institute for Humane Studies (George Mason University), 193
Institute of International Education Scholar Rescue Fund (IIE-SRF), 101
instrumental approach to higher education, 22, 158
Inter-American Principles, 16, 92, 102–4
Intergovernmental Panel on Climate Change (IPCC), 184
International Association of Universities (IAU), 255n5
International Covenant on Economic, Social and Cultural Rights (CESCR), 103, 261n3
International Institute for Education, 100
international law, 103, 261n3
International Monetary Fund (IMF), 163–64, 198, 227

intersectionality, 116
Iraq Qar, 178
Israel–Hamas war, xix, 69, 95, 209
Ivory Coast, 127–31

Jackson, Ketanji Brown, 43
Jackson State University, 154
Jaffer, Jamell, 42
Japan, 207
Johns Hopkins University, 209
"Joint Statement on Academic Freedom," 104–5
journal rankings, 172

Kalven Report (University of Chicago), 18, 49, 62–63
Kamola, Isaac, 145, 165, 192–93
Kaufman-Osborn, Timothy, 19
Kaye, David, 7–8
Kent State University, 153–54
Kerr, Clark, 151–52
Keyishian v. Board of Regents, 83–84
Khalid, Amna, 87
King, Jennie, 196–97
King, Martin Luther, Jr., 149, 227
knowledge production: antidemocratic fears of, 65–68; in antidemocratic vs. democratic regimes, 64–65; as borderless, 16; in Brazil, marginalized, 114–15; commoning and, 82–83, 97; decolonization and, 224–25; Einstein, lessons from, 74–80; epistemic justice, 94–96; evidence-based, 218; free speech and, 83–89; as global and local, 230–31; global economy of knowledge, 61–62; human–nature binary and, 231–33; human rights and, 68–71; meaning and definitions of, 71–74; nonhuman relations and, 231–32; past vs. current fascism and, 80–82; pluriversalism and epistemic diversity, 224–25; "profits over people" logic and, 180; universities as political and, 61–64; universities as site of critique of, 90
Koch, Charles, xvii, 35, 192–94

Koch Industries and family foundations, 35, 47, 84, 192–94, 197, 266n14
Kone, Cheikh, 127–31
Krenak, Ailton, 232–33
Krugman, Paul, 181

labor precarity, 174–76
land-grant universities, 138–39
Landin, Jennifer, 190
Lat, David, 88
Latour, Bruno, 185
lawfare strategies: about, 28–30; antiprotest laws, 209–10; book bans and burnings, xiv, 55–59, 75, 75, 163; defined, 257n5; Florida's "Stop Woke Act" and "Don't Say Gay Act," 57–59; gag order measures, 57–58, 183; in Hungary, 110–11; against US higher education, 41–43
Lawlor, Mark, 212
Lee Hsien Loong, 29
Leff, Laurel, 260n11
Leininger, Liz, 126
Levine, Arthur, 257n11
LGBTQ+ community: bills against, 204; book banning and, 56, 70; campus police and, 213; CNP and, 166; New College of Florida and, 57; Trump's executive order and, 203
libertarianism, 35
Lincoln University, 77–78, *78*
López, Francesca, 203
Lynk, Michael, 40

Macalester College, 86–87
Mack, Arien, 100
MacLean, Nancy, 47
Maher, Geo, 226–27
Maira, Sunaina, 10
Manhattan Project, 76, 158, 260n8
market logics. *See* neoliberalism and free-market ideology
"marketplace of ideas" narrative, 83–85
Martin, Grady, 205–7
Martinez, Jenny, 88

Massachusetts Institute of Technology (MIT), 69, 159, 165, *191*
Mbembe, Achille, 224, 232
McCarthyism, 76–80, 141–42, 181, 263n4
McElroy, Kathleen, 199–200
McInnes, Gavin, 85
McInnis, Maurie, 213–14
McNinch, James, 222
Medeiros, Débora, 113–18
Merry, Sally, 265n18
microaggressions, 249–50
Mignolo, Walter, 226
Milei, Javier, 28
militarization of campuses, 45–46, 208–14
militarization of research agendas, 268n34
military-industrial complex, 264n10
Modi, Narendra, 28, 55, 101
Monbiot, George, 186
monitoring organizations, 99–105
Moore, MariJo, 94
moral panics, 56–57, 181, 218
Morrill Act (1862), 139
Morrish, Liz, 171–72, 174
Mulvey, Irene, 59
Murdoch, Rupert, xvii, 185
Musk, Elon, xvii, 48

NAACP, 41, 77, 203
Nabulsi, Karma, 95
Naím, Moisés, 27
Nakatsu, Penny, 146
Nash, Margaret, 139
National Environmental Education Act (1990), 188–89
National Guard, 146, 153
Native Americans, 138–39, 232–33, 263n3
Nazi Germany, 71, 74–76, 80, 100, 208
Nelson, Anne, 166
Nelson, Cary, 194
Nelson, Gaylord, 151
neoliberalism and free-market ideology: capitalism and, 264n13; crisis of, 2, 51; economic and legal ideology, 35–36; interference in universities, 47; Koch Foundation and, 193–94; market logics and reshaping of higher education, 164–67; questioning of, 179; universities' roles in, 159–64. *See also* capitalism
Neo-nationalism and Universities (Douglass), 50–51
Netanyahu, Benjamin, 29
Network for Education and Academic Rights (NEAR), 93
New Agenda for Peace, A (UN), 180
New College of Florida, 57, 126, 213
Newfield, Christopher, 167
New Left Movements, 148, 149
New University in Exile Consortium, 100, 128, 131–33
Ngũgĩ wa Thiong'o, 228–30
Nichols, Tom, 32
Nixon, Richard, 148, 153–57
Nobrega, Camila, 113–18
Norman, Peter, 264n12
Northern Ireland, 118–22
nuclear weapons, 76

O'Donnell, Catherine, 84
Office of Environmental Education (OEE), 188
Ohio, 183
oil industry, 184–87, 190–96, *191*
Okihiro, Gary, 146
Operation Condor, 28, 162, 256n3
Oppenheimer, J. Robert, 76
Orbán, Viktor, 54, 109–13, 132
Ortega, Daniel, 55

Pasquerella, Lynn, 205
Passavant, Paul, 209
Patrick, Dan, 37
Patriot Front, 260n7
Pedagogy of the Oppressed (Freire), xiv, 55
Pelt, Scott, 257n11
PEN America and PEN International: *America's Censored Classrooms*, 57–58; Case List, 99; exiles and, 128

PEN America Principles on Campus Free Speech: calls to punish speech, 247–48; campus climate, 242–43; campus speakers, 245–47; campus speech legislation, 252–53; education and language, 251–52; faculty speech and expression, 248–49; hateful speech, 244–45; microaggressions and language of harm, 249–50; overview, 241–42; safe spaces, 250–51; speech and sexual harassment, 251; trigger warnings, 250
Pennsylvania State University, 85
performance measurement, 170–74
persecution of scholars: about, 98–99; Afghanistan, 106–7; Brazil, 113–18; civil society response, 99–105; escalation of, 100; Ethiopia, 107–8; exile stories, 122–33; Hungary, 108–13; Ivory Coast, 127–31; legal protections of academic freedom, 102–5; Northern Ireland, 118–22; stories (overview), 105–6; Syria, 128, 131–33; United States, 124–26; violent and nonviolent acts, 101–2
Philipp Schwartz Initiative, 100
Pike, John, 169
Pillar of Shame (Galschiot), 67–68, *68*
Pinochet, Augusto, 162
Planck, Max, 76
pluriversalism, 224–25
Poland, 208
"Polarizing Times Demand Robust Academic Freedom" (AAUP), 63, 220–21
policing: about, 44–46; monitoring and violence, 46–47; political economic destabilization and, 53; self-censorship, 47–48, 122; social media and digital surveillance, 48–50; of speech, escalating, 98; through corporatism and precarity, 167–70. *See also* censorship; surveillance
political economy: destabilization of, 2, 11, 53–54, 178–79, 220; inequality in, 52–53; of neoliberal populism, 124

Popović, Milica, 95, 175
Post, Robert, 83
Powell, Lewis F., Jr., 160
Prager University Foundation ("PragerU"), 195
Prashad, Vijay, 28, 175–76
Price, Richard, 148–49
Princeton University, *191*
Professor Watchlist (Turning Point USA), 49–50
profit-driven logic, 22, 185–86. *See also* capitalism; neoliberalism and free-market ideology
Project 2025 (Heritage Foundation), 187
protests and activism: anticolonialism, 143–47, 263n5; antiprotest laws, 209–10; antiwar, 148–49; civil rights movement, 143, 147–48, 149, 156; conservative backlash, 151–58; environmentalist, 151; Free Speech Movement, 142–43; invited speakers and, 246–47; militarization and, 208–14; policing of student protests, 45–46; Szabad Egyetem (Free University), Hungary, 109–13; tuition hikes and, 168; women's movement, 149–50, 157–58
Proud Boys, 85, 260n7
public opinion, 37–38, *38*, 69–70

Quebec, 262n5
Queen's University, Belfast, 118–22
Quinn, Robert, 48, 101, 104, 106, 113–22

Rachman, Gideon, 27
racism: Black female scholars and, 199–200; in Brazil, 116; campus police and, 211, 213; DEI attacks, 204–7; far right and, 200–202; GI Bill and, 138; Great Replacement conspiracy theory, 231; history denialism and recolonizing minds, 197–200; King assassination and, 149; land-grant universities and, 263n1; McCarthyism, Einstein, and, 77–78; Reagan and, 153; slavery, censorship of, 198–99, 229
Randeria, Shalini, 66

rankings: journal, 172; university and college, 173, 265n18
Reagan, Ronald, 37, 152–53, 157, 163, 165–66, 188
Red Squads, 143
Reichmann, Henry, 71
Renteln, Alison, 257n11
Republican Party: academic freedom, free speech, and, 85–86; activism, backlash against, 151–58; authoritarianism and, xvi–xvii, 31; climate denialism and, 183, 187–90; CNP and, 166; CRT and, 203–4; DEI programs and, 204–7; higher education, criticism of, 37–38; history denialism and, 229; lawfare tactics and, 42, 257n5; MAGA movement, xvi, 10–11, 70, 264n7; McCarthyism and, 80; objectives of, 182; oil industry and, 187, 217; racism and, 200–204; science and, 64; social responsibility in face of, 219; state control efforts, xviii, 47, 55–59, *58*, 85, 125, 197, 199–200, 212–13; Supreme Court cases and, 43, 83–84; Turning Point USA, 49–50; tyranny of the minority and, 32; weaponization and, 181, 235. *See also* Florida
responsibility. *See* social responsibility
Rhoades, Gary, 165
Rhodes, Cecil, 226
Rice University, *191*
Robeson, Paul, 260n9
Robinson, David, 59
Robinson, William, 53–54
Roe v. Wade, 150, 158
Roy, Arundhati, 98
Rufo, Christopher, 202, 205, 260n6
Russell, Barry, 50

safe spaces, 250–51
Said, Edward, 123
San Francisco State University, 145–46, *147*
Sanger, Margaret, 150
Santa Barbara oil spill (1969), 151, *152*, 188
Santos, Boaventura de Sousa, 26, 81, 225

Sayen, Jamie, 76–77
Scheppele, Kim Lane, 30
Scholars at Risk (SAR): about, 101; *Free to Think*, 39, 40, 106; *Inter-American Principles* and, 102–4; role of, xviii–xix; on social responsibility, 14
scholasticide, 95
Schrecker, Ellen, 45, 90, 156, 160–61
Schwartzburg, Rosa, 108–13
science denialism, 182–83, 184
Scott, Joan Wallach, 72–73, 84
sexual harassment, 251
shadow academy, 160–61
Shelton, Jon, 22
Sinanan, Kerry, 50
Singapore, 207
Sitze, Adam, 84
1619 Project, The (Hannah-Jones), 198–99, 201
Slaughter, Shiela, 165
slavery, censorship of, 198–99, 229
Sleeter, Christine, 203
Smith, Tommie, 264n12
Snyder, Jeffrey, 87
social justice, 18, 89–94, 96, 236, 242
social media, 48–49, 80–81, 119, 220, 248
social responsibility: academic freedom reframed as, 12–18; across national borders, 230–31; beyond the Euro-American academy, 223–28; to collective futures, 234–35; as duty, 14, 218–21; human–nature binary and, 231–34; with inclusive student communities, 228–29; to whom?, 222–23, 235–36
solidarity, 110, 112
Solidarity for Academic Freedom in India (InSAF India), 100–101
Soon, Willie, 184–85
Sotomayor, Sonia, 207
South Africa, 14, 144–45
Spooner, Marc, 222
Stanford Law School, 87–88
Stanford University, 159, *191*, 191–92
State of Play of Academic Freedom in the EU Member States (European Parliament), 15

Steiner, H. Arthur, 28
STEM research, 22, 62, 171
Stony Brook University, 213–14
strongman leaders, 27–28, 200–201
student loans, 43
Students for Fair Admissions v. Harvard, 42–43, 207
Supreme Court, US: *Biden v. Nebraska*, 43; *Brown v. Board of Education*, 157; *Keyishian v. Board of Regents*, 83–84; packed by Trump, 158; *Roe v. Wade*, 150, 158; *Students for Fair Admissions v. Harvard*, 42–43, 207
surveillance: audit culture, 170–74; digital, 48–50; by FBI, 142–43; militarization of campuses, 45–46, 208–14; sensationalized, 49. *See also* policing
Syria, 128, 131–33
Szabad Egyetem (Free University), 109–13

Takriti, Abdel Razzaq, 95
Talepasand, Taravat, 86–87
Talloires Network, 15–16
Teays, Wanda, 257n11
Tessier-Lavigne, Marc, 88
Texas A&M University, 139, *191*, 199–200
Thatcher, Margaret, 56, 163, 165–66
Thelin, John, 158
Third World Liberation Front (TWLF), 145–46
Third World Liberation studies, 146–47
Thunberg, Greta, 195
Title IX, 150
Toscano, Alberto, 4
transnational capitalist class, 52–54
trigger warnings, 250
Trump, Donald: authoritarian states and, 132; Executive Order 13950 (on CRT), 202–3; fascism and, 31–32; oil industry and, 186–87; racism and, 200–201; style of, 28; Supreme Court and, 158
Tufts University, 196
tuition, raises in, 167–68

Turkey, 82, 123–24, 207
Turning Point USA, 49–50

UK Council for At-Risk Academics, 100
Uncensored America, 85
UN Educational, Scientific, and Cultural Organization (UNESCO), 15
UN Human Rights Council, 104–5
Universal Declaration of Human Rights, 103, 261n3
Universidad Nacional Mayor de San Marcos, Lima, 55
universities. *See specific universities and topics*
universities as political, 18–20, 61–64
University in Exile, 100. *See also* New University in Exile Consortium
University of California: fossil fuels divestment, 195–96; land-grant system and, 139–40; UC Berkeley, 139–40, 151–52, 153, *154*, 168, 191, *191*; UC Davis, 168, *169*, 233; UC Irvine, 140; UCLA, 203; UC Santa Barbara, 153; UC Santa Cruz, 211
University of Cambridge, 196
University of Cape Town, 226
University of Chicago, 213
University of Illinois, *191*
University of Mississippi, 202
University of North Carolina (UNC), 199
University of Pennsylvania (Penn), 69, 260n6
University of Pittsburgh (Pitt), 194, 266n14
University of Texas, Austin, *191*
University of Toronto, 196
University of Virginia, 205–6
UnKoch My Campus, 195
Utah State University, 193–94

Vatansever, Asli, 123–24, 128
V-Dem, 26
Vietnam War, 148
violence: campus violence panics, 212–13; in Hungary, 111–12; invited speakers

and, 246; militarization of campuses, 45–46, 208–14; policing mechanisms of control, 46–47; trends on campuses, 41. *See also* policing
Voting Rights Act (1965), 143, 264n7

Walters University, 41
war on terror, 178
weaponization: in Brazil, 113–14; of facts, 64; of identity, 98; of universities in 2020s, 181–82
West, Cornel, 166–67
West Virginia University, 193–94
White nationalism, 199–200, 207
Wilks, Farris and Dan, 195, 197
Williamson-Lott, Joy Ann, 143
Wilson, Ralph, 192–93
"woke" ideology, 1, 37–38, 182
women's rights movement, 149–50, 157–58
women's studies, 149–50
Woollacott, Angela, 264n9
World Bank, 163–64, 165, 198, 227
World Trade Organization (WTO), 164
Worth, Katie, 190

Xi Jinping, 67

Yacovone, Donald, 201
Yale University, 140–41, 159, 212
Young, Neil, 154

Explore other books from HOPKINS PRESS

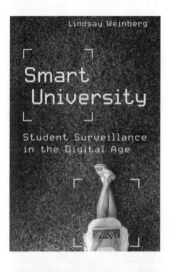

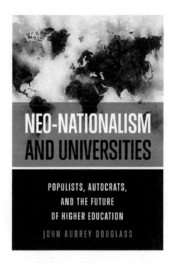